CLASSICAL MUSIC

TOP 40

ANTHONY J. RUDEL

A FIRESIDE BOOK

PUBLISHED BY SIMON & SCHUSTER

NEW YORK   LONDON   TORONTO

SYDNEY   TOKYO   SINGAPORE

FIRESIDE
Rockefeller Center
1230 Avenue of the Americas
New York, New York 10020

Copyright © 1995 by Anthony Jason Rudel

FIRESIDE *and colophon are registered trademarks*
of Simon & Schuster Inc.

Designed by Marysarah Quinn

Manufactured in the United States of America

10   9   8   7   6   5   4   3   2   1

Library of Congress Cataloging-in-Publication Data
Rudel, Anthony J.
     Classical music top 40 / Anthony J. Rudel.
       p.   cm.
     "A Fireside book."
     1. Music appreciation.   2. Compact discs—Reviews.   I. Title.
II. Title: Classical music top forty.
MT90.R8   1995
781.6'8—dc20   94–23109
                                                         CIP
                                                         MN

ISBN: 0-671-79495-7

TO MY WIFE,
KRISTY RUDEL,
WHO INSPIRED ME
TO WRITE THIS BOOK.
WITH LOVE.

CONTENTS

PREFACE BY BILLY JOEL

I am one of the lucky ones. Not only because I have had a wonderful, extended career in popular music, but also because when I was a child I had parents who introduced me to classical music. The treasure that is the classics has stayed with me, influenced my writing, and has continued to be an inspiration throughout my life. To this day, I sit down at the piano and play through classical works by ear, perhaps some Debussy or an ersatz rendition of a Rachmaninoff piece. It serves to remind me what a shame it is that our schools have been forced to cut back on music education; too many kids today grow up without being introduced to Beethoven, Mozart, Chopin, Bach, or other great composers.

When I started taking piano lessons at age four, I often found the music I had to practice to be somewhat tedious, but I had a good ear and could imitate the styles of the great composers. So instead of doing my scales, I would make up pieces that sounded like easy Mozart sonatas, each day improvising another movement. By the end of the week, I had created an entire piece, but I couldn't play my assigned lesson. When I got to high school I made another interesting discovery, thanks to my classical training: At parties I would find a piano and sit alone, improvising lonely melodies. Soon I would notice one girl standing there and listening, and then another, and another. It dawned on me that music was like an aphrodisiac, but this was a motivation that Beethoven, Mozart, Liszt, and countless other composers had understood long ago.

As a composer, I have learned many lessons from the classical masters. In fact, solutions to all songwriting problems can be found in the classics. Beethoven said it all and conquered all. The key to all good music, whether it be classical, popular, jazz, or Broadway is composition. The elements of composition are chords, melody, and rhythm, but especially melody. When you hear a popular song for the first time and like it, what you are reacting to is the melody or, as the Music Biz calls it, the hook. The truth is that classical music is filled with hooks. Beethoven's Pastoral Symphony (no. 6) is one great melody after another, blending to paint a large picture. Melody itself can be so evocative that it can dictate the subject matter of the lyric or libretto.

When I write a song, the melody comes first. Once I have the music, the words seem to fall into place, inspired by the mood and character of the music itself. Classical music is no different: The melodies create emotional images, but the literary scope of these words is much larger than the minutes allotted to a popular song.

Whenever I hear a melody, I have to listen. Even when I am standing in an elevator and hear some god-awful Muzak version of one of my own songs. The great classics require even keener listening, and I am thrilled when I can introduce friends to this music. I might start them on Mozart, and then gradually move to Beethoven, and then on to the Romantics like Schumann or Dvorak. Just having played classical music on the stereo has had an obvious influence on my daughter. It has been a joy to watch her absorb these treasures, and to pass it on to her so that her life may be richer for it.

I am often astounded by how many times I find my own compositions being influenced by the classical music I love. In the original version of "The River of Dreams," there was a blend of classical-style lullaby, some Ambrosian chant, and a bit of Schumannesque Romanticism (until it was edited to its present version). My song "This Night" utilizes Beethoven in its chorus, while "For the Longest Time" evolved from a Mozartian piano piece into a late 1950s doo-wop piece. But I shouldn't be surprised, because the power of the past is immense. We could not write the songs that become the popular hits of today if it hadn't been for the composers who came before us.

What you have to realize is that the satisfaction we seek in contemporary music can also be found in the classics. If you are looking for revolutionaries and romantics, consider that Beethoven tore up the original dedication of his Third Symphony because he was so anguished that his proletarian hero, Napoleon, had named himself emperor. Surely, this was a more sincere form of protest than a rock star who sells millions of albums dramatically ripping up a picture of the Pope on television. If you love today's music because of the bohemian nature of its musicians, you should be looking at the classical musicians who struggle for years to learn their craft and then survive from job to job on the hope they might at least make a living from their music. And even if they don't, they continue in their craft purely because they love the music itself. Classical musicians make today's rockers seem pretentious. Let's face it: Rock musicians are no longer outlaws or starving artists, especially those of us who have nice fat recording contracts (which most classical musicians do not have).

With today's contemporary music in rather poor condition, the continuity provided by the classics is reassuring, especially when you take time to really absorb all there is. Power, passion, sex, angst, libido, stimuli, sorrow, joy . . . it can all be found in classical music. If you want to hear the blues, listen to Barber's Adagio for Strings; there ain't no blues *that* sad. If you want to dance, try moving to the wild rhythms of Ravel and Stravinsky, or the exciting melodic propulsion of Brahms and Chopin. These syncopated compositions are much more challenging than today's rote, 4/4 time, *Yo! MTV Raps* dance drivel.

Let yourself become familiar with classical music and it will please you for the rest of your life in a way that fads and fashions simply cannot. Beethoven, Mozart, Chopin, Debussy, Bach, Brahms, Tchaikovsky, Prokofiev, Copland, Mahler, and all the other greats who speak to us from the grave are sharing with us the secrets of their souls. We owe them a huge debt. Perhaps I can repay a part of my own debt to them by introducing you to this terrific book and, in turn, the music it will bring into your life.

Billy Joel

INTRODUCTION

Once at a performance of Verdi's *Don Carlo* in Cincinnati I was seated behind a middle-aged couple who had never been to an opera before. They sat motionless observing every detail, absorbing what they could while trying to follow the intricacies of the plot. Roughly two hours into the evening, just as the trombones dramatically intoned a very powerful phrase the husband turned to his wife and said in an animated whisper: "I don't know what's going on, but something bad's going to happen!" It was at that moment that this book was conceived.

In recent years classical music has become more and more distant for people who would like to enjoy this wealth of beauty but have not been introduced to it and therefore feel intimidated. Too often I am confronted by the comment: "I would like to enjoy classical music but I don't understand what it is I am listening to." My usual response is to ask if the person can enjoy a gourmet meal even if they don't understand how it is prepared. Classical music should be no different; it is an exquisite form of entertainment that can and should be enjoyed on a variety of levels. And, when prodded most people will admit they have heard classical music in their everyday lives; in movies, television commercials, elevators, and even used and abused in show and pop music. Music is everywhere, and classical music can be a very rewarding part of anyone's entertainment fare; you just have to let it. What this book attempts to do is to break down the barriers and make great music accessible to those who have been afraid to venture into its realm.

The very first thing to know is classical music is nothing more than a language used by composers to convey emotions, moods, pictures, landscapes, and even outer space. Don't say you can't appreciate music because you don't know the language; music is a universal language that speaks directly to the soul. The emotions conveyed are feelings each of us has; you will know when something is sad because it will sound sad! The problem most new listeners face is not one of understanding but rather of insight; they can hear the music but are often frustrated by the feeling they must be missing something since they did not study this art form. The point they miss is classical music is *entertainment* and need not be *education*.

However, they are correct in the belief that the music will be more interesting if they understand it in some detail, a concept that applies to most forms of entertainment. For example, have you ever watched a sport without having any idea of what was going on? All around you other spectators are enthralled by the action while you stare blankly wondering what you missed; this is boring and not entertaining. Then someone starts to explain the basic rules: who is doing what and when; how play starts and stops; what constitutes an error or a foul; the role of each player on the field; the degree of difficulty in each act, and on and on. Suddenly, what had been boring and meaningless starts to make sense; you notice a fine play by one athlete, an exciting moment that thrills you. You have become a fan. Now in place of the sporting event we have classical music without all the foreign phrases and classroom terminology, and before you know it, what was once a boring listening experience is transformed into stirring entertainment. If you are one of those people who finds classical music difficult because you don't understand it, then this book will be that considerate sports spectator who showed you the way and turned you into a fan, because once you have experienced the fantastic entertainment provided by over three centuries of composers you too will become a fan.

THE LANGUAGE FACTOR

First of all do not be put off by the foreign terminology used by classical musicians and critics; these terms are important for the accurate performance of a composer's creation, but not for being able to listen to and enjoy the work. The only language you need to appreciate is the universal language of music without need of interpretation or translation; there is no known emotion that cannot be conveyed by music.

As you begin to enjoy classical music you will find yourself describing pieces using everyday adjectives: lively, sad, slow, loud, exuberant. This is the beginning of a vocabulary of words you may use repeatedly, and will enable you to group pieces and to identify those that please you most. However, sometimes the words will not be enough to accurately convey exactly what comes across in the music; in essence the "translation" from music to words may not always be exact. The task of describing classical music is daunting not because one needs to be educated in its fine points, but because the music describes itself better than any combination of words possibly can. But, with the forty masterpieces included in this volume I have tried to give the reader a sense of what each work is about so as you approach the music the barriers of language will have been removed. You will see words repeated in an attempt to be consistent, so as your ear develops you will recognize types of melodies and what the adjectives used "sound" like.

HOW TO USE THIS BOOK

Each of the chapters in this book is devoted to a single piece of classical music culled from countless "Top Ten" lists. (If you put five classical music fans in a room and asked each for a list of ten favorite works you would receive at least ten such lists!) Each chapter is divided into five distinct sections:

1. A brief introduction to the composer and the work, including references designed to place the piece in historic context, and a description of the size of the forces required to perform the work.

2. Using a "reference recording," the piece is described movement by movement pointing out some of the highlights by using the digital time readout provided by compact disc technology. Since each recording of the same work is different, these time references are accurate only for the reference recording. However, this section is still useful even if you are using another recording in order to give a sense of when things occur within the work.

3. Musicians and record producers familiar with the works give brief, personal insights into the piece with the hope that the reader will be able to benefit from the performer's perspective.

4. Three recordings of the work are recommended and reviewed so you have some choice and guidance as you build your CD collection.

5. A list of other works either by the same composer or similar in nature to the featured piece, the logical next step to take to build knowledge and a collection.

The second of these sections in each chapter is where the earlier sports analogy is most apt; here we are able to point out signposts along the musical journey giving the first-time listener some landmarks to listen for. Of course selecting the most important moments to point out is a highly subjective undertaking, and for every moment highlighted here there are probably five others of equal import that could be mentioned. The key is, using these select moments as a guide, the novice listener will be able to listen for specific details that will clarify what is going on and will help develop the ability to recognize similar effects in other works. This is especially true in terms of the sounds of the instruments; once aware of the sound an oboe makes, you will eventually be able to pick out its sound in other pieces and will then be able to identify your own signposts, much the way that once you have seen a curveball pitched in a baseball game and had it pointed out you can recognize it again in another game.

It is critical to hear these instruments in the context of performance so the relationships among them is clear; hearing an oboe in isolation does not have the meaning of hearing it blending with the other woodwinds. Similarly, in isolation an apple may taste very sweet, but when compared to a chocolate it may not. Remember, music is aimed at our senses, our emotions— react, don't analyze!

Another important factor is the role of interpretation. Very often the question of why there are so many recordings of a particular classical work arises, and fans of pop music are surprised to find out two recordings of the same piece can be so dramatically different. How can that be when the conductors are reading the same notes in the same score? The answer is interpretation: musicians choose the elements they wish to bring out in performing the work, much the way two actors may stress different words or aspects in the same Shakespearean monologue.

In selecting the "Reference Recording" for each piece I have tried to introduce the reader to a wide range of artists, styles, and sounds. Fortunately there is no shortage of fantastic recordings from which to choose. However, in each case I sought a recording that allowed the listener the best opportunity to hear the critical moments. Further, compact disc technology not only affords the opportunity to point out specific moments by using the digital time readout, but also gives an incredibly clear sound, making it easier to highlight the role of the inner voices in a work, the music supporting the melody that gives texture and richness to the sound. Often, as you will see, it is the interplay among these inner voices that will take a simple melody and transform it into a glorious sound sending shivers up your spine. But don't be frustrated if at first you can't identify all the details highlighted in these pages; always try to first get the overall sense of the work and then go back and track the specifics. Also, repeated listenings will make the journey through the work more familiar and gradually you will recognize musical landmarks, those indicated here and your own.

LEARNING TO LISTEN

Don't! Listening to classical music should be a form of entertainment and it does not require careful study. It is far more important to *experience* a piece of music; allow it to speak to you in its language, always remembering there is no right and wrong. Great music requires purely subjective reactions; if something sounds joyful to you then that is what it is. Remember there is no human emotion that cannot be portrayed through great music. Don't be afraid to react to what you hear; remove the shackles, laugh, cry, smile, admire, and even dislike what you hear, but react! It will make the listening experience much more fun.

Great music has the ability to conjure up very powerful images in the mind, much the way a good movie soundtrack enhances the visual images on the screen. Try to imagine a movie without the music; in all cases the movie would be less evocative and interesting. It is my belief that in some cases it is the music which can take a good movie and make it exceptional, as was the case with the Robert Redford movie *The Natural*; it was the music that accentuated the beauty of the American heartland or the supernatural quality of the hero's final home run. If you are not convinced, watch the final scene with the sound off; the power of the visual images is greatly diminished without the music.

As you listen to these forty pieces, or any other great works, allow the music to create images in your mind, whether they be of elegant European courts, outer space, flowing natural wonders, or anything else you can come up with. Great music will transport and relax you, if you let it. It can also be haunting, passionate, disturbing, grim, and anger invoking. If it wasn't you would be disappointed!

WHY THESE FORTY WORKS?

Among the hardest tasks in putting this book together was the selection of the pieces. While the first twenty, pieces like Beethoven's Fifth Symphony and Handel's *Messiah*, are clear favorites, the other twenty were more difficult to select. The final mix is designed to give the reader a blend of different eras, national styles, instrumentation, size of forces required, and moods. In this way the new listener might develop the ability to identify styles such as the Baroque sound of Bach, Handel, and Vivaldi, or nationalistic sounds such as the Russian power of Tchaikovsky and Mussorgsky, traits and qualities apparent not only in these pieces but in all music. These works should serve as a starting point from which one can use bits of newly gained information and apply it to the thousands of pieces of the classical repertoire. For example, the brooding intensity of Mahler's First Symphony is apparent in all of his later symphonies and once its distinctive sound is in your ears you will be able to identify his style more easily.

Some of the other works were selected because of popularity gained through pop-culture, making them more recognizable and therefore more accessible. But, it is safe to say there is no work among the forty that is not a great composition. In fact, as I listened to these pieces over and over again their greatness became more and more apparent. You will notice the span of three centuries of music covered by these pieces. Try, at some point, to listen to these works in chronological order; you will be struck by the steady progression and development leading seamlessly from era to era. While for convenience' sake we refer to eras such as Baroque or Romantic, it is important to remember that each era sprang out of its predecessor, growing more complex, much as the world itself did. Listen to Handel's *Messiah* followed by Mozart's Requiem and then Orff's *Carmina Burana;* try to grasp the development occurring over the more than two hundred years separating Handel from Orff. Then, listen to the rock opera *Tommy* and see if there are any points of comparison; I think you will be surprised by the debt *good* pop music owes to the classics.

SOME FINAL THOUGHTS BEFORE YOU GO

Listening to classical music should be a rewarding experience. For too long the trappings of this art have prevented potential listeners from "getting into it"; the barriers of language and culture have stood firm protecting the historical legacy and muffling the passionate message composers sought to deliver through their music. "Let us entertain you!" they call from their graves; "Let us educate you," the guardians of the past have implored, "then you will be able to hear what the great masters intended." Nothing could be further from the truth. Great music speaks to the willing listener, and for some the ability to appreciate classical music comes with little or no effort. But, for others there is a need for some guidance, for some signposts along the route making the journey a little more understandable and therefore enjoyable.

This book is intended for those listeners, like the couple in Cincinnati, who aren't really too sure what is going on, but don't need to know precisely because they are able to feel the passions within the music; they let the music speak to them. Each chapter is designed to open the ears to some of the details that combine to form the whole sonic tableau, to enable the listener to read the conductor's score, not in notes or Italian directions, but in simple English using words inspired only by the sound of the music. As you experience these forty works you will develop likes and dislikes, discover styles and composers you love, instruments whose sound inspires you, melodies you need to hear over and over. Before you know it *you* will be that avid fan guiding some neophyte through the rousing "Ode to Joy" or the sublime beauty of Mozart's Clarinet Quintet.

Music is powerful stuff; let it transport you to another era or another state of mind. But, by all means do not be afraid of it. These great composers would be appalled to find out there are people who find their melodies and passions inaccessible, in the same way a great writer would be saddened to learn his words did not speak to the vast majority of readers. Music is "emotions"; you have them, now simply feel the music.

Before you go any further keep in mind these words from the greatest composer in the English language, Shakespeare, who wrote in Act V, Scene 1, of *The Merchant of Venice:*

For do but note a wild and wanton herd,
Or race of youthful and unhandled colts,
Fetching mad bounds, bellowing and neighing loud,
Which is the hot condition of their blood—
If they but hear perchance a trumpet sound,
Or any air of music touch their ears,
You shall perceive them make a mutual stand,
Their savage eyes turn'd to a modest gaze
By the sweet power of music.

Enjoy the music!

—Anthony Jason Rudel
Chappaqua, New York

Please note: At the time this book was written, all of the recordings cited were available and in print. However, record companies have been known to delete titles over time. It is our hope that most if not all of the recordings referenced will be available for many, many years.

BACH

*B*RANDENBURG CONCERTO NO. 2
IN F MAJOR

The six concertos written by Johann Sebastian Bach (1685–1750) known as the *Brandenburg* Concertos, were composed between 1718 and 1721, then grouped together and presented by the composer to the margrave of Brandenburg on March 24, 1721. Interestingly, Bach did not call the concertos "the *Brandenburgs*" nor did he compose them specifically for the margrave. In essence he took six random concertos each using a different combination of solo instruments with a small orchestra accompaniment and grouped them together, in the process creating wonderfully varied works that have become an integral part of the standard repertoire both as a set and as individual pieces.

The *Brandenburgs* were created at the height of the baroque period, as composers such as Handel, Scarlatti, Corelli, Vivaldi, and Bach were at their peak. In 1721, Peter I was proclaimed emperor of all Russia, regular postal service between England and New England was begun, and Pope Innocent XIII was elected.

Each of the six *Brandenburg* concertos features a different grouping of solo instruments. For example, the Third Concerto is

scored for three violins, three violas, three cellos, bass, and harpsichord, while the Fifth Concerto uses a solo flute, solo violin,
harpsichord, and strings. While all six are mainstays of the concert repertoire, the second concerto is our focus because of its
highly unusual solo instrumentation, the familiarity of the last
movement, and the almost jazzlike nature of sections of the work.

The first element of importance in the *Brandenburg* Concerto No. 2 is the way all four solo instruments—trumpet,
recorder, oboe, and violin—have rather high ranges. While listening, it is fun to try to follow how the solo instruments play off
of each other and exchange themes and parts, and how they go
from being in the foreground as soloist to returning to the background as a part of the accompanying ensemble. To further the
jazz analogy, think of the soloists as members of a band, each of
whom steps out for a quick solo, then immediately steps back
into the "band" to serve as backup.

One further point: the final movement of the *Brandenburg*
Concerto No. 2 may sound familiar because it has been used as
the theme for the public-television series *Firing Line*.

REFERENCE RECORDING: PHILIPS 412 790
I MUSICI CHAMBER ENSEMBLE
TOTAL TIME: 11:06

FIRST MOVEMENT   (4:55)

The opening phrase is brisk and soaring with the solo instruments and the accompanying string orchestra and harpsichord
all playing the theme together. Bach establishes the melody in
the very opening and maintains it throughout the movement. Although everyone is playing together, the trumpet seems
to soar above the rest. The first solo is taken by the violin (0:22),
followed in sequence by the oboe, the trumpet, and then
the recorder. There is a continuous interchange of voices with
different solos coming out, and sometimes two of the solo

instruments stepping forward together. Every so often the distinct solo lines blur (2:00), but it always clears up as the trumpet regains the lead (2:17).

The tone changes to a slightly mysterious version of the opening theme (2:45) accentuated by the accompanying harpsichord. This section definitely seems less settled and somewhat busier. But then there is a sudden, split-second stop (4:10) when all the activity ceases, then quickly resumes (4:11) and reestablishes the order of the opening. One final section of interplay (4:20) leads toward the final drive for the ending as all the instruments, solo and accompanying, come together with one last repeat of the theme.

SECOND MOVEMENT: Andante   (3:28)

In this movement Bach eliminates the solo trumpet and the accompanying strings, leaving only the three other solo instruments, the harpsichord, and the cello continuo playing together. The movement is like a piece of intimate chamber music for five players. The phrases are long melodic lines, but the style of stepping out and withdrawing seen in the opening movement is still evident here.

After the briefest of introductions by the harpsichord and cello, the solo violin establishes the theme, quickly picked up by the oboe and then the recorder. Listen for how the three solo lines exchange the melody while overlapping so that there is an unbroken line. This continues until they all end a phrase together (1:10), the continuo harpsichord and cello filling the gap until the solo instruments again take over. In essence, the exchanges are like bits of a three-way conversation, each statement answered and then altered by the subsequent response (1:44). In a series of three-note phrases (2:20) it is especially interesting to listen for the way the three instruments always appear two teamed together against one alone. The final, almost dissonant moment (3:14) leads to a totally resolved, unison conclusion.

THIRD MOVEMENT: Allegro assai   (2:43)

In this final movement the trumpet and the strings return. Be sure to watch how the four solo instruments are split into teams, with the trumpet and the oboe playing against the recorder and the violin.

In the opening the trumpet is back immediately in a solo of the rousing new theme, soon joined by the oboe, and together they make an exhilarating sound. The violin joins in (0:25), followed by its teammate the recorder (0:31). When played properly, this opening solo section with its harpsichord and cello accompaniment should really rock; the beat should be irresistible, moving propulsively. When the orchestra finally comes in (0:55), it further accentuates the relentless beat.

The key to this movement is the fabulous passagework Bach makes the soloists perform; it is like intricate filigree. However, as free-flowing as it is, it must remain within the parameters established by the work's structure and enforced by the solid, repetitive beat. Be sure to enjoy and appreciate each soloist's technique in the intricate sections. During this interplay the trumpet must repeatedly take control to reestablish the movement's theme (2:20). The final seconds (2:31) highlight the importance of the repeated notes as the trumpet soars above everyone else for one last jazzy solo.

PRINCIPAL TRUMPET OF THE ORCHESTRA OF ST. LUKE'S, CHRIS GEKKER:

"I had a teacher who told me that every trumpet player has only a limited number of Brandenburg 2s in them. His advice was to not rush into playing the piece too soon because of the difficulty of the very high solo part. In fact, the trumpet player for whom Bach wrote the work died while playing a similar passage in the Christmas Oratorio!"

COMPARATIVE RECORDINGS

I MUSICI
PHILIPS 412 790   TOTAL TIME: 11:06

An extremely solid performance with every soloist exceptional. A perfect introduction to the *Brandenburgs*. This conductorless ensemble spent decades specializing in performance of
baroque masterpieces, and their years of experience shine
through in this recording.

HOGWOOD/ACADEMY OF ANCIENT MUSIC
L'OISEAU-LYRE 414 187   TOTAL TIME: 11:28

Played on period instruments, this historically correct
recording has some excellent moments, but is only for those
interested in hearing the sound of the period instruments. A
good second recording.

SMEDVIG/LING/SCOTTISH CHAMBER ORCHESTRA
TELARC CD 80227   TOTAL TIME: 12:03

Featuring the trumpet artistry of Rolf Smedvig, this is an
excellent, exciting recording that places the focus squarely on
the trumpet. The accompanying ensemble is fine, and the sound
is exceptional.

IF YOU ENJOYED THIS PIECE. . .

The first thing to do is to listen to the five other concertos
that make up the complete *Brandenburgs*. The variety of the solo
instrumentation will keep you interested throughout the set.
Then to expand your appreciation of Bach's tremendous output,
listen to some of the keyboard works, especially the **Goldberg
Variations**. Finally, for something grander, the large-scale choral
works are truly great listening experiences. Start with the **Christmas Oratorio** and then go on to **The Saint Matthew Passion**.

BACH

ORCHESTRA SUITE NO. 2
IN B MINOR, BWV. 1067

Johann Sebastian Bach's (1685–1750) Orchestra Suite No. 2 is one of four such suites that he composed. When Bach wrote them is a matter of some disagreement, since he did not keep accurate records of the composition dates of his works. The most likely periods for their composition are between 1717 and 1723 or 1729 and 1731, and it is possible that they were written during the earlier period and recopied or reedited during the latter. Regardless of which of the periods is correct, it is safe to say the suites or Overtures were composed as the baroque era was at its apex; Bach and Handel were the leading composers among dozens of masters whose works have come down to us; Voltaire, Defoe, and Fielding were writing; Watteau, Wren, and later Canaletto were creating the art and architecture that defined the era. Simply put, it was a period of tremendous creative ferment.

The term *orchestra suite* can be interchanged with *overture*, or more accurately *Ouverture* since the works are written in the French baroque style. The key is each of the four suites is written as a series of movements all in the form of dances. The use of the word "orchestra" is also somewhat deceiving since that conjures up images of a large group of musicians. While these works can be (and have been) played by large orchestras, Bach intended for them to be played with one or two players to a part, thus limiting the size of the orchestra to the forces available in Bach's day.

While there are movements in each of the suites that are recognizable, such as the famous air that is part of the Third Suite, the Second Suite is probably the most frequently performed of the four. Its exact title is Overture in B Minor for flute, two violins, viola, and cello. In addition a continuo harpsichord plays throughout the work. What makes this work particularly appealing and interesting is Bach's use of the solo "traverse" flute. This work has become an important part of the solo flute repertoire, much like a flute concerto, and is a mainstay of the repertoire of flutists everywhere.

The Second Suite is written in seven distinct dance movements with the flute playing a critical role in each movement. An important element to be aware of is the frequent repeats, which are part of the baroque style. In each movement of the suite certain sections will be heard two and sometimes three times. What makes listening to the piece particularly fascinating is to note how the performers find ways to alter the repeated sections, thus keeping them interesting.

REFERENCE RECORDING:
RCA VICTOR RED SEAL 60900
GALWAY/FAERBER/WÜRTTEMBERG CHAMBER
ORCHESTRA   TOTAL TIME: 20:46

FIRST MOVEMENT: Ouverture   (7:22)

At the outset, Bach divides the orchestra into two distinct teams: the flute and the first violins are one team, and the second violins, violas, cellos, and bass make up the other team. The harpsichord continuo is a constant, independent force, and occasionally the cellos and bass will join the first team. There is an elegance to this introduction; the opening stately, slow, and pompous, with sustained passages made more interesting by the liberal use of trills. The importance of the flute becomes evident right at the outset as its sweet tone soars above the strings and harpsichord. The mood is strangely ambiguous, neither happy nor sad, but rather a contemplative mix of mild strain and gradually surging pomp.

This continues until the first team sets a faster tempo (3:06), and the feel of the work suddenly becomes lighter. The new melody quickly turns into a "round" with the second violins (3:10), the violas (3:16), and the cellos and bass (3:20) all entering quickly one after the other. This fugue keeps the pace moving, and the flute gets its first true solo (3:42) while the strings play a choppy, rhythmically precise accompaniment. This initial solo is just the first of a series in which the flute alternates with the orchestral accompaniment, a pattern repeated throughout most of the movement. At one point (6:00), albeit ever so briefly, the flute and first violin have a sustained note while the other instruments play the tricky passagework. Then, as quickly as it arrived, the bouncy melody stops and turns into a recapitulation of the sustained, trill-filled, slow opening (6:15). The opening movement is, in essence, an introduction to the entire suite, and it closes as it opened with the same stately, pomp-filled theme decorated by graceful trills.

SECOND MOVEMENT: Rondeau   (1:30)

This dance is filled with grace. It is slightly more cheerful than the opening of the first movement. Structurally, the teams established earlier remain together. In this short movement, the melody is established immediately and keeps returning throughout with only slight changes in volume or intensity. It is especially interesting to listen for sustained notes played by the flute and violins, while the violas briefly take the melody (0:33). This movement calls for excellent ensemble playing because, even though the flute does stand out, its solos are much less significant than in the first movement. Here, each instrument must be able to lead and then quickly return to be part of the overall sound.

THIRD MOVEMENT: Sarabande   (3:59)

The mood of this movement can be best described as sullen, a sad lullaby. It is somewhat plaintive and should be performed at the pace of a leisurely stroll. It is filled with instruments' melodic lines overlapping each other. It is important to listen throughout for the flute and first violins playing their phrases against the lower voices. Notice how the flute initially all alone (0:54) takes the main theme and restarts it quieter and more pensively. This movement in particular is filled with repeats, and since the pace is fairly slow, it presents the perfect opportunity to examine how the performers vary the music, through changes in ornamentation, phrasing, and volume. An excellent example of this occurs when the flute recapitulates the main theme (2:03) softer and more pensively than any of the earlier renditions. Joined by the strings and the harpsichord they all play in unison toward the movement's quiet, almost depressed end.

FOURTH MOVEMENT: Bourrée I–II   (1:41)

This dance is the first truly cheerful movement. It is brisk and bouncy, yet is not overly fast. Again here, the flute and first violins have the primary role, with the lower strings playing the accompaniment. In the second phrase (0:16), the second violins add some interesting solo passages. It is important to listen for the alternating of phrases with Team I again playing against Team II, especially evident in the first bourrée.

The second bourrée (0:47) continues right out of the first and features an elongated flute solo superimposed over the strings' quiet background. This is extremely demanding passage-work requiring the ensemble to be very precise so they can stay together. The end of the second bourrée (1:11) goes directly into a reprise of the first bourrée.

FIFTH MOVEMENT: Polonaise   (3:39)

The mood is stately; one can imagine courtiers in a baroque palace gracefully moving to this elegant dance. The feeling is set up primarily by the precise beat provided by the second violins, violas, cellos, and bass. Of particular interest are the three-note phrases played by the cellos and bass and harpsichord ending each of the movement's many sections (0:12, 0:27, 0:42, 0:54, 1:23).

The double (1:25) is truly a fantasy for flute. During this entire section, the violins and violas do not play, while the flute plays a fanciful series of passages accompanied only by the cello, bass, and harpsichord. Be sure to notice the contrast between the flute's high range and the heavier, lower range of the accompaniment. Following this fanciful flute solo (2:51), the movement returns to the beginning of the Polonaise for a final reprise.

SIXTH MOVEMENT: Menuet   (1:19)

This typical minuet is graceful and elegant, conjuring images of fancy-clad courtiers with powdered wigs moving in unison following the strict structure of the baroque minuet. Each section is played through twice, as all the repeats are taken. Throughout this brief movement Bach exploits the two-team structure, clearly dividing them, although occasionally the cellos do defect and join the flute and first violins. Once again the qualities of grace and elegance so integral in a formal dance are provided by the flute seeming to dance right along with the courtiers.

SEVENTH MOVEMENT: Badinerie   (1:16)

This is by far the most famous movement in the entire suite. Extremely fast, it is a true tour de force for the solo flute. In fact, the *Badinerie* is often played by itself as an encore at concerts. The key to the flute's solo is great passagework; in essence, for every note the strings have to play, the flute has to play two. Since the movement is virtually nonstop, it is interesting to try to notice when the flutist has time to take breaths. The initial phrase sets the pace as the flute has to attack this difficult passage work. The pace is constant and relentless even when the mood shifts slightly (0:28). Be sure to focus on the flute and note the exciting cross-play that occurs between the flute and the first violins (0:39). One final rush through the melody (1:01) races us toward the suite's thrilling conclusion.

JAMES GALWAY:

"The greatest challenge is to make the flute the solo instrument and a member of the ensemble in the course of the same piece."

COMPARATIVE RECORDINGS

GALWAY/FAERBER/WÜRTTEMBERG CHAMBER
    ORCHESTRA
RCA VICTOR RED SEAL 60900   TOTAL TIME: 20:46

A stunning recording that puts the flute front and center where it should be. Galway's agility in the fast passages combined with his warm tone in the slower ones makes this a first-rate recording. He receives excellent support from the fine chamber orchestra.

MÜNCHINGER/STUTTGART CHAMBER ORCHESTRA
LONDON 430 266   TOTAL TIME: 19:59

A precise recording that blends the best elements of modern instrument performances with much of the baroque style needed to make the piece sound good.

PARROTT/BOSTON EARLY MUSIC FESTIVAL
    ORCHESTRA
EMI CLASSICS 54653   TOTAL TIME: 23:10

This recording using instruments of the period is absolutely thrilling. It avoids the pitfalls of thin sound and bad intonation, so often a part of period instrument recordings. The sound is excellent and the interpretation keeps every movement interesting and exciting.

IF YOU ENJOYED THIS PIECE . . .

The three other orchestra suites by Bach are equally great pieces and are good companions to this one. Additionally, the **Magnificat** is a perfect introduction to the wealth of choral music Bach composed. Finally, for more intimate fare, try the delicate **Sonatas for Flute and Harpsichord.**

BARBER

ADAGIO FOR STRING ORCHESTRA

While the American composer Samuel Barber (1910–81) may have written greater or more significant works, no single composition of his has gained the fame or popularity of the Adagio for String Orchestra. Originally the Adagio was part of Barber's String Quartet in B Minor, which was written in 1936, the same year that Margaret Mitchell completed her epic novel *Gone with the Wind* and *Life* magazine began publishing. In 1937, Barber expanded the Adagio by arranging it for string orchestra, creating a short concert work that could stand alone without the other movements of the quartet. The string orchestra version was premiered by Arturo Toscanini and his NBC Symphony Orchestra on November 5, 1938.

Possibly due to its American source and its solemn, sorrowful serenity, the Adagio was broadcast on national radio after the announcement of President Roosevelt's death. It has been played at many memorial concerts for other world-renowned figures, including at the concert in observance of Barber's own death. It was also used extremely effectively at the very end of the Anthony Hopkins movie *Elephant Man* and became the repeated theme in the Vietnam War movie *Platoon*.

REFERENCE RECORDING:
DEUTSCHE GRAMMOPHON 431 048
BERNSTEIN/LOS ANGELES PHILHARMONIC
TOTAL TIME: 10:02

With its quiet, sustained opening notes the mood of the Adagio is set within the first ten seconds. Initially the sad melody is played by the violins while the cellos and basses supply a heavy bottom of sustained notes. The phrases are long and drawn out, and there is no doubt that this is a melancholy, yet peaceful work.

This exposition continues for almost two minutes. Then the different sections of the orchestra start to change roles, and with this shift the intensity of the piece grows. It is as if one is striving against all odds to climb a mountain, and with every two steps up you slip back one. This slow climb continues as the music grows in intensity until it reaches a searing climax (7:10). The climax is followed by a brief silence; the struggle to reach the pinnacle is now replaced by the calm and quiet of an exhausted trip down the mountain. The music returns to its solemn, peaceful beginning theme. The Adagio ends with sustained chords that are held until they fade away into silence.

PRINCIPAL CELLO OF THE NEW YORK PHILHARMONIC, LORNE MUNROE:

"Even if you are not familiar with Barber's Adagio, you will know that you have heard a good performance when the music moves you. A good performance of this piece is like a religious experience for the musicians as well as the audience.

"It is music like the Adagio that makes Barber one of my favorite composers. As a student of his I admired his intensity and intellect. He was a terrific inspiration."

COMPARATIVE RECORDINGS

BERNSTEIN/LOS ANGELES PHILHARMONIC
DEUTSCHE GRAMMOPHON 431 048   TOTAL TIME: 10:02

This is possibly the slowest performance on disc. Bernstein milks the work for everything it's got and it works. The playing is sensitive and the sustained phrases come through well.

LEVI/ATLANTA SYMPHONY ORCHESTRA
TELARC CD-80250   TOTAL TIME: 8:12

Not nearly as passionate, yet more pastoral with wonderful recorded sound.

SLATKIN/ST. LOUIS SYMPHONY
EMI CLASSICS 49463   TOTAL TIME: 8:56

Leonard Slatkin is one of the finest interpreters of American music, and he has trained the musicians of the St. Louis Symphony to play this music with a style that is constantly appropriate. An absolutely first-rate reading, filled with pathos but not sappy.

IF YOU ENJOYED THIS PIECE. . .

The Adagio certainly does stand on its own as an orchestral piece. However, it is equally beautiful and moving when listened to as one of the movements of the **String Quartet.** Another work by Barber that will move you is the ballet suite for voice and orchestra known as **Knoxville: Summer of 1915.** Further, there is another Adagio composed by Albinoni more than two centuries before Barber's that captures much of the same mood.

BARTÓK

CONCERTO FOR ORCHESTRA

When Béla Bartók (1881–1945) received the commission to compose a Concerto for Orchestra during the summer of 1943, he worried his greatest compositions were already behind him. It is ironic that this work, composed so late in his life, would be the one that would secure Bartók's place among music's greats. The Hungarian-born Bartók wrote this while living in the United States, a self-exiled refugee from Nazi-occupied Hungary.

It is impossible to listen to the Concerto for Orchestra and not think of the world in which it was composed. On the European continent, 1943 was the year of Hitler's "scorched-earth policy" and of the Warsaw-ghetto uprising. In the United States, where rationing was begun, the year saw *Casablanca* win the Academy Award, Rodgers and Hammerstein's *Oklahoma!* open on Broadway, Aaron Copland compose the *Lincoln Portrait*, and William Saroyan write *The Human Comedy*, all while the jitterbug became a national craze.

Though clearly a composition of the twentieth century and therefore often thought of as difficult to listen to, the Concerto for Orchestra is actually a dynamic work that shows off the virtuosity of the modern symphony orchestra. It is a demanding piece to perform, filled with exposed solos all taken by members of the orchestra. However, it also requires the orchestra to play some very fast passages as a unit, staying together through the tricky rhythmic patterns Bartók used.

The Concerto for Orchestra received its premiere on December 1, 1944, at Carnegie Hall, with Serge Koussevitzky, who commissioned the work, conducting the Boston Symphony Orchestra. The piece is scored for three flutes, piccolo, three oboes, English horn, three bassoons, bass bassoon, four horns, three trumpets, two tenor trombones, a bass trombone, a tuba, timpani, a snare drum, a bass drum, tam-tam, cymbals, a triangle, two harps, and strings.

REFERENCE RECORDING:
RCA LIVING STEREO 61504
REINER/CHICAGO SYMPHONY ORCHESTRA
TOTAL TIME: 37:15

FIRST MOVEMENT: Introduzione: Andante non troppo; Allegro vivace   (9:55)

At the outset only the cellos and double basses play, quietly rumbling through a slow, lugubrious sequence of sustained notes. The violins enter tremulously (0:20), contrasting with the lower strings, creating a mystery-filled sound. The flutes sneak in and all alone finish the phrase, leaving it hanging, incomplete. The lower strings start again and this pattern is repeated.

The first extended solo in this concerto belongs to the flute (1:42), hesitantly unveiling a melody, supported by the sustained lower strings and the tremulous violins. The lower strings and the timpani (2:00) take over, now faster, but still lugubrious. The addition of the trumpets (2:14), emerging from the murky sound, awakens everything. Strain dominates when the violins, oboes, and flutes pierce through (2:54), louder and definitely dissonant, filled with struggle and pain. As the intensity decreases, the speed steadily increases (3:31). There is a sudden stop (3:48), and then the violins launch into the faster Allegro vivace section.

The violins carry the melody supported by a series of one-note pulses played by the other instruments, the strain, though lessened, still evident. There is a shift in melody (4:04); it is now less angular and more flowing, yet still sounds uncomfortable and unresolved. The trombone has a brief solo (4:36), popping out of the busy-ness of the violins, then handing the melody to the flute, which continues the phrase until the music slows to a stop.

The next section is tranquil: the violins and cellos set a rhythmic pulse as a base for a haunting oboe solo; occasional notes from the harp add an exotic tinge. When the clarinets assume the oboe's line (5:12), the exotic becomes distinctly bohemian; the melody then becomes cheerful as the flutes play their variation of it (5:28). The lower strings end this section by rumbling calmly. It is a false calm, because the moment they stop, there is an eruption (6:05) led by the violins and trumpets, fast and wicked, filled with nasty sneers and snarls. Then, just as the strain seems about to burst out, there is another sudden halt.

The clarinet fills the void (6:36), its meandering solo accompanied by the strings. The English horn, sounding somewhat ducklike (6:52), takes the solo line and creates a calm, pastoral image. It is short-lived, as the lower strings launch another furious attack (7:16) leading to the trumpets and trombones blasting angrily at each other. The pace is relentless; eventually the strings join and there is an explosive cymbal crash (8:04) preceding a quieting down as the strings reestablish an unsteady pulse, and the clarinet returns for another bohemian-sounding solo (8:12). The melody is taken over by the flutes and oboe, remaining sinewy and calm.

The lower voices start to rumble (9:09), shattering the peace and slowly rebuilding the strain and anger that filled the earlier sections. As it builds, it seems to become uncontrolled, leading to a blasting climax (9:43) played by the horns, trumpets, and trombones. One final snipe from the whole orchestra abruptly ends the movement.

SECOND MOVEMENT: Giuoco delle coppie: Allegretto scherzando   (5:58)

The most interesting element of this movement is the way Bartók pairs the solo instruments: each solo is played by two of the instruments at a time. In other words, two bassoons are together and so on; a sort of "Noah's ark" of the orchestra.

The snare drum begins alone, establishing an uneven rhythm as the two bassoons, accompanied by pizzicatos, play a jaunty, yet quirky melody. While the overall tone is calm, an unmistakable uneasiness permeates, as if waiting for a struggle to erupt. Next, two oboes (0:33) are the soloists while the strings provide occasional sniping comments; the pace quickens, growing slightly more animated and anxious.

The clarinets are next (0:58), more strident and seeming to be laughing nastily. As they complete their solo, the lower strings respond with steadily paced, angry retorts, until the flutes interrupt (1:19) with a more carefree, airy pass at the solo melody. The trumpets' turn is next (1:59), their solo eerie and macabre, verging on the bizarre, played quietly and somewhat off in the distance. At the end of this section, the strings join the trumpets for a jazzy, more harmonious few moments concluding with a series of repeated beats from the snare drum.

Rich harmony is the hallmark of the next solos (2:44), as the trombones, trumpets, and tuba team up joined by the snare drum, whose occasional beats lend a militaristic sound. The four horns take over (3:20) joined by the tuba. As their sustained notes fade away, the oboe and flute toss in a series of three-note comments, quietly leading to a brief pause and a return to the bassoons' solo from the movement's beginning (3:46). Now, however, the third bassoon adds a contrasting line making everything less stable. A little more agitation appears when the clarinets and oboes all play together (4:06), with sporadic comments from the strings. When the flutes replace the oboes and join the clarinets (4:29), the pace slows slightly, the music reminiscent of clowns' laughing in the circus, with an audible sneer.

Gossamerlike trills in the violins accompany the trumpets' solo (5:09), distant and haunted. But as the trumpets move to the foreground, the tone becomes more resolved and harmonious. The flutes, oboes, clarinets, bassoons, and horns join for one final sustained chord, and the movement ends with the lone snare drum tapping out its rhythm as it did at the outset.

THIRD MOVEMENT: Elegia: Andante non troppo   (7:54)

Again there is a creepy, slow beginning, this time played by the timpani and basses, introducing the harp and the other strings. After this heavy opening, the clarinet's serious yet flighty solo (0:35), copied by the flute, stands out. The thick layers of sound provided by the strings contrast with the little phrases in the winds to yield an exotic, sexy sound. It conjures up images of smoke-filled rooms, alluring dancers, and mystery.

The clarinet and oboe pierce the haze (1:10) with sharp, sustained notes, before the piccolo emerges with the solo (1:46) standing out above the strings. The quiet is shattered (2:07) as the strings busily strain, while the brass blasts through. The struggle in the strings intensifies (2:52), now filled with pleading and anguish.

A dissonant, distant chord played by the four horns (3:27) returns the mystery, and the violas and harps (3:57) unsettle everything still more, brewing greater difficulty and discomfort. But the flutes, oboes, clarinets, and bassoon valiantly try to establish some harmony (4:35), an uplifting series of harp glisses and chords from the brass helping. This cannot be sustained, and the English horn, clarinets, and bassoons (5:05) lead to another strained outburst from the upper strings.

Trumpet and horn blasts, fierce timpani beats, and biting violins (5:34) push the strain to its greatest point yet, violent, bordering on the ugly, before subsiding and stopping. Now (6:01), the violas, cellos, and double basses return and reprise the movement's opening. However, after hearing all the preceding dissonance, this section sounds downright melodic, especially when the clarinet and flute whisper their flighty phrases. The tremors are still there, just temporarily dormant. But surprisingly, the violins, oboes, and clarinets play a calm section (6:42), the strain and struggle seemingly resolved, until the lower strings and timpani angrily rumble again (7:12). A distant, lonely horn adds its voice, as the piccolo, now accompanied only by the quiet timpani, meekly ends the movement.

FOURTH MOVEMENT: Intermezzo interroto: Allegretto   (4:13)

Angry strings cut through the silence, their sound ugly and nasty, but brief, as they pause to let a single oboe play its comparatively cheerful, dancelike melody. The flute, clarinet, and bassoon (0:16) take over this intoxicating melodic line, supported primarily by sustained notes in the strings. The flute and harp (0:26) vary the melody, making it sound even more perky, and when the horn takes over (0:36), the mood turns romantic. The oboe reestablishes itself (0:46), this time countered by the flute playing a more sustained line as a contrast to the original melody's somewhat jerky nature.

The next melody is rich, harmonious, and romantic. The violas lead (1:01), but it is the harp that makes this a truly lush-sounding section, becoming even fuller when the violins take the melody (1:18). The mood is broken by the English horn (1:35), playing a short solo that seems almost out of place, like a duck wandering into a romantic setting! This leads to the oboe and flute taking over again, but now their solos sound strange and disjointed.

The strings emerge to reestablish some direction (2:04) as they launch into a happy, bouncy pattern introducing a jaunty clarinet solo, interrupted by angry snipes from the brass. Humorous blats from the tuba and trombone (2:21) start the orchestra again on a cheerful, laughing path, still with an uncomfortable undercurrent. Total calm replaces the jollity (2:55) as the violins quietly reprise the romantic melody. But this, too, disintegrates into a series of scattered oboe, flute, and clarinet notes as the English horn bravely tries to establish the melody (3:25), eventually turning it over to the flute. Ultimately the energy disappears, as the oboe, followed by the bassoon and then by the piccolo, each play one last phrase. Exhausted, the movement ends with three notes played by the oboes and bassoons.

FIFTH MOVEMENT: Finale: Pesante; Presto (8:58)

Four horns announce the final movement sustaining their final note. Then the violas and cellos begin a rapid rumble (0:08), and the second violins begin to scurry, kept in check only by sustained notes in the horns and steadying timpani beats. During this brisk section, as the first violins join the second violins, the wind instruments occasionally stir, adding punctuation to this flight. The volume increases steadily and leads to a respite where the scurrying stops (0:38) just long enough to catch one's breath. Then the oboes and bassoons establish a new, equally fast pulse (0:43), and the strings again scurry about. There is a joyful freedom to this frantic activity, and it all explodes exuberantly (1:01). But trouble is not far off as the trombones and tuba interrupt the strings' flight with ugly burps of sound (1:11), and an angry series of exchanges begins.

Some calm is restored when the flute, triangle, and harp play a delightful, flowing passage (1:19), leading to another series of fast passages. The difficulty here for the performers is keeping everything together through this musical minefield of entrances, solos, and ensemble sections, all played at breakneck speed. Out of all this intensity the second bassoon suddenly emerges (2:02) playing another quirky melody, soon joined by the first bassoon, and the other wind instruments. The pace slows, and the mood becomes calm as the flute plays a dreamy passage (2:19) echoed by the bassoons.

The oboes and clarinets accelerate the pace (2:44) and launch into a charming peasant dance. When the strings join, the frenetic quality returns as the pace quickens. In the midst of all of this, try to listen for the trumpet heralding this carefree section, and as the other brass instruments are added, the sound grows in celebration. But the joy is interrupted by a piercing alarm (3:31) indicating trouble is once again on the horizon, and a rumbling timpani roll confirms this. Calm does take over, however, and we are confronted with the violins and harps joining for what sounds like a musical visit to the Orient. Then the strings break into a comedic fugue, seemingly laughing at each other.

The next section is disjointed, as if unable to determine which way to go. Throughout, the sections of the orchestra toss in their comments, each in its place, yet sounding somewhat random. A distinct timpani beat (5:38) launches the strings into another furious, fast flight, and the whole orchestra picks up this pace, becoming absolutely wild, eventually winding down to a tranquil, sexy section featuring the violins (6:31).

When the haunting, sustained notes in the wind instruments fade away (7:09), another rumble begins to brew, even faster than before. Trouble is clearly returning, and the distant trumpets only heighten the feeling of impending doom. Building steadily, the explosion ultimately comes from the brass instruments (8:00), while the strings forcefully play in unison. When the brass instruments stop (8:16), the strings launch into a frenzy, faster than ever. A single cymbal crash amid the confusion (8:43) cues a series of unison trumpet and horn blasts, and a final, ferocious climax using the entire orchestra.

MAESTRO ADAM FISCHER:

"Bartók's Concerto for Orchestra has a strong claim to be considered the most popular symphonic orchestral score of the twentieth century; it is full of brilliantly colorful sounds and memorable tunes permeated with the strong tug of the composer's nostalgia for his native Hungary. Some of the movements are haunted by the shadows of folk songs, but the final impression is of life-affirming exhilaration. It is so sad to think that Bartók died of leukemia within two years of the work's composition. My players in the Hungarian State Symphony Orchestra responded instinctively to the Hungarian dimension of the score and brought out all the distinctive nuances of Bartók's idiom in an authentic way."

COMPARATIVE RECORDINGS

REINER/CHICAGO SYMPHONY ORCHESTRA
RCA LIVING STEREO 61504   TOTAL TIME: 37:15

Fritz Reiner was one of Bartók's champions in the United States, and his recording from 1955 of this masterpiece is one of the greatest ever made. The Chicago Symphony is a well-tuned machine, and they meet every one of the work's demands.

FISCHER/HUNGARIAN STATE SYMPHONY ORCHESTRA
NIMBUS NI 5229   TOTAL TIME: 42:02

This recording from 1989 has the sonic advantages of digital technology, and therefore each instrument comes through fabulously. Further, the Hungarian musicians play Bartók's music with tremendous feeling and passion.

VON DOHNÁNYI/CLEVELAND ORCHESTRA
LONDON 425 694   TOTAL TIME: 37:42

A stunning 1990 recording in which Dohnányi gets to show off the virtuosic instrument that is the Cleveland Orchestra. The interpretation is excellent and is equaled by the sound.

IF YOU ENJOYED THIS PIECE. . .

While certainly a unique composition, the angular sound of Bartók found in the Concerto for Orchestra can also be heard in his **First Violin Concerto,** the **Piano Concertos,** or his demanding **String Quartets.**

BEETHOVEN

TRIO FOR PIANO, VIOLIN, AND CELLO
IN B-FLAT MAJOR, OP. 97
ARCHDUKE

Beginning in 1809, Ludwig van Beethoven (1770–1826) was the favorite composer of Austria's Archduke Rudolph (1788–1831) and benefited from his generous patronage. Living in Vienna, the archduke studied piano with Beethoven, and the composer dedicated fifteen compositions to him, among them the Trio for Piano, Violin, and Cello in B-flat Major, Op. 97, an absolute gem of the chamber-music repertoire filled with delicate passages, noble melodies, and even some humor.

Composed between March 3 and March 26, 1811, the Trio was Beethoven's only major work of that year, a year of turmoil as the Napoleonic struggles continued. Austria was forced to declare bankruptcy; in England, King George III was declared insane and was forced to relinquish the throne. In the creative world Jane Austen published *Sense and Sensibility*, and Franz Liszt, a pianist/composer who would later transcribe Beethoven's symphonies for solo piano, was born. The *Archduke* Trio was Beethoven's last complete composition for this combination of instruments, and he performed the work several times in the years immediately following its creation.

There is a nobility to the Trio—each movement captures the elegance of the Austrian royal court. (After all, the archduke's brother was the Emperor Franz.) As you listen to the piece, try to visualize the splendor and grandeur of the Austrian capital, especially of the royal palaces, and note how it translates into Beethoven's melodies, especially the fantastic piano part. Further, it is interesting to observe how each of the three instruments has an individual character yet simultaneously plays a distinct role as a member of the ensemble. Finally, be sure to appreciate how Beethoven was able to vary the nature of each movement: noble and powerful one moment, charming and tender the next, all while using only three instruments.

REFERENCE RECORDING:
SONY SM4K 46738
ISTOMIN/STERN/ROSE TRIO
TOTAL TIME: 40:32

FIRST MOVEMENT: Allegro moderato   (13:42)

The piano introduces the stately melody, elegantly unveiling the steady, flowing phrase until interrupted by the violin and cello (0:12) and their brief, cadenzalike interjections. The violin reestablishes the melodic line (0:29) with the other instruments accompanying; listen especially for the contrast the cello provides. The regal quality is suddenly tinged with mystery (0:44) as the piano quietly echoes the violin. But a swell of sound returns the original mood, leading to a tender section (1:01) begun by the piano followed immediately by the first more powerful sounds (1:11) as the cello and violin play forceful, sustained notes against a bold piano romp over the keys.

Delicately, the piano begins a new melody (1:51) filled with grace, the theme copied by the strings weaving around each other building to a unison outburst (2:41) that suddenly retreats. With just a wisp of sound the violin and cello gradually rebuild the power (3:01) accompanied by steady beats from the piano, followed by a series of almost raucous, fun-filled passages leading to a repeat of the movement to this point (3:31).

The piano leads out of the repeat (6:57), its bouncy phrases mimicked by the strings; something new is developing, and while the piano continues its jagged background, the cello and violin soar over it with tender reminiscences of the original melody (7:18). As the piano continues to quietly meander, the cello nobly restarts the original theme (8:14), then leaves it in midphrase as the violin takes over and completes it (8:24). But this development is cut short, replaced by the piano softly chopping the phrase into a series of two-note sections (8:34); mystery abounds heightened by the cello and violin plucking the melody out on their strings (8:39). Initially this part sounds like music to accompany someone stealthily creeping around, trying to go unnoticed. But this extended pizzicato section grows confident, even forceful before stopping (9:41) as the piano asserts its power and takes over. A trill (9:49) brings the strings back briefly; the movement seems to be trying to "refind" itself, evolving into a recapitulation of the noble opening theme played by the piano with sustained support from the strings (10:12). Much of this section revisits the earlier part of the movement; note especially the soulful rendition of the theme played by the cello (10:42).

A delicate duet for the piano and cello (11:54) is followed by the violin alternating flowing passages with the cello as the piano plays a steady background. As before, a wisp of sound starts the gradual reenergizing leading to a forceful outburst (12:38) overflowing with joy and exuberance. Then, suddenly, the energy wanes (12:51); but this is a ruse as the power instantly returns unveiling the movement's original theme now in its most noble, stately guise (13:00). Enjoying each other's company, the three partners set off jauntily for the movement's excited, unison conclusion.

SECOND MOVEMENT: Scherzo: Allegro (7:08)

This fairly fast-paced movement opens with a bouncy, delicate melody begun by the cello and immediately taken over by the violin. The piano assumes the theme (0:16), soon joined by the strings' resonant pizzicato accompaniment. A new elegant phrase that seems to be filled with contentment is unveiled initially by the piano (0:30) and then the violin (0:38) as the trio glides along rapidly.

The cello (1:20) gives the theme a sonorous warmth that evolves when the piano takes over (1:25) with romantic elegance. The volume begins to diminish (1:50), the tone growing more tentative; but this is nothing but a fake because the piano immediately rebuilds the strength leading to two abrupt chords (1:58).

Muddled and uncertain, the cello quietly opens a new section (2:07); as the piano imitates the cello, some dissonance is heightened even further by the addition of the violin (2:15). The instruments seem to be lying in wait, looking for the opportunity to pounce with something loud and definitive, an opportunity that arises with a forceful outburst (2:35) led by the piano's power brilliantly displayed. The musical quagmire returns (2:55) again led by the cello, joined quickly by the others; but this time the outburst occurs sooner (3:09). The next sections are a series of these muddled parts linking the dramatic outbursts, the final one leading to a reprise of the original theme played by the cello (4:33) and continued by the violin.

We are firmly returned to the elegance as the piano takes the theme (4:49) accompanied by the pizzicatos (4:57); the subdued joy is captured by the violin (5:11), then by all three instruments as the happiness overflows. With great tenderness the violin and cello join (6:08), calmly relaxing the mood before two chords (6:32) abruptly stop the gentle flow and bring back the murkiness, swelling and receding until, seemingly out of nowhere, the cello boldly steps forward to reannounce the first four notes of the original theme (6:57). The violin continues the phrase, handing it over to the piano before all join to complete the line and cheerily end the movement.

THIRD MOVEMENT: Andante cantabile, ma non però con moto   (12:25)

A pensive, expressive piano solo steadily unfurls, filled with dignity heightened when the violin and cello join (0:29). While the pace is slow, a singing quality carries the theme seamlessly from phrase to phrase; because of its calm nature, this is great music to clear one's head of troubling thoughts. A slightly busier part for the piano blends with a rich cello solo (1:58) played softly, like a whisper, a tone carried through as the violin teams with the cello (2:27).

The first departure from the total calm occurs when the cello breaks into a comparatively bouncy passage (3:37), copied by the violin, adding a lighthearted delicacy, like a cheerful exchange of comments. A brief digression into a lyrical, passionate cello line (4:22) is echoed by the violin then quickly reverts to the cheerful bounciness. The piano, as if made bold by the cello, further increases the pace, getting busier and busier (4:58), the happiness now mixed with nervous excitement. Within this section try to pick out the movement's original melody; it's there, only now hidden by the increased activity surrounding it.

Against a background of sustained string lines, the piano fills in the sonic voids with its sonorous chords (6:25); the pace is broader and the original pensiveness returns, the sound swelling and receding through each phrase. Eventually the piano plays what sounds like the movement's opening theme (8:34), but in midphrase the cello interrupts (8:40) filled with sadness but still elegant; the speed slows, halting, as it moves through the theme with caution. When it seems the movement has worn itself out and cannot go on, a sudden mild burst (9:38) reenergizes the trio leading to a gorgeous, dreamy section filled with romantic tenderness. Note how the piano serves as carrier of the theme *and* as accompanist, yielding some ravishing duets for violin with piano, and cello with piano. Once again, the pace slows, tired and sleepy; amid this total calm, the violin and cello hold one note, which gradually fades away. As the piano adds its voice, there is a distinct chord change (12:19) ending the third movement and launching us directly into the finale.

FOURTH MOVEMENT: Allegro moderato; Presto
(7:17)

The attack beginning the movement starts immediately with single beats from the violin and cello launching the piano on a joyful romp; this is a happy "wake-up" call snapping us out of the dreamy world of the third movement. After the exposition, during which the violin and cello served mainly as accents for the piano, they become more important, forcefully alternating with the keyboard (0:43). The piano continues the fast-paced filigree contrasted by a lyrical line played by the cello (1:03). But the piano wins out as the violin and cello mimic its jerky propulsive phrases (1:13), a bit of tension and mystery infiltrating the buoyant nature of the movement.

A recapitulation of the opening (1:31) brings back all the delicate humor and charm, slowly growing forceful and leading to a confident, dramatic outburst (2:18). But this power soon starts to corrupt, the cheerfulness tending toward anger (2:30) filled with strain. As it quiets (2:51), there is a sense of mystery, like the music for a creepy movie, trouble brewing until suddenly there is a musical "Uh-oh!" (3:09) as the cello pulls away from the piano bravely reestablishing the original theme. The violin joins (3:19) creating a beautiful harmony and an even more spirited rendition of the melody.

The piano is constantly busy, moving gracefully through its intricate passages, a fabulous contrast to the sustained, lyrical lines of the cello (4:17) and the violin (4:22). The brewing mystery returns (4:27), copying the earlier section with its power and anger, eventually fading away, as it slows, too tired to continue. Then, suddenly aroused, the piano trills excitedly as the violin and cello launch into a joyful, giddy, dancelike melody much faster than anything we have heard thus far; this is the beginning of the Presto (5:21).

The trilling piano coupled with the ebullient bouncing of the strings yields a melody that giggles uncontrollably until a relatively horrific outburst shatters the mood (5:43). But this is only a brief darkness that calms quickly, leaving the pianist to fly giddily over the keys accompanied by steady pulses played in unison by the strings. Another outburst (6:38), this one joyful, briefly breaks the continuous flowing line, eventually quieting and slowing down as if spent. The movement grinds to a calm stop (7:03). But don't be lulled because before the sound can fade away the piano restarts the flow, now even faster, and the three instruments romp happily together to the movement's exuberant conclusion.

PIANIST EUGENE ISTOMIN:

"*Among piano trios the Archduke is the Mount Everest, with several close runners-up including others by Beethoven himself. When I begin the first movement I have in my mind's eye a view of the harmonic world from on high. B-flat major asserts itself in that unique Beethovenian way that brooks no contention. The message is: 'The triad is good; man is good and must prevail.' It builds arches and girders as great over- and under-pinnings to resonate the variety and immensity of goodness. You may doubt everything else, but not Beethoven.*

"*There is also wit, both subtle and even slapstick, in the last movement. (Only in music can you have changes of mood from sublime to rowdy in an instant.) But, it is the majestic serenity of the slow movement whose overpowering beauty surpasses all in this incomparable masterpiece.*"

COMPARATIVE RECORDINGS

ISTOMIN/STERN/ROSE
SONY SM4K 46738   TOTAL TIME: 40:32

These three artists played together as a trio for decades, and the fruits of that collaboration are revealed in this extraordinary performance filled with life, fun, tenderness, and passion. Recorded in Switzerland in 1965, the sound is crystal clear and rich.

KEMPFF/SZERYNG/FOURNIER
DEUTSCHE GRAMMOPHON 415 879   TOTAL TIME: 45:19

Another excellent performance by three legendary artists of the Middle European school. The playing and interpretation are fine, only the sound lacks some clarity.

ASHKENAZY/PERLMAN/HARRELL
EMI CLASSICS 47010   TOTAL TIME: 37:12

Three first-rate soloists each brings his artistry and skill to this magnificent trio. Unlike the other recordings the blending of styles is not well ripened, but the technical skill of each musician is a wonder. The digital sound is by far the best of the three recordings.

ＩF YOU ENJOYED THIS PIECE. . .

First, listen to the **other Beethoven piano trios,** especially the **Ghost,** a beautiful underperformed work. Then try some of the **string quartets** from Beethoven's early period. If you like the sound of the piano trio, be sure to listen to the works of Beethoven's contemporaries Mozart, Haydn, and Schubert, each of whom gave the trio a slightly different sound. Finally, for a great listening experience try Beethoven's exquisite **Quintet for Piano and Winds, Op. 16.**

BEETHOVEN

*P*IANO CONCERTO NO. 5

IN E-FLAT MAJOR, OP. 73

EMPEROR

Ludwig van Beethoven (1770–1826) wrote five piano concertos, composing the last one in 1809 while firmly ensconced in Vienna, the musical capital of the era. There is no certainty as to who gave this concerto the name *Emperor*, but it was definitely not Beethoven, who had by this point in his life grown disenchanted with Napoleon in part because the conqueror had named himself emperor and had thus seemingly stopped representing the average man.

Given Beethoven's passionate championing of the common man, the irony of the name *Emperor* is evident. Nonetheless, there is an audible reason for the subtitle. Put simply, Beethoven's Fifth Piano Concerto contains some of the most regal music ever written. Every passage conveys an image of grand elegance conjuring up images of the Viennese royal court.

The year 1809 was fascinating, especially in the Austrian capital. In that year the French army led by Napoleon occupied

Vienna, and the newly crowned emperor annexed the Papal States. It is amazing, given the upheaval around him, that Beethoven was able to compose a work of the beauty and elegance of the *Emperor*. Far away from the Continent and its wars, Abraham Lincoln was born.

The Fifth Piano Concerto is scored for strings, two flutes, two oboes, two clarinets, two bassoons, two horns, two trumpets, and timpani. While listening to the concerto, try to identify what it is in this music that makes it seem so regal and elegant. Also, take note of how rarely the piano and full orchestra actually play together; instead they alternate melodic phrases.

The *Emperor* had its premiere at the Leipzig Gewandhaus on November 28, 1811.

REFERENCE RECORDING:
RCA 09026-61260
RUBINSTEIN/KRIPS/SYMPHONY OF THE AIR
TOTAL TIME: 38:32

FIRST MOVEMENT: Allegro   (20:14)

The opening of this concerto is unusual: a sustained chord is played by the entire orchestra followed immediately by a rhapsodic piano solo. Then a second chord and another piano solo, and a third chord followed by another piano solo, the piano solos serving as intricate bridges linking the chords together. Finally, the strings establish a melody (1:13) and are soon joined by the winds. The solo piano remains silent during this exposition. The music is extremely regal, yet not pompous and filled with tremendous energy.

The initial melody is replaced by a new, more mysterious-sounding section (2:09) featuring the clarinets and bassoons playing against the string instruments. But soon the horns and timpani join (2:24) and the regal quality returns. The orchestra plays alone through this section; except for the fact that the piano is sitting on the stage, at this point one would think this is a Beethoven symphony, and not a concerto.

Out of the excitement emerges a jerky three-note phrase, initially in the entire orchestra, but then only in the woodwinds and horns (4:10); this reintroduces the solo piano, beginning with a scale going up the keyboard (4:14). At the end of the scale there is a trill, and then finally the soloist gets to play the melody the orchestra has been playing for the last four minutes.

One of the beauties of this concerto is the way Beethoven uses the sections of the orchestra individually, so that stretches of music resemble intimate chamber music. A duet between the bassoon and the piano (5:14), soon joined by the flute and oboe, is a striking example of this. The next section (5:41) has the piano jousting with the strings in what feels like a precursor of jazz, a quality heightened by the off-the-beat piano solo and the accompanying plucked strings.

The calm is broken by a series of harsh, curt notes (6:18) in the orchestra; they are forceful, almost militaristic, yet the regal quality is still evident, but now in a more powerful guise. The piano returns (6:33) for an extended solo, aided by the orchestra sometimes playing short interjections and sometimes longer passages equal in importance to the solo piano. The piano is replaced by the full orchestra for a return of the initial melody (8:13), and a series of short notes in the winds (9:17) leads to the return of the piano solo. This time, however, instead of playing the melody, the piano part meanders, leading to a mysterious-sounding section (9:45) dominated by the clarinets and bassoons. This entire section is a great example of chamber music for piano and wind instruments. (Be sure to try to identify each solo woodwind phrase, especially the haunting one played by the oboe [10:02].) The addition of the strings (10:20) adds to a mounting tension leading to a somewhat angry explosion (10:40) with the piano and orchestra alternating outbursts.

Calm eventually returns (11:32), the strings playing sustained notes, while the piano plays a dreamy phrase echoed by the winds. When the piano moves into the very high range playing against the lower strings (12:10), the tension rebuilds. The rumbling lower strings are joined by the rest of the orchestra and a recapitulation of the movement's opening, with the orchestra playing chords while the piano provides the bridges (12:34). As in the beginning, the orchestra takes the melody first (13:17), but the piano joins in sooner and there is more chamber-music-style playing. (Be sure to listen for the brief horn and piano duet [13:57].)

During the latter portion of this movement, much of what is heard is a copy of earlier sections and will sound familiar, including another pass at the jazzy section (14:23). This recap leads to the orchestra taking the melody once more (16:55), this time broken up by occasional bridges from the piano. This leads to the cadenza (17:26), a brief piano solo in many ways a microcosm of the whole movement. While the piano is still in the midst of its cadenza, it is joined by the horns and pizzicato strings (18:10), and the regal quality shines through once again. From this peaceful section, there is one last repeat of the original melody (18:37), now with the piano alternating with the orchestra, a final reminder of the energy and regal bearing that have dominated the movement.

SECOND MOVEMENT: Adagio un poco mosso
(8:26)

The hallmark of this movement is calm, romantic elegance. From the opening phrase, played by the muted strings accompanied by the pizzicato bass, one gets the image of a leisurely stroll. The piano's entrance (1:34) heightens the mood, its phrases played against the sustained notes in the strings. The piano's second solo phrase (2:50) is juxtaposed with sustained notes in the oboes and horn; it is even dreamier than the first.

A new solo phrase (4:22) in the piano is now positioned against plucked notes in all the string instruments, with occasional entrances by the woodwinds adding color; but the focus remains on the piano. Eventually the melody is taken by the flute, clarinet, and bassoon (5:51), while the piano provides an accompaniment resembling fine, detailed filigree. The strings' sole function during this part is to provide the steady pulse. Over time there is less and less intensity, until finally it winds down to only sustained notes in the bassoons and horns (7:50). But out of this total calm, the piano emerges with a new phrase, giving the impression the piano is trying to figure out what direction to take (8:05) as it layers one phrase on top of the other. Suddenly, there is a distinct attack, and we are in the third movement.

THIRD MOVEMENT: Rondo: Allegro   (9:47)

As indicated, there is no pause between the second and third movements. Rather, the noodling the piano seemed to be doing explodes into a fast, energetic romp, beginning joyfully with the piano solo accompanied only by sustained notes in the horns. Soon the orchestra picks up this melody (0:21), led by the winds and the first violins. A new piano solo (0:58) takes over, and the piano and orchestra alternate brief phrases.

A semblance of jazz again appears as the piano seems to be playing an improvisation against sustained notes in the violins and a pizzicato bass line (1:39). As in the first movement, the piano plays many intimate sections with only one other instru- ment in a form of chamber music. When the piano resumes the initial melody (2:06), the horns supply a distinguished-sounding accompaniment.

A bit of tension appears (4:40) as the piano plays against angry notes in the strings. This evolves into an almost mysterious passage (5:15) similar to the transition that led from the second to the third movement. Once again, we are left wondering how this is going to develop. But soon, the piano reprises its original theme and the orchestra takes it over, returning all the splendor and energy from the movement's initial phrases (5:50).

The next moments are recapitulations of the movement's development. When the piano again plays the movement's opening phrase (7:35), the orchestra answers immediately, a pat- tern repeated until the orchestra takes over completely (7:58), now more energized than ever. Out of this excitement emerges a brief bassoon solo (8:13) signaling the return of the solo piano. Then the piano and timpani team up (8:59) for a short duet, slowing down progressively, eventually coming to a split-second halt (9:29). The immediate reentrance of the solo piano, now completely reenergized, leads to the orchestra's reentrance (9:35), and together they play the final, excited moments of the concerto.

PIANIST MISHA DICHTER:

"In the more than thirty years that I have been playing Beethoven's Fifth Piano Concerto, I have continued to be struck by the extraordinary demands placed upon the pianist to produce a sense of loftiness in the performance of a work whose piano part is, with few exceptions, Mozartean in its linearity. Yes of course there are stretches of octave and double-note writing, and indeed the last movement does burst forth in gloriously chordal writing, but a simple overview of the score reveals how rare these passages are. And although we know that Emperor was a name Beethoven did not apply to the work, after so many years we are simply stuck with the label and play to ears expecting a 'grandiose and noble' sweep of sound. Our fingers must struggle to create this image with Mozartean filigree; this, to me, is the great challenge of the piece."

COMPARATIVE RECORDINGS

RUBINSTEIN/KRIPS/SYMPHONY OF THE AIR
RCA 09026-61260   TOTAL TIME: 38:32

While this is a monophonic recording, and the sound transfer to CD is not ideal, the elegance of the performance transcends the technical limitations. At once it is exciting, passionate, and supremely musical. Although Rubinstein recorded the *Emperor* again later in his career, this is the recording to hear.

ASHKENAZY/MEHTA/VIENNA PHILHARMONIC
LONDON 411903   TOTAL TIME: 39:49

One of the most elegant recordings of this concerto ever made. Ashkenazy's playing is matched breath for breath by the exquisite sound of the Vienna Philharmonic. The recorded sound is warm, allowing the instruments room to develop.

PERAHIA/HAITINK/CONCERTGEBOUW ORCHESTRA
    OF AMSTERDAM
CBS MASTERWORKS MK 42330   TOTAL TIME: 38:43

An exquisite recording featuring a first-rate pianist with an orchestra and conductor who accompany with silklike tone and style. Excellent sound makes this a recording to add to any collection.

*I*F YOU ENJOYED THIS PIECE. . .

The first thing to do is listen to the four great piano concertos that preceded this one. Then try the **Violin Concerto** and the **Concerto for Piano, Violin, and Cello.** Each is an exciting concerto requiring a great accompanying orchestra and first-rate soloists. If the Beethoven mastery of the piano is what appeals to you, listen to the **Moonlight Sonata** and any of the other piano sonatas.

BEETHOVEN

$\int$ YMPHONY NO. 5

IN C MINOR, OP. 67

It is possible that the four most well-known notes in all of classical music are those that begin Ludwig van Beethoven's (1770–1826) Fifth Symphony. The phrase, three short notes followed by one long note, is almost a cliché. Yet when it is heard, whether for the first time or the one-hundredth, it is riveting and powerful. One of the amazing things about the Fifth is that the drama with which it begins is sustained throughout the piece's roughly thirty-minute duration. The trick is to listen to the rest of the symphony without being overwhelmed by its opening.

Beethoven probably began working on this symphony sometime in 1803, shortly after completing the *Eroica* Symphony, and finished it at the end of 1807 or early in 1808. The Fifth premiered on December 22, 1808, in a concert pairing it with the next symphony in the cycle, the Sixth (*Pastoral*). Europe in 1808 was dominated by Napoleonic issues; Napoleon captured Madrid; Goethe met Napoleon and completed the first part of his drama *Faust*, while Goya painted the *Execution of the Citizens of Madrid*. Beethoven, upon completing the Third Symphony, destroyed its title page, changing the symphony's name from the *Napoleon* to the *Eroica* as a protest against Napoleon's naming himself emperor. It is important to keep this in mind as one listens to the rage that is so prevalent in the Fifth Symphony.

The strength and power that Beethoven packs into the Fifth Symphony is delivered to the listener by a relatively small orchestra made up of strings, flutes, oboes, clarinets, bassoons, horns, trumpets, and timpani. (In the fourth movement a piccolo, a contrabassoon, and three trombones are added.) It is the use of this compact ensemble that gives us a particularly good opportunity to listen for the inner voices and how they add to the sound. But most of all, be certain to keep the opening four-note pattern in mind, three shorts and a long, because it will reappear in various guises throughout the symphony.

REFERENCE RECORDING:
TELDEC 9031-77313
MASUR/NEW YORK PHILHARMONIC
TOTAL TIME: 36:22

FIRST MOVEMENT: Allegro con brio   (7:29)

It has been likened to fate knocking at Beethoven's door or the first musical salvo of the Romantic Revolution. Whatever it might be, the opening of Beethoven's Fifth Symphony is visceral and powerful. The incredible musical intensity of three short notes followed by one long note is initially created by just the strings and a clarinet. While you might expect to hear trumpets, horns, or the timpani, this fabulous opening is made more incredible by its sparse instrumentation.

The movement seems to have trouble getting going. The first loud attacks are followed by the strings furtively passing the melody around—quietly at first but eventually getting louder. There is a pause, and then another ferocious attack as in the beginning (0:19), only now the strings are joined by the flutes, oboes, clarinets, bassoons, and horns. As before, the melody gets passed around, mysteriously building with the addition of the timpani until there is another stop (0:45). The horns break the brief silence with a noble version of the four-note theme, which introduces a delightful, calm melody played by the violins and echoed by the clarinet and then the flute. As this calm develops, the violas, cellos, and basses sneak the four-note theme into the background, slowly increasing the tension until it overpowers the calm and leads to an excited outburst by the violins supported by the woodwinds. The next section is propulsive and leads to a series of four-note phrases that end abruptly (1:28). At this point the entire first part of the movement is repeated.

After the repeat (2:54) the horns and clarinets in unison blast the four-note phrase one more time before the strings take it over accompanied by the clarinets and bassoons. The theme is passed among the instruments rapidly: the winds, second violins, violas, and cellos take the short notes (3:15) while the first violins play a sustained chord. Here, for just a few seconds, one feels as if the movement may free itself and begin to soar, but the sustained line disappears as the four-note phrase again dominates and the tension and drama rebuild. Where before there was fierce power, now we are confronted with intense anger (3:25) as the whole orchestra unites.

The winds begin a calming with a two-note phrase (3:42) that is tossed back and forth between the winds and the strings. This gradually diminishes the intensity and creates an exhausted peace that is shattered (4:05) by an attempt to return to the four-note theme. But, as if panting for breath, the labored exchange between winds and strings returns. Power wins out (4:13) with an absolute eruption that returns to the movement's opening phrase intensified by the addition of the timpani. As earlier, mystery replaces the power, only now when the pause is reached (4:25), there is a plaintive, slow oboe solo.

Not to be deterred, the strings return to the four-note phrase (4:51) and steadily rebuild the intensity. When the second pause is reached (5:13), the bassoons, with a somewhat hollow sound, restart the four-note phrase and introduce a return of the lyrical calm melody. But, as before, the four-note theme begins to creep into the mix and the power comes back with a jubilant explosion spearheaded by the trumpets (5:41). This propulsive section feels as if it could be ridden endlessly like a powerful wave, but suddenly the brakes are applied (6:06) and everything stops. The clarinets, bassoons, and horns meekly interject a four-note phrase, only to be snarled at by the full orchestra reprising the propulsion that was interrupted.

These last few moments have been jerky, filled with stops and starts. Suddenly, as if no longer able to remain earthbound, the violins launch into a flying series of phrases, supported by a steady pulse in the winds and contrasted by a series of four-note phrases in the violas and cellos (6:14). This section has a distinctly tortured quality, as if the struggle has been too great a burden, a feeling heightened by a series of exchanges between the strings and winds (6:39). This seemingly benign exchange leads to a ferocious drive that culminates with a powerful reprise of the movement's opening pair of four-note phrases (7:03).

An eerie quiet takes over (7:11). The violins play the four-note theme as the bassoon, clarinet, and oboe each add a more lyric line. But this calm is nothing more than a ruse as there is a final explosion (7:16) with the whole orchestra blaring the four-note phrase. They play in unison until the movement's end.

SECOND MOVEMENT: Andante con moto (9:59)

A gracious melody played by the violas and cellos with elegant pizzicatos from the basses starts out the second movement. Its steady, stroll-like pace and lyrical melodic line are a sharp contrast to the power and jerky nature of the opening movement. The woodwinds interject a response to the opening phrase (0:26) that is copied by the strings. When the clarinets and bassoons take over (0:56), the rich sound increases the elegance. At this point try to listen for the interesting accompaniment played by the violas.

The stately theme is tinged with mystery, but quickly becomes jubilant and turns triumphant as the horns and trumpets joyously take the lead (1:19). The energy wanes and is replaced by unsettled mystery (1:36). Emerging from this musical fog, the violas and cellos dominate (2:04) with a graceful flowing phrase. The clarinets and bassoons (2:55), again with a great accompaniment from the violas, take the theme, blending richness with grace. After a short return to the mystery, the horns, trumpets, and timpani break out jubilantly (3:17) as if announcing something of great importance. Once their announcement is complete, we are again confronted with the quiet and mystery.

The violas and cellos emerge with a recapitulation of the flowing, stately melody (4:02) with the flute, oboe, and bassoon sustaining notes that provide a nice contrast. The violins assume the flowing line next (4:20) while the bassoon and clarinet alternate quirky two-note comments. The cellos and basses next take over the flowing line (4:39) while the rest of the orchestra aggressively articulates a loud, steady pulse. But everything is stopped (5:03) virtually in midphrase and slowly restarts, almost like a train beginning to chug out of the station. A peaceful, melodic section is played by the flutes, oboes, and clarinets (5:27), serving as a bridge to the horns determinedly reenergizing the movement (5:58) with six strong repeated notes just before the whole orchestra joins in a burst of jubilance.

The strings are left alone (6:33) insecurely fitting bits and pieces of the melody together like parts of a puzzle. Into this, the flutes, oboes, and clarinets weave the melody (6:50). It seems that the energy is gone, but a series of short phrases rebuilds the power and leads to the strongest explosion of the entire movement (7:29). Yet this one is not totally jubilant, but rather tinged with a distinct element of strain.

After another pullback, the bassoon has a jaunty solo (8:17) during which the pace picks up slightly. A brief recharge is followed by another slowdown and a calm solo for the woodwinds (8:41). It seems that the movement is winding down and is going to end completely out of energy, but one more resurgence (9:29) leads to the movement's final two, forceful unison chords.

THIRD MOVEMENT: Allegro   (8:19)

The cellos and basses growl out the opening phrase, filled with mystery; it sounds like music written to conjure up the image of someone sneaking around. The strings dominate this quiet introduction and give no indication of the explosion that is about to come. The shroud is lifted when the horns blast out with three short notes followed by one long (0:21), a familiar pattern that the rest of the orchestra quickly adopts. The movement's creepy opening returns (0:40), leading directly this time to the whole orchestra triumphantly announcing the four-note theme.

Everything stops (1:48); the cellos and basses start a forceful, fast fugue that is joined in sequence by the violas and bassoons, then the second violins, and finally the first violins. With the addition of each instrument, the sound grows. This section is then repeated. At the repeat's conclusion (2:20), the cellos and basses restart the fugue, which grows ebullient. Following another stop, it is the cellos and basses that again start (2:48) the fugue, which grows almost uncontrollably and then pulls back to return to the dark mystery of the movement's opening (3:18) and a repeat of what we have heard thus far.

Following the repeat (6:19) the cellos and basses are again left to play their murky opening theme. This time, however, the bassoon takes over, joined only by the cellos playing pizzicato. This wonderful solo seems to creep around; clearly something is brewing, and something satanic is mixed in the music throughout this section. When the timpani beats out its steady rhythmic figure against sustained notes in the first violins, violas, and cellos, the mystery is at its greatest level (7:35). Like water in a cauldron slowly coming to a boil, the intensity starts to rise as the violins weave in and out of the pattern. Suddenly there is a dramatic spurt of energy (8:14); the volume increases rapidly and goes right into a tremendous explosion that is the beginning of the final movement.

FOURTH MOVEMENT: Allegro   (10:35)

(Note: Some recordings may not have a track separation between the third and fourth movements.)

The excitement is overwhelming, as if all the pent-up energy has suddenly been released with the trumpets, horns, and trombones leading the surge. The horns, oboes, clarinets, and bassoons play a solo (0:36) that seems to soar above the rest of the orchestra. Occasionally the surge abates for brief moments (1:07), but with each pullback the energy quickly rebuilds, fast and confident.

As a contrast the clarinets, bassoons, and violas attack a phrase and then instantly retreat (1:34), seeming to sting the melody. But this is nothing more than a respite before another jubilant eruption (1:46) that speeds to a repeat returning us to the beginning of the movement (2:05).

Following the repeat (4:09) the fast pace continues, heightened by a continuous tremolo in the violins and violas. Thus far in the final movement the mood has been cheerful, but Beethoven wouldn't be Beethoven if there weren't some darkness, and soon anger creeps in (4:33). The trombones, calling out (4:41), cut through like foghorns valiantly trying to reestablish the joyful mood, but the ferocity prevails. (In the midst of all this fierce action, try to find a four-note pattern, three short and one slightly longer note, featured in the horns and trumpets [4:55].) The jubilance eventually wins out, replacing the darkness with triumph (5:06) in an outpouring of excitement that seems as if it will never end.

The energy suddenly wanes (5:38) leaving the violins alone; they start to creep again, returning to the mysterious mood heard earlier. Again note that the pattern the violins evolve ends up being four notes, although these are all even in length. Listen also for the plaintive, sustained note played by the oboe. Gradually the other instruments add their voices and the power rebuilds to a new explosion (6:18) of unbridled joy as in the movement's beginning. Throughout this next section, much of what is heard is a recapitulation of the movement's earlier part.

Listen especially for the increases in power followed by retreats, although the general feeling will always be of forward propulsion.

A series of individual forceful chords (8:41) are little more than powerful accents or punctuation that serve to reduce the volume. From this the bassoon emerges with a brief solo phrase (8:48) that is immediately copied by the horn. The flute then takes this short phrase and extends it (8:54) bringing the rest of the orchestra back in. When the strings in unison play their version of the bassoon's melody (9:10), it suddenly takes on tremendous weight and import. But this is a prelude to a return to the excited passages that have been the hallmark of this movement.

Almost unbelievably, the speed begins to increase (9:29), snowballing and racing ahead, gradually getting louder and louder, erupting in a joyful explosion led by the horns and the trumpets (9:56). An extended series of powerful, short chords played by the entire orchestra (10:04) seem to be taking us to the movement's conclusion. But another flourish of rapid repeated notes interrupts. Finally, when the single-note chords return (10:20), they lead to one jubilant sustained chord that is the symphony's ultimate statement.

MAESTRO KURT MASUR:

"Beethoven's Fifth Symphony is always a piece where anybody who is involved in the performance must identify himself totally with the music, especially in the first movement with its sparkling and philosophical spirit."

COMPARATIVE RECORDINGS

MASUR/NEW YORK PHILHARMONIC
TELDEC 9031-77313   TOTAL TIME: 36:22

Masur brings out the inner voices without sacrificing any of the symphony's power or drama. The sound is exceptional and the New York Philharmonic shines in this superb recording.

REINER/CHICAGO SYMPHONY ORCHESTRA
RCA RCD1-5403   TOTAL TIME: 30:57

One of the truly classic recordings of this too frequently recorded symphony. Reiner defines every detail and lets the music soar. The sound in this transfer is excellent, especially in the way it captures the sound of the Chicago Symphony's brass section.

NORRINGTON/LONDON CLASSICAL PLAYERS
EMI CLASSICS 49656   TOTAL TIME: 33:43

This performance has as its claim to fame theoretical historical accuracy. Norrington researched the Beethoven performance practices extensively, and his knowledge makes this an interesting recording. However, be sure to familiarize yourself with a modern instrument recording before expanding into this one.

*I*F YOU ENJOYED THIS PIECE. . .

The problem with the Fifth Symphony is that because of its famous opening it can seem to be a cliché. But, when you listen to it repeatedly, it gets more exciting and more interesting! The place to begin to expand your listening is with the **other Beethoven symphonies,** especially the odd numbers (**1, 3, 7, and 9**), which are the most powerful. For a beautiful contrast, try the **Sixth Symphony, the Pastoral,** a symphony that tells a story and describes nature in musical terms. Also, the **Violin Concerto** is a work of melodic brilliance that should be added to any collection.

BEETHOVEN

SYMPHONY NO. 9
IN D MINOR, OP. 125
CHORAL

Ludwig van Beethoven's (1770–1826) Ninth Symphony is one of the most staggering compositions in the repertoire, a work that reveals something new with each listening regardless of how many times it is heard. Perhaps one reason for this is that each of the first three movements is a complete work unto itself, and when heard together, they form the perfect introduction to the overpowering final movement. It is in the fourth movement that Beethoven broke ground and altered the traditional classical style by including a chorus and four solo voices in a symphony. Attracted by its pleas for brotherhood, it had been Beethoven's lifelong desire to set Friedrich von Schiller's poem "Ode to Joy" to music, and in the final movement of his last symphony he fulfilled this wish.

Beethoven began composing the Ninth Symphony in 1817, but did not complete it until 1823. Among the more than two dozen other works he wrote during that period, two stand out as pivotal: the *Hammerklavier* Sonata (1819) and the majestic *Missa Solemnis* (1823). Although virtually deaf, Beethoven conducted the premiere of the Ninth Symphony at the Kärntnertor Theater in Vienna on May 7, 1824. Further, the Ninth Symphony, a massive, difficult work, was not alone on that program, as Beethoven also included three movements from the equally demanding *Missa Solemnis*. At the time Beethoven was one of the most famous musicians in Vienna. It was in 1824 that Anton Bruckner, who half a century later would also dominate Vienna's musical life, was born, while in the United States John Quincy Adams was elected president by a vote of Congress when none of the four candidates could get a majority, a solution that would have pleased Beethoven's republican sensibilities.

The *Choral* Symphony is scored for flutes, oboes, bassoons, four horns, trumpets, timpani, and strings. In addition three trombones are used in the second and fourth movements, and a contrabassoon, piccolo, triangle, cymbals, and bass drum are incorporated into the final movement where Beethoven introduced the four vocal soloists and the full chorus augmenting the symphony orchestra.

REFERENCE RECORDING:
EMI CLASSICS 49493
MUTI/SOLOISTS/PHILADELPHIA ORCHESTRA/
WESTMINSTER CHOIR   TOTAL TIME: 71:52

FIRST MOVEMENT: Allegro ma non troppo, un poco maestoso   (16:25)

The first movement can best be described as a series of beginnings in search of an ending; one can imagine Beethoven beginning the piece, developing it somewhat, returning to the opening theme, then trying a slightly different development, and doing this over and over until he got it just the way he wanted it to unfold, finally bringing it to its conclusion.

The quiet opening belies the musical explosions filling this work; mystery abounds. The second violins and cellos play tremulously, while the horns sustain a distant chord. This opening is like a slow awakening as the first violins, followed by the violas and basses, play a distant two-note phrase. Note this pattern because it is the crux of the movement and will be heard repeatedly. With each passing moment the sound builds, slowly but steadily until there is an explosion (0:33) led by the timpani with the whole orchestra playing in unison. However, it quickly backs off and we are returned to the tenuous awakening of the opening moments (1:09) in turn rebuilding to a second explosion (1:39). It feels as if Beethoven were struggling with getting the movement going, especially when this second eruption also dissipates, evolving into a lyrical section (2:19) led by the woodwinds. Eventually, the lyricism turns mysterious (3:20), and the next section sounds like a puzzle in which the pieces do not quite go together. When they do all fall into place (4:34), there are a series of forceful unison passages. This, too, ebbs, and we return to another rendition of the movement's opening (4:55), only this time Beethoven sustains the mood, trying to find a new path.

After a sustained attempt at continuing the opening theme, the woodwinds interrupt (5:50) and slow everything down, sapping the momentum. The strings try again to reenergize the movement, but are thwarted by the woodwinds (6:22), who slow the pace. After a split-second pause, the strings, angrier and more determined, start a drive they are able to sustain, passing it to the woodwinds (8:00). But this time instead of slowing down, the wind instruments accelerate the pace, leading to uncertainty, trying to find a direction. Led by the timpani (9:00), the orchestra unifies and erupts into an explosive version of the movement's opening theme, loud, angry, and absolutely thrilling!

The energy begins to wane (10:00), like steam escaping, as the flute and oboe emerge from the fray playing lyrical lines. The other parts of the orchestra add their voices, and soon the angst starts to rebuild, taking us through much of the same music already heard. As before, the pattern of pushing ahead and pulling back to slowly rebuild the power is repeated, as are the sections of mystery and struggle. A ray of musical sunshine emerges (13:53) as the horns and oboe join forces to play an almost cheerful, albeit brief, melody. This, too, dissolves into mystery and uncertainty, in turn replaced by growing anger.

The woodwinds interrupt the developing ire (14:55), replacing it with a listless interlude slowing the pace, grinding almost to a complete halt. But this is deceptive, because from this exhausted state, a new rumble begins as the timpani provides the pulse for a funereal, dark passage. Slowly, the intensity grows while the pace quickens until one final explosion (16:04) leads to an intense struggle and the movement's end.

SECOND MOVEMENT: Molto vivace   (14:42)

For those readers who watched television during the 1960s this movement will be familiar because it was used as the opening theme of the *Huntley-Brinkley Report* every weekday evening on NBC. It is fast, with a great deal going on at most times, making it difficult to pick out the details at first hearing. Therefore, when listening initially, try to get a sense of the movement's overall shape, rather than the details.

The strings launch the movement, answered forcefully by the timpani mimicking their opening salvo. After the punctuated beginning, the second violins begin rapidly sneaking around (0:04), the pace pushing forward, propulsive but quiet. One by one the other string sections join in, each adding to the scurrying. Eventually the whole orchestra plays the theme (0:27), now loud and more established, the scurrying becoming a gallop that turns almost raucous (0:44). A total stop (1:13) precedes a repeat that goes back to the beginning of the rapid sneaking section.

Following the repeat (2:24) the movement continues haltingly as the strings and horns alternate with the flutes, oboes, clarinets, and bassoons playing as a unit. The bassoons reestablish the sneaking-around melody (2:39) joined by the flutes, oboes, and clarinets, the line interrupted by a series of isolated timpani crashes. Once over the timpani's interruptions, the propulsive force keeps increasing the intensity and volume until the whole orchestra joins together for another explosive gallop (3:25), turning somewhat raucous as before, only this time tinged with anger. A series of stops and starts (4:22) leads to another repeat.

The stops and starts lead to the end of the repeat, and once the scurrying gets restarted, it moves faster and faster, leading to some beautiful, jaunty solos for the oboes, clarinets, and bassoons (6:41). The strings take over (6:55) and provide a lyrical, forgiving melody that leads to sustained phrases in the horns accompanied by delicate passages in the violins. The oboe then assumes the strings' part (7:25) in an exquisite solo accompanied only by the other winds, before the whole orchestra joins together for another pass at this "good mood" melody (7:44). This whole section is then repeated.

Following the repeat (9:04) the flute plays the delicate melody, and the jauntiness slowly diminishes, evolving into an ever-increasing lethargy and calm, shattered (9:49) as we suddenly find ourselves back at the riveting opening of the movement, and a long repeat. This repeat ends (14:19), and then the violins and horns start the scurrying again, getting faster and faster, galloping away. Suddenly (14:29), the strings play sustained chords while the woodwinds return briefly to the happy melody from the movement's center section. This, too, stops (14:34), and then the entire orchestra launches into one final propulsive drive to the movement's brusque end.

THIRD MOVEMENT: Adagio molto e cantabile (16:04)

Although this movement opens with a discordant solo for the bassoons and clarinets, it quickly resolves and turns into a calm, lyrical composition, a striking contrast to the two previous movements.

The strings start the slow, sustained melody (0:19); the mood is calm and reflective. One should luxuriate in the seamless flow of the sustained melodic lines. When the winds take the lead (2:14), their rich sonorities combined with occasional timpani beats create a regal, elegant sound, leading to the movement's second part (Andante moderato) (2:55) as the second violins begin a new melody. The pace is a little faster, but still calm, the mood is unstrained, relaxed, and pastoral, like a gentle breeze, and when the first violins establish another new melody (4:22), it evokes images of a gently flowing brook.

A distinct chord change (6:18) brings another slight tempo change, and the winds chance to assume the melodic lead. (Listen for how the melody heard earlier in the violins translates to the winds.) The pace slows even more (Adagio) (7:43) as the clarinets, bassoons, and horn blend sounds. Something is brewing in this slow section, and eventually the horn pulls away with a solo (8:55), just before the violins (9:14) launch into another elegant flowing section. Ultimately, the violins stop (10:45) and the winds carry on.

The endless flow is interrupted by a regal call from the horns and trumpets (11:22), a bit of force in an otherwise totally calm scene. The interruption is brief as the violins quickly reestablish the long flowing lines; somehow it is evident that the outburst was not an isolated occurrence, and the horns and trumpets again break the line with another salvo (12:33). As it fades away, a distinct sadness remains, even though the violins do manage to reestablish the calm, flowing line again (13:20). At the end the first violins and the woodwinds carry the line, and the movement ends quietly.

FOURTH MOVEMENT: Presto   (24:31)

This is one of the best-known movements in all of music, having been used in countless television commercials and motion pictures, including the Tom Hanks film *The Money Pit*. Because of its popularity, it is natural that most first-time listeners expect the movement to begin with the chorus singing the "Ode to Joy." But before that point is reached, there is a great deal of fascinating music. (Note: Before listening to this movement be certain to read a translation of the text.)

The fourth movement opens with a ferocious explosion: the timpani crash, and the wind instruments launch into a chaotic frenzy, stopping as suddenly as it began. Then the cellos and basses try to establish a melody, but it just gives an opportunity to catch one's breath before another equally fierce explosion, followed again by the cellos and basses providing a respite. This leads to a brief recapitulation of the first movement's opening theme (0:48) with tremulous strings and sustained chords in the winds. Another bridge from the cellos and basses takes us to a fleeting revisit of the scurrying second movement (1:30). Yet another cello and bass bridge leads to the now expected reminder of the lyrical third movement (1:55), out of which emerge the cellos and basses, this time leading us to new territory as the oboes, clarinets, and bassoons (2:33) play a delightful new melody. But they have trouble sustaining it and are interrupted.

Quietly the cellos and basses, as if to prove they are the only ones who can get this thing going, begin almost tentatively to play the new melody (3:05); this is the "Ode to Joy" melody. Gradually the other instruments join in, as if they have been shown the way and can now add their voices. The building of sound is steady, and with each new voice the richness increases. Finally, the whole orchestra explodes (5:16), unable to hold back any longer; there is a joyful feeling, the trumpets soaring above the rest of the orchestra creating an atmosphere of heavenly excitement. The controlled pace cannot be maintained, and suddenly it breaks away (5:54), yielding the image of wild abandon. It slows, and the control seems to be reestablished, but then chaos returns (6:33) with a recapitulation of the movement's frenzied beginning.

"O friends, no more of these sounds": with the German equivalent of these words, the lone angry voice of the solo baritone sets the true tone of the "Ode to Joy" (6:42). It is important to note that Beethoven wrote these words for the baritone preceding the part of the movement that uses Schiller's poem. This introduction is in the form of a sung recitative, with the orchestra providing occasional punctuation. When done properly, this brief solo should make you sit up and take notice, as it was Beethoven's way of musically halting the chaos.

When the "Ode to Joy" begins (7:47), it is unmistakable, the baritone singing the famous lines accompanied only by pizzicatos and passagework in the oboe and clarinet. Be sure to listen for the contrast of the baritone's strong voice against the delicate sounds of the clarinet and oboe. Once the line has been established, the whole chorus echoes the baritone's initial song of joy (8:12), musical exuberance at its utmost.

The solo alto and tenor along with the baritone (8:31) replace the chorus and are quickly joined by the solo soprano, their lines interwoven with the delicate passages of the flute and bassoon. This is intimate yet still powerful, the intimacy intensified when contrasted with the explosive sections sung by the chorus. This alternating of solo versus choral voices continues until the pace suddenly broadens (9:57) when the chorus sings: ". . . *und der Cherub steht vor Gott*" (and the angel stands before God). As they loudly sustain the final *Gott* (10:14), a powerful timpani roll brings everything to a rumbling halt.

An entirely new section (Allegro assai vivace) is hesitantly begun by the bassoon, contrabassoon, and bass drum (10:23). It is hard to imagine, but this jerky beginning will develop into a march, and when the piccolo, cymbals, and triangle are quietly added, along with the distant sounds of the woodwinds and trumpet (10:34), it is clear this is a march with militaristic overtones. The solo tenor forcefully sings *"Froh"* (glad) (11:04), beginning a short solo accompanied by the military-style march.

This interlude ends abruptly (11:59), and the orchestra accelerates the pace, flying through some passages. Gone is the strong confidence established by the march; in its place is a frenzied, almost skittish race. When the fury abates and the pace slows (13:17), the horns are left alone (13:22) as if everyone else is regaining strength. Suddenly, after this momentary respite, the chorus resumes (13:40), joyfully returning to the opening lines of the Schiller poem; this is wildly exciting; it, too, ends abruptly.

After a brief silence, a slower section begins (Andante maestoso) (14:30) introduced by the bass trombone, cellos, and basses, the tenors and basses of the chorus intoning the words *"Seid umschlungen, Millionen!"* (Be embraced, ye millions!). The upper voices led by the violins (14:57) add an ethereal quality, and the mood quickly turns prayerful, as if calmly beseeching. Here they tell their "brothers" that beyond the stars there lives a loving Father. This is some of the most hopeful, inspirational music ever written. Then, a beautiful transition (Adagio ma non troppo, ma divoto) (16:20) played by the flutes, clarinets, bassoons, violas, and cellos yields a mysterious-sounding interlude, its intimacy sounding like chamber music in the midst of these huge forces. Soon the chorus returns (16:40) whispering their prayerlike lines, then growing louder and more intense. When they stop, the orchestra sneaks back in (17:43) extremely quietly. But gradually layers of sound are added, and the chorus returns, totally delicate, like gossamer as the sound seems to evaporate.

A sudden outburst (18:14) led by the women in the chorus shatters the silence and launches another fast section (Allegro, energico, sempre ben marcato). When the tenors and basses add their lower voices (18:25), and the orchestra adds its power, the energy is released in an unbridled outburst of joy. This is sustained until a mysterious whisper sung by the basses replaces the excitement (19:38), the mood becoming forgiving as we, all brothers, are reminded of the heavenly Father; everything seems to be resolved and at peace.

But the violins start another section (Allegro, ma non tanto) (20:32), playing a rapid, yet steadily paced introduction to new solos sung by the tenor and bass alternating with the soprano and alto: "Freude, Tochter aus Elysium" (Joy, daughter of Elysium). The chorus joins the soloists (21:04) and the mood becomes ebullient, straining to pull away. Then, in another outburst (21:15), the chorus launches into a series of "Alle Menschen" (All mankind), again reminding us we are all brothers. While it feels as if the momentum is straining to pull the movement constantly forward, ever louder and ever faster, there are moments of sudden pullback, as if the brakes were applied. One such stoppage (22:00) has the four solo voices taking over for the chorus again reiterating that "all mankind are brothers," this extended solo ending quietly, prayerfully, with the voices fading away.

The strings, sounding somewhat like the ticking of a clock (22:52), hesitantly begin a transitional section (Poco allegro, stringendo il tempo, sempre piu allegro). But this is nothing more than an introduction steadily increasing in speed until it explodes into a furious eruption (23:00) at breakneck speed (Prestissimo). Complete with crashing cymbals, ringing triangles, and beating drum, the orchestra, and the chorus, this is the ultimate cry of joy. But, Beethoven cannot resist one last slow-down, reveling in the majestic phrase *"Tochter aus Elysium, Freude schöner Götterfunken"* (23:50). This turns out to be the last choral phrase, and once it is complete, the orchestra, led by the trumpets, flies into the final, frantic musical explosion taking us to the symphony's exultant end.

BASS JAMES MORRIS:

"When asked about my thoughts on the entrance of the bass soloist in Beethoven's Ninth, one word comes to mind: panic! *I know of no other role in the repertoire that makes a singer display practically his whole range, volume, breath control, and agility in the first few bars. Also, because the part is so short, there is no chance to redeem yourself if you mess up. Add the fact that usually you are made to sit onstage for the first three movements while your throat gets drier and drier, and you have a great case of nerves. But it's worth it."*

COMPARATIVE RECORDINGS

MUTI/STUDER, ZIEGLER, SEIFERT, MORRIS/
    WESTMINSTER CHOIR/PHILADELPHIA ORCHESTRA
EMI CLASSICS 49493   TOTAL TIME: 71:52

This is by far one of the most exciting performances of the Ninth ever recorded. Muti seems to set every tempo perfectly and is aided by superb soloists, a powerful chorus, and a glorious-sounding orchestra.

WALTER/CUNDARI, RANKIN, DA COSTA,
WILDERMAN/WESTMINSTER SYMPHONIC
CHOIR/COLUMBIA SYMPHONY ORCHESTRA
CBS MASTERWORKS MK 42014   TOTAL TIME: 71:15

Recorded in 1959, this performance stands the test of time purely because of Bruno Walter's excellent interpretation. This is a solid reading, filled with passion and tremendous depth. The soloists are good and the chorus and orchestra exceptional. The recorded sound is acceptable.

ABBADO/BENACKOVA, LIPOVSEK, WINBERGH, PREY/
CHORUS OF THE VIENNA STATE OPERA/VIENNA
PHILHARMONIC
DEUTSCHE GRAMMOPHON 419 598   TOTAL TIME: 72:31

An excellent performance, although it lacks some of the drive found in the Muti recording. The soloists are good, but what makes this recording special is the sound of the Vienna-based chorus and orchestra.

IF YOU ENJOYED THIS PIECE. . .

Few pieces have the dramatic power combined with the great familiarity of the Ninth Symphony. However, one should listen to all the Beethoven symphonies in sequence so the developmental progression of his style becomes clear. Three other works of interest are the **Choral Fantasy,** scored for piano, soloists, chorus, and orchestra, the **Missa Solemnis,** and Beethoven's only opera, **Fidelio.**

BERLIOZ

SYMPHONIE FANTASTIQUE, OP. 14

FANTASTIC SYMPHONY

Hector Berlioz (1803–69) was the picture of the passionate, tormented, Romantic creative spirit, and in his *Symphonie Fantastique* he painted a musical self-portrait. Berlioz himself described
this large-scale work as: "Episode from the life of an artist, fantastic symphony in five parts." The impetus for the symphony
was a Paris performance in 1827 of Shakespeare's *Hamlet* by a
visiting company from England. Berlioz became infatuated with
the lead actress, Harriet Smithson, and in true Romantic style
his infatuation quickly became obsessive, unrequited love.

Berlioz channeled his burning desires into creative energy
and wrote this mammoth, autobiographical symphony. The *Fantastic* Symphony conjures up the image of the tortured creative
spirit, driven by demons and consumed by unfulfilled dreams,
and even though Berlioz was twenty-four years old when he saw
Harriet Smithson perform, there is a distinctly adolescent quality to the story of this piece. To describe it as a perfect representation of the Romantic ideal would not be an overstatement.

The *Fantastic* Symphony premiered at the Conservatory of Music in Paris on December 5, 1830. That was the year that saw Louis Philippe, known as the Citizen King, become king of the French, assuming the throne in a city still torn by revolutionary strife. But it must have been an inspirational environment because it was in France during 1830 that Victor Hugo penned *Hernani* and Stendhal wrote his classic tale of Romantic passion and unrequited love *Le Rouge et le Noir* (*The Red and the Black*).

Berlioz, insuring the listener would understand the story he tells in the *Fantastic* Symphony, took the unusual step of writing descriptive paragraphs describing each movement of the piece and had these program notes distributed to the audience. (We will paraphrase his words prior to each movement.) In addition to his descriptive words, Berlioz used a large orchestra to paint his musical autobiography. In the first movement the orchestra is made up of a piccolo, flutes, oboes, clarinets, bassoons, four horns, valved cornets, trumpets, timpani, and strings. In the subsequent movements he introduces two harps in the second, an English horn and another set of timpani in the third, trombones, tubas, bass drum, snare drum, and tambourine in the fourth, and bells in the final movement.

The best way to appreciate the *Fantastic* Symphony is to get into the ultra-Romantic mood, read the text of the story, and then let the powerful passion of the music draw you into Berlioz's tormented world.

REFERENCE RECORDING: LONDON 414 203
DUTOIT/MONTREAL SYMPHONY ORCHESTRA
TOTAL TIME: 54:37

FIRST MOVEMENT: REVERIES-PASSIONS: Largo (15:47)

Our Romantic artist/composer sees the ideal woman, the woman of his dreams, and falls hopelessly in love. Obsessed by her image, every time he thinks of her he hears a musical phrase that is at once passionate, noble, and shy, reflecting the characteristics of his beloved. The melancholic reverie of the movement's opening is transformed into frenzied passion, furious rages of jealousy, and the wide range of emotions that love can evoke. Ultimately, the movement returns to tenderness, tears, and religious consolation.

The flutes and clarinets, joined almost immediately by the oboes, bassoons, and horns, play a series of quiet, steady moving notes leading to a melancholic chord that slowly fades away. The first violins, accompanied by the other string instruments, then play a phrase that oozes with romantic longing. The mood and sentiment are absolutely unmistakable, and the slow unraveling of this introduction only heightens the unrequited yearning. There is also a distinctly operatic quality to this opening in the sense that one can easily imagine a tormented character in an opera brooding onstage while the orchestra plays this music. When the violas, cellos, and basses rumble quietly through a sustained phrase (1:42), it seems as if we have reached the depths of a depression. Suddenly, out of this darkness the first violins (1:50) launch into a cheerful, fast passage that is the antithesis of the movement's introduction. Gone is the heavy operatic brooding, replaced by a gay balletic lightness.

Gradually the fast pace is picked up by the other instruments and the joy spreads. After a sustained buildup, a retreat yields a beautiful, languorous section (2:15) featuring the flute and horn. Melancholy returns (3:19) as the violins play another phrase filled with longing that seems to mimic the silly pangs of an adolescent heart torn by passion and love. Slowly the movement loses all energy, exhausted by the emotions, and almost grinds to a complete halt (4:30). Like a reawakening, the violins start again (4:37) aided by the rich sound of the horn and the more delicate accompaniment of the flutes and clarinets. Here the music is absolutely balletic as it serves as an introduction to a rude jolt provided by the timpani (5:54). Suddenly everything becomes agitated, and though it starts slowly, it trembles and rumbles until the flutes and violins launch into a beautiful melody (6:01), which symbolizes the "beloved." Take careful note of this melody because it is crucial to how the story unfolds as it reappears in each movement.

The excitement of this "discovered love" grows and grows until it explodes into unbridled rapture (6:42). In the midst of all the fervor, occasional reminders of the beloved theme appear, most notably played by the flutes and clarinets (7:17). Then there is a repeat (7:33) back to the moment when the flute and violins first launched into the melody. After the repeat the violas, cellos, and basses play their version of the beloved theme (9:03) and the mood swings return: joyful one moment and filled with terror the next. A single timpani stroke (9:58) echoes into an eerie silence.

A single, sustained note played by the third horn (10:02) introduces quiet comments initially by the violins before the flute, clarinet, and bassoon restate the beloved theme. Then a tense duet between the violins and cellos (11:19) begins and the string instruments argue, each group of strings entering and then quickly quieting down. This tense part eventually calms as the oboe emerges with a solo filled with longing (12:14). But this is just a brief respite as the passions again take over, restoring the frenzy that becomes absolute unbridled excitement (13:11) played with total abandon by the whole orchestra; the pace is relentless and seems to take off, unable to stay earthbound. Out of a terrific explosion led by the timpani (13:47) the flute returns to the "beloved" melody.

One more time the strings create a frenzy (14:00), which builds into a series of explosions (14:10) summing up the uncontrolled passion experienced by our protagonist. But then the mood becomes sad (14:30) and quiet, and the violins, now all alone, sadly play a deliberate, energyless version of the "beloved" theme (14:51). The mood has become introspective; there is a distinctly religious quality, and the movement ends with quiet sustained chords.

SECOND MOVEMENT: *UN BAL* (A BALL): VALSE
Allegro non troppo   (6:30)

In this "scene" we are transported to an elegant ball at which our hero finds himself surrounded by the noise and excitement of the party, but at every turn he is haunted by the image of his beloved.

Shimmering violins and violas introduce an elegant ascending phrase played by the harps. There are periodic, angry interjections from the growling cellos and basses, creating a contrast between these phrases and the harps'; tension versus calm. After this brief introduction, the waltz starts (0:40) with the second violins, violas, cellos, and basses providing the unmistakable pulse. Once the beat is established, the first violins launch into the waltz melody; it is light and airy and makes the more graceful among us want to get up and dance. The harps join the strings (1:00), making the dance even breezier, and it seems to move faster, and when the violins reestablish the waltz theme (1:42), the wind instruments add their support.

The elegant airiness of the waltz somehow dissolves into tension and mystery; the strings begin to tremble and the flute and oboe emerge from the haze playing the theme of the beloved (2:11). Evidently obsessed by the vision, our hero sees his beloved. Musically that theme is then absorbed into the strings' effort to reestablish the pulse of the waltz, but the conflict of the two moods only serves to heighten the tension, and it soon becomes clear more trouble is on the horizon (3:00). But then, just when everything has fallen apart, the waltz resumes (3:15), busier and more frenzied than before.

A calmer, more elegant version of the waltz (4:15) dominates, with the flutes, oboes, and clarinets playing the theme. A brief pause (4:45) precedes a galloping section; the joy of the dance overcomes everything, giddily speeding up wildly. Then the strings stop (5:26), and where there had been their excitement there now is the flute, clarinet, and horn flashing back to remind us of the "beloved" theme. But the excitement of the ball cannot be denied, and the other winds, harps, and strings interrupt the melancholy (5:51) with an excited, but steadily paced buildup leading to the cellos and violas whirling the group back to the frenzied waltz melody. Unbounded excitement flies us to the end of the movement.

THIRD MOVEMENT: SCENE IN THE COUNTRY:
Adagio   (17:01)

A bucolic evening visit to the countryside begins with our hero hearing two shepherds far in the distance cooing to each other with their pipes. The pastoral beauty, his newfound love, his love of being in love, all bring him an internal peace, until he starts to wonder about whether his beloved is deceiving him. His happiness is now clouded by dark premonitions. Then, as if to further trouble him, he again hears the shepherd's piping, only this time it goes unanswered. He is left with the distant rumbling of thunder, silence, and loneliness.

The parts of the two shepherds exchanging calls are taken by the English horn and the oboe. Their exchange is peaceful, evocative of nature's beauty, and filled with the yearning sound of two lovers. The flute and first violins take over (1:56), playing a delightful duet extending the peaceful opening. The clarinet (3:03) and horn (3:18) quietly add their voices, lending richness to the sound. This slow development continues with the addition of the other strings, clarinets, horns, and bassoons (4:00), yielding the first relatively big sound of the movement.

A lovely little interlude played by the flutes, oboes, and clarinets (4:29) changes the pace slightly, yet these phrases seem to heighten the "nature" in this scene. When the strings accompany twitters played by the oboe, flute, and clarinet (5:59), the outdoor setting appears clearly in the music. These short chirps contrast with the cello and bassoon solo (6:07) that features longer, flowing phrases. The pastoral setting becomes troubled (6:51), then grows suddenly quiet, but still strained, especially the repeated notes played by the violins. Clearly trouble is brewing until the bassoons, cellos, and basses establish a forceful solo that takes control (7:34). Suddenly, out of the rumbling, the flutes, oboes, and clarinets sneak in the "beloved" theme (7:47).

The delicacy of this theme played against the power of the rumbling lower voices makes the melody stand out, but ultimately the power wins out.

The mood becomes agitated and nervous and erupts into a ferocious storm (8:54), screeching, and exploding with loud timpani beats. The storm dies down, replaced by a gracious, calm section featuring the flutes and oboes (9:27). A beautiful, languorous clarinet solo (9:55) fully restores the pastoral atmosphere that began the movement. Gradually the volume builds as more instruments join in, all leading to another explosion (11:42) that instantly pulls back, revealing another elegant phrase first in the woodwinds and then in the strings. The flute and clarinet, alternating, restate the "beloved" theme (12:22). It is peaceful until a dark cloud comes into the picture (13:09) illustrated by the rumbling of the timpani. But through it the flutes continue to chirp (14:10) and the pastoral calm is restored.

The English horn representing the shepherd returns (14:38) and pipes its call. There is no response, only the horrible distant rolls of thunder played by the timpani. Repeatedly the English horn, growing more intense with each passing call, sadly longs for the reply of its beloved. The movement ends quietly with a single horn sounding its lonely note.

FOURTH MOVEMENT: MARCH TO THE GALLOWS: Allegretto non troppo   (4:52)

This scene is based in the hallucinations of our hero, who dreams that he has killed his beloved and has been condemned to be executed. A ferocious march accompanies the procession. At the final moment, our hero thinks of his beloved only to have the thought cut short by the fall of the executioner's ax.

Two sets of timpani quietly set the tone, introducing the muted horns, eerily leading the procession unceasingly toward a ferocious explosion (0:26). Then the cellos and basses enter with great determination. The violins take the melody (0:53) while the timpani play on unhaltingly, this march interrupted by occasional ugly outbursts. A fabulous bassoon solo (1:19) played over pizzicatos adds an element of frivolity that evolves into a stirring march featuring the brass and winds (1:40). There is a distinctly regal quality in this section. But this dissolves into a strained march (3:01), now unstoppable, filled with a series of horrific explosions.

The strings establish a steady pace (3:34), which becomes furiously driven. Suddenly the clarinet, all alone, reprises the "beloved" theme (4:17), but is interrupted by a sharp cut, the ax falling. The snare drum and winds, loudly and slowly, draw the movement to its depressing end.

FIFTH MOVEMENT: DREAM OF A WITCHES' SABBATH: Larghetto   (10:27)

Groups of ghouls, monsters, and sorcerers have gathered for our hero's funeral. Hellish shrieks of laughter and distant cries abound. Through it all the "beloved" theme appears bereft of its nobility and shyness, now trivial and grotesque. "She" has come to the witches' Sabbath and joins the diabolical orgy. Suddenly the funeral bells sound along with a burlesque of the Dies Irae. The witches dance, and the sacred and profane melodies combine in a strange marriage.

Mystery abounds at the outset of the final movement; the violins and violas tremble while the cellos and basses, strengthened by the occasional timpani beats, angrily growl. Then the violins and violas break into a repeated phrase reminiscent of the music from the shower scene of Hitchcock's *Psycho*, while the oboes, clarinets, and bassoons blare a sustained chord. The clarinet and flute pierce through (0:32) seeming to call everyone to attend the Sabbath. A solo horn quietly echoes the call (0:43) just before the movement's opening is reprised. When the solo horn is heard again, it leads into a faster section (Allegro) started by the unusual combination of a clarinet, timpani, and bass drum (1:40).

This brief interlude is the calm before the storm, because suddenly an explosion (1:49) lets the furies fly; all hell breaks loose as the full orchestra cavorts wildly. But as quickly as it began, it ends, and the oboes and clarinets dance wickedly (1:59). This particularly descriptive music, as ugly and grotesque as it is, is the "beloved" theme, now imbued with the wickedness of the underworld. As the other instruments join in, the frolic becomes more demonic and wild. Another sudden break (2:54) leaves the bassoons, cellos, and basses heavily slowing the pace and creating a calm. The sound is initially rich, then steadily fades away yielding to the bells (3:12) solemnly intoning their repeated, hollow chime. Occasionally, sections of the orchestra try to restart the wild dance, but instead the trombones and bassoons (3:37) join the bells' intoning. This is the Dies Irae, and the ritualistic nature of the ceremony is all too apparent in the somber tones of the trombones. This pseudoreligious atmosphere is disturbed by the piccolo, oboes, flutes, and clarinets interrupting (4:10), their annoying perkiness sneering at the solemnity of the moment.

This pattern of contrasted solemnity and frivolity becomes more tense and scary and leads to another sudden stop followed immediately by the section known as the "Ronde du Sabbat" (5:35). This "round" begins with the cellos and basses, then the violas, and then the violins. It is a demonic, somewhat erotic dance played primarily by the strings with occasional interjections from the winds. The dance grows wild, but is slowed by a solid interruption from the brass (6:40) temporarily calming the festivities, although a series of angry explosions intermittently keeps the fury present. As it quiets, the power is but a shadow of itself. Then the cellos (7:41) restart the "round" and the wild dance begins anew, instruments adding their voices until it regains its former fury.

The strings continue their wild dance countered by the wind instruments solemnly reprising the Dies Irae (8:32). In addition to hearing the two sections of the orchestra playing against each other, this section also gives the opportunity to hear the rapid strings playing against the slow, steady winds. Out of this controlled chaos the solo flute emerges (8:53). But the strings cannot be denied, and they resume their wild dance, now even stranger because the wood portion of their bows are used, creating sonic pinpricks.

The flutes, piccolo, oboes, clarinets, and bassoons start to fly (9:17), furiously heading toward some demonic end. Everything becomes totally wild; the full orchestra furiously races; explosions are frequent, featuring the bass drum, timpani, and cymbals. This angry, wild orgy carries until the final explosion that concludes the symphony.

THEODORE BASKIN, PRINCIPAL OBOE OF THE MONTREAL SYMPHONY ORCHESTRA:

"One must understand that Hector Berlioz was a writer as well as a composer. Symphonie Fantastique is a programmatic work that is autobiographical, highly theatrical, and revolutionary in its historical context. This is shown in the unprecedented sounds that the composer wrote for the orchestra; the florid harp, strident clarinet, the dialogue between the English horn and the off-stage oboe, glissandi in the flute and oboe, solo timpani, nasal 'stopped' brass, ponticelli strings. Once the descriptive image of the piece is clear in the performer's mind, realizing the technical aspects of the orchestration becomes the challenge. The interpreters must understand the function not only of each individual's line with its expressive purpose, dynamic definition, and tone color, but must fit it into a complex multilayered orchestration. In reference to the oboe in particular, the technical requests made by Berlioz are of an extreme nature in regards to dynamics, awkward registers, mixed articulations, rapid trills, and highly atypical glissandi."

COMPARATIVE RECORDINGS

DUTOIT/MONTREAL SYMPHONY ORCHESTRA
LONDON 414 203   TOTAL TIME: 54:37

A superb recording that enables the listener to pick out the voices of the orchestra. Dutoit and his Montreal orchestra have a definite affinity for this piece.

TEMIRKANOV/ROYAL PHILHARMONIC ORCHESTRA
RCA 61203   TOTAL TIME: 54:09

A fine recording that is a little angrier and more ferocious. It is exciting, but the solo instruments in the orchestra could be a little better. The sound is superior.

DAVIS/LONDON SYMPHONY ORCHESTRA
PHILIPS 422 253   TOTAL TIME: 55:22

Sir Colin Davis is considered to be one of the great Berlioz interpreters of all time, and while the sound of this recording is somewhat dated, the interpretation is an important one to hear.

IF YOU ENJOYED THIS PIECE . . .

The *Symphonie Fantastique* is a unique composition, and it is hard to find another that has its overall power. However, if Berlioz is of interest his **Harold in Italy** is certainly worth exploring. On a larger scale, Berlioz's opera **Les Troyens** requires lots of time, but it contains some fabulous vocal and orchestral music.

BRAHMS

ᔍYMPHONY NO. 1
IN C MINOR, OP. 68

To say Johannes Brahms (1833–97) struggled to write his First
Symphony would be a great understatement. This symphony,
which we now know as his "first," was begun in 1862 and completed some fourteen years later. (As early as 1854, Brahms had
begun work on another symphony, which he put aside, eventually turning it into the first movement of his First Piano Concerto.) However, 1862 to 1876 was not a fallow period for Brahms
since during those years he did compose two orchestra serenades,
the F Minor Piano Quintet, the Alto Rhapsody, and the *German
Requiem*, to name just a few.

It is not surprising therefore that the work now known as the
First Symphony is a mature-sounding piece lacking the youthful
joy so evident in the early symphonies of many of Brahms's predecessors. Brahms was forty-three years old when he finally completed the symphony, the work premiering in Karlsruhe on
November 4, 1876. It was the year the famed Wagner Festival
House at Bayreuth presented its first complete *Ring des Nibelun-
gen;* Mallarmé wrote his poem *L'Après-midi d'un faune,* which De-

bussy would later make famous (see chapter 12); and in the United States, Alexander Graham Bell invented the telephone.

Brahms's First Symphony is a big, romantic work, filled with sections of strain and tremendous joy. It depicts struggle and success using a large orchestra to create dramatic sonic images. It is scored for large string sections, two flutes, two oboes, two clarinets, two bassoons, contrabassoon, four horns, two trumpets, and timpani. Then in the final movement Brahms adds three trombones.

REFERENCE RECORDING: DEUTSCHE GRAMMOPHON 431 790 ABBADO/BERLIN PHILHARMONIC
TOTAL TIME: 45:26

FIRST MOVEMENT: Un poco sostenuto–Allegro (14:13)

The opening moments of this movement seem to capture the essence of Brahms's struggle to compose this work; from the outset the tone is strained, slow, almost tortured. It is important to listen for the timpani's steady, rhythmic beat fighting to get from one pounding note to the next against the rest of the orchestra's expressive sustained phrases filled with strain. It is a staggering beginning, continuing until a sudden calm interlude (0:46), played first by the woodwinds and then the strings, changes the mood. This calm is temporary, as Brahms rebuilds to a reprise of the opening (2:04); this time an oboe solo (2:25) emerges from the struggle and then passes the melody to the flute. The tension abates to the point where everything seems to come to a complete stop.

A single beat, heard clearest in the timpani (3:08), announces the fast section of the movement with its distinctly frenetic, angry quality. A calming (4:38) occurs yielding a new, pastoral sound filled with wonderful exchanges among the woodwind instruments (5:05) until the strings take over (5:49) rebuilding the tension with a mystery-filled theme. When it gets back to speed, there are some exciting moments as the horns play against the strings (6:13), seeming to argue angrily, a constant mood save for an occasional triumphant phrase brought out primarily by the strings (7:20).

Another section of exhausted calm is brought to an end by the return of the mystery theme (8:36), introduced by the lower voices initially represented by the basses and the contrabassoon. The other instruments join, layering the sound, growing louder and louder, leading to a tremendous explosion (9:18) started by the horns, trumpets, and timpani blaring four repeated notes. This then takes us to another frenetic, angry section recapitulating much of what was heard earlier, and as before, it eventually runs out of energy and returns to the exhausted calm (11:27) before returning to mystery (11:48) and a rebuilding of the energy; listen especially for some wonderful passages for the horns (12:15).

The drive toward the finish begins with a series of choppy start-and-stop sections (12:39) turning into sustained phrases that gradually slow down (13:15). Throughout the final moments of the movement, listen for the return of the timpani's slow repeated notes played quietly against the sustained phrases. This combination, so reminiscent of the opening, except now without the strain, takes us to the movement's quiet close.

SECOND MOVEMENT: Andante sostenuto (9:39)

The second movement is best heard initially with one's eyes closed, allowing the romantic beauty of the music to simply flow over the listener. The strings take the lead in the opening romantic and lyrical section, serving as an introduction to a beautiful oboe solo (1:22). An expressive, soaring theme played by the first violins (2:14) is held back only by the steady pulse provided initially by the lower strings and later by the horns and bassoons. This is the first of a series of pushes and retreats, almost like the ocean rolling in and out as the tide comes in, each time a little farther up the beach. These passionate buildups lead to a climax (4:07) exploding with emotion heightened by its undercurrent of anguish. Relief is ushered in by a quiet timpani roll (4:50) as the tension dissipates.

The next buildup (5:19) starts with a wonderful pizzicato phrase in the strings played against the wind instruments. A violin solo (6:19), played by the concertmaster, puts the movement's distinct romanticism in the hands of a single instrument. This solo continues through to the end of the movement, echoed and joined by an equally haunting French-horn solo (7:18). Throughout this section the wind instruments have critical parts. The movement's peaceful ending gives the solo violin one last ascending phrase leading to extremely quiet, sustained notes.

THIRD MOVEMENT: Un poco Allegretto e grazioso   (5:06)

The cheerful, graceful opening of the third movement features melodic solos played by the clarinets and horns against a pace-setting series of pizzicatos in the cellos. The violins take the melody over (0:29), and now the clarinet provides a sped-up pulse in addition to one pulse still provided by the cellos.

The tone becomes mysterious (1:08) with a new melody initially played by the clarinet then followed by the oboe and the flute against a somewhat erratic pulse provided by the strings. Out of this evolves a return to the original melody (1:35) played by the clarinet now against a flowing, rivuletlike pulse in the first violins and the violas.

When this eases, there is a three-note call (two short, followed by one long) played initially by the flutes, oboes, and bassoons (1:48). This innocent beginning develops into an exciting, almost raucous outburst with the three-note phrases constantly returning and ultimately signaling a retreat (3:15) and another mood change; the somber tone is transitional as the clarinet again returns to the original melody (3:25). The final sections of the movement are another series of brief buildups and retreats. The ending is extremely tranquil and reprises the three-note call in a relaxed guise.

FOURTH MOVEMENT: Adagio–Piu Andante–Allegro ma non troppo, ma con brio   (16:28)

This movement, though one composition, is in clearly divided sections distinguished by abrupt changes in speed. The beginning is slow and brooding, the first notes played by the lower voices, immediately interrupted by the higher voices. The tortured quality of the first movement has returned. This is soon followed by an unusual segment in which the string instruments play everything pizzicato (0:43), heightening the mystery, creating great dramatic tension.

When the violins resume using their bows, they have a series of fast-moving passages that give the impression of the tide ebbing and flowing (2:10). A loud burst followed by a crisp timpani roll (2:36) leads to the Piu Andante section (2:45) and a regal horn solo played against shimmering strings. The flute then assumes the melody (3:15) leading to a chorale (3:47) played by the bassoons, contrabassoon, and trombones. It is an unmistakable, rich sound that, even though not very loud, should rumble the ground. Another horn solo (4:06) begins the sonic buildup leading into a split-second pause and the Allegro ma non troppo portion of the movement (4:42). The tone is stately, the strain and struggle gone, replaced by one of the most uplifting melodies ever written, played initially by the strings and the horns. Eventually the winds, led by the flutes, take the melody (5:15) supported by crisp pizzicatos and a restrained roll in the timpani. But then, seemingly nothing can contain this buildup any longer; it explodes (5:42) yielding an animated section occasionally showing traces of the earlier strain. An oboe solo (6:42) leads back to some of the mystery, and a series of struggling, brief starts and stops.

When the violins (8:21) valiantly return to the regal melody, order seems to be restored; but, it is short-lived, followed by a section of incomplete phrases, the struggle and mystery alternating with attempts to reestablish the regal melody. This develops into a warring, fuguelike section (10:29), building to an angry release (11:08) and a quick resolution (11:33) with the horns and the strings leading the calming.

Mystery again returns (14:15), highlighted by a series of swells rebuilding the tension. Suddenly, the speed increases and starts to gallop away. The movement's final section, Piu Allegro (14:58), accelerates the pace again, yet is controlled by the distinct undercurrent provided by the unified strings, bassoons, and timpani. A glowing resolution (15:15) bringing all the orchestra's forces together launches the joyful flight to the end of the movement. Here there is some strain in the upper voices, but it is pure excitement and brings the symphony to its energetic, joyful conclusion.

ROLAND KOHLOFF, PRINCIPAL TIMPANIST OF THE NEW YORK PHILHARMONIC:

"The timpani beat at the opening of the symphony is often considered to symbolize a human heart. However, I don't think of it as the heart of a human, but as the heart of the universe. Possibly, Brahms was contemplating his own universe as he turned to composing symphonies, which he started to do late in his career."

COMPARATIVE RECORDINGS

ABBADO/BERLIN PHILHARMONIC
DEUTSCHE GRAMMOPHON 431 790   TOTAL TIME: 45:26

A first-rate recording in every way. The performance is true to the music, the playing superb, and the sound is dynamic.

BÖHM/VIENNA PHILHARMONIC
DEUTSCHE GRAMMOPHON 413 424   TOTAL TIME: 47:11

Though a much broader, slow reading, Böhm's care and evident love of this score makes this a recording worth hearing. The Vienna Philharmonic is also splendid.

TOSCANINI/NBC SYMPHONY ORCHESTRA
RCA 60257   TOTAL TIME: 41:22

This is a typical Toscanini performance: driven and highly dramatic. Despite the sound of this 1951 recording, the excitement comes through loud and clear and is interesting to study from a historical perspective.

IF YOU ENJOYED THIS PIECE . . .

The first place to start is with the three other symphonies that make up the cycle of Brahms's symphonies. Also, be sure to listen to the **Variations on a Theme of Haydn,** the two **piano concertos,** and the **Violin Concerto.** Each of these works shows off Brahms's fabulous use of the Romantic orchestra. For a more intense experience, work your way up to the staggering **German Requiem.**

COPLAND

*A*PPALACHIAN SPRING
BALLET FOR MARTHA

When Aaron Copland (1900–1990) was commissioned in 1943 to compose a ballet score for Martha Graham, he was concerned about the amount of time required to write the piece because traditionally, ballet scores were forgotten soon after the initial performances. Nonetheless, Copland completed the ballet score in 1944, but one year later wrote a symphonic synthesis of the piece and the resulting suite quickly became part of the standard concert repertoire, a position it has maintained ever since. The ballet was originally scored for a chamber ensemble of thirteen instruments. However, it is the full symphonic version that has become best known.

The *Appalachian Spring* symphonic suite was premiered by the New York Philharmonic on October 4, 1945. The work achieved instant popularity and was awarded the Pulitzer Prize for 1945, the same year that John Hersey's *A Bell for Adano* was awarded the Pulitzer for Best Novel. In the same year, T. S. Eliot's *Four Quartets*, Sartre's *No Exit*, and Tennessee Williams's *The Glass Menagerie* were published.

Copland's music, due to his use of rhythms and melodies evocative of an American ambience, has a "folksy" American sound. In addition, Copland used the Shaker tune " 'Tis the Gift to Be Simple" as the melody for one section of *Appalachian Spring*. The ballet's title was chosen by Martha Graham, who borrowed it from the heading of a Hart Crane poem. *Appalachian Spring* is the story of a pioneer housewarming party in the Appalachian Mountains for a young, soon-to-be-married couple. The simple story notwithstanding, one way to listen to the piece is to let the music create pictures in your imagination, and since the music is so evocative, it is sure to conjure up distinct images. Sections of the suite may sound familiar to those who watched the news series *CBS Reports* during the 1960s as that program used a section of the suite as its opening theme.

The symphonic version of *Appalachian Spring* is scored for flutes, oboes, clarinets, bassoons, horns, trumpets, trombones, timpani, percussion, harp, piano, and strings. Although the suite is one long piece, it is divided into eight sections, each one telling another part of the story.

REFERENCE RECORDING:
DEUTSCHE GRAMMOPHON 431 048
BERNSTEIN/LOS ANGELES PHILHARMONIC
TOTAL TIME: 26:34

There is calm as the second violins and violas set the mood with a slow, quiet, sustained opening. In this part we are introduced to the characters of our story, the first represented by the clarinet (0:07), who stirs calmly. (Try to remember this phrase because it will appear several times throughout the suite.) There is an unmistakable innocence to the music, heightened by the clarinet's sound. One by one the other instruments add their voices, like people slowly gathering together. A high-pitched violin solo (0:57) conveys a feeling of peaceful yearning; there is no strain here. The flute (1:53), then the oboe (2:06), and then the bassoon (2:18) quietly announce their arrival, while the violins and violas provide a sustained base that is constant. Listen especially for the "colors" of sound created by the blending of the strings' notes. The opening scene ends much as it began with the harp (2:52) quietly providing a rich, ringing chord introducing a reprise of the clarinet's initial phrase.

Directly from the clarinet's last sustained note, there is a burst of excitement (3:09); the action has begun with the violins, violas, xylophone, and piano unleashing a perky, angular melody. The pace quickens, each instrument now fitting its phrase into the overall picture, like the pieces of a jigsaw puzzle. Initially this section starts and stops, ultimately launching into a more frenzied passage filled with activity (3:27). The flutes, over the steady strings, play a dancing duet that bounces jauntily along (3:38). Steadily the volume increases until the full orchestra joins together for a joyful ensemble; here the piano, violins, and violas happily race, while the winds forcefully remind us of the more sustained opening section. As the celebration quiets down, the flute and triangle emerge (4:21) with a delightful little musical comment. Eventually everything comes to a standstill, but just briefly, as the joyful activity resumes anew (4:31). Calm is restored when the violas, cellos, and basses provide a rich, sustained series of chords as a base for the flute twittering like a happy bird watching the contented pioneers from above (5:18). This section ends as the passages disintegrate, chopped into little more than a series of three-note phrases exhaustedly grinding to a halt.

The third section (5:58) (Moderato) is a duet for the engaged couple. It is pensive, even somewhat deliberate, with the harp, trombones, trumpets, and horns creating a heavy base for the bassoons and clarinet. Once again the clarinet reminds us of its innocent opening passage, a phrase that is now taken by the solo oboe playing it even slower. The first indication of any disharmony among our pioneers suddenly raises its head (6:55) with a harsh chord in the horns and strain in the first violins and violas. The discord resolves (7:45), replaced by mystery; the strain is diminished and some calm has returned, but there is still a hint of the "argument" that has just occurred. The oboe plaintively restores the earlier mood (8:44), calm introducing the clarinet, and then the flute. A sleepy peace returns.

The fourth section, depicting the revivalist and his followers, is very fast and begins (10:12) with snippets played in sequence by the oboe, the second flute, the clarinet, and the first flute. It is light and happy, a mood heightened by the wood block and first violins (10:30) playfully racing. Excitement grows when the snare drum and trumpet set off together (10:55) in a stately trot. Here the "folksy" quality is particularly evident, and a single timpani beat (11:22) starts the violins on a more deliberate path, as if announcing the beginning of a country dance. Others join in, and the stately becomes slightly raucous, in a friendly American way. The dance takes on different guises filled with catchy rhythms that keep the pace moving and varied. Just as the celebration grows wilder, there is a sudden stop (12:45) and a more regal, loud resolution takes over. The steady strength at this point is created by the timpani, trombones, trumpets, horns, bassoons, and strings blending their sounds in a swell of harmonic sunshine. Calm is restored as the oboe pensively restates the opening clarinet theme.

Suddenly, everything comes alive again (13:52) with a laughing, jerky section that gets going slowly but steadily. Then the flute and first violins take off at a furious clip (14:12) (Presto). This is the fifth section, a solo dance for the bride-to-be, flitting along at its breakneck pace even when the bass drum adds its force (14:51). The pace grows more deliberate (16:35), and the tone becomes a little strident just before the oboe, one first violin, and the harp calm the frivolity. Led by the flute, bassoons, and the strings (17:20), a forgiving, romantic series of chords, like a musical sunset, create the most peaceful environment yet. A restatement of the opening clarinet theme, now slowed down, is played by the flute over a quiet bed of sustained string chords (18:58). This reminder of the introduction is the brief sixth section.

Accompanied by the first flute and the harp, the first clarinet calmly unveils its innocent rendition of the Shaker melody "Simple Gifts" (19:14). This is the seventh part of the suite and depicts the daily activities of the bride and her farmer husband. Copland's use of this melody, which is passed around the orchestra, captures the pioneer spirit and oozes with the "goodness" of the American heartland. When the violas take the melody (20:13), the tone becomes jauntier, and the charming chimes of the glockenspiel add their distinctive perkiness. Gradually the whole orchestra gets involved, but somehow the simplicity of the melody remains prevalent. A more boisterous variation shines through (21:04) when the trumpets and trombones take the Shaker melody, and the excitement grows further with the addition of the oboes, clarinets, and horns. The woodwinds quickly restore the peace and simplicity, but this is the calm before the storm, as suddenly the whole orchestra launches into a broader, statelier rendition of the Shaker theme (21:49).

Like a prayer, or final "Amen," the strings restore the calm as the final section of the suite begins (Moderato) (22:25). An absolutely peaceful quality abounds. The oboes, clarinets, bassoons, and eventually the flutes replace the strings (23:25) and are then rejoined by the strings, creating a wonderful sonority. As the piece began, so it ends, the flute reprising the clarinet's opening melody (24:18). But now, instead of sounding like an awakening, it sounds tired, as if it were time to go to sleep. To complete the symmetry, the clarinet itself plays the final solo phrase (25:43) with quiet accompaniment from the strings. The phrase fades away leaving only the sustained, quiet strings joined by the harp and glockenspiel for the last three chords of the piece. All is quiet; everyone has enjoyed their day, and peaceful contentment abounds.

MAESTRO DENNIS RUSSELL DAVIES:

"*I have always been moved and excited by the extraordinary range of colors in the original version, and my loyalty to it reminds me of the experience of being disappointed in the film version—even a good film version—of a book or play which I passionately loved in the original form.*"

$\mathcal{C}$OMPARATIVE RECORDINGS

BERNSTEIN/LOS ANGELES PHILHARMONIC
DEUTSCHE GRAMMOPHON 431 048   TOTAL TIME: 26:34

This is a pensive, exquisite performance that conveys every mood to the fullest and presents a beautifully clear portrait of the American spirit. Recorded in concert in 1983.

DAVIES/ORCHESTRA OF ST. LUKE'S CHAMBER
   ENSEMBLE
MUSICMASTERS 7055 C   TOTAL TIME: 24:48

This is a superb reading of the suite as performed by a thirteen-piece chamber ensemble. Each musician plays the part of a soloist, making it possible to clearly identify the instruments in every section. The digital sound heightens the crystal clarity.

COPLAND/LONDON SYMPHONY ORCHESTRA
CBS MASTERWORKS MK 42430   TOTAL TIME: 24:38

It is hard to argue with the composer's interpretation of his own work, so this is a historically interesting recording. The performance by the London orchestra is very good, and the sound is acceptable.

IF YOU ENJOYED THIS PIECE . . .

Copland's output was tremendous, but few of his works have had the lasting impact of *Appalachian Spring*. However, Copland's **Music for the Theater** and **Music for the Movies** are two suites that capture the same American spirit. On a larger scale Copland's **Third Symphony** is a fabulous, exciting work that is more dramatic than these other compositions. Also, Copland's adaptation of **The Old American Songs,** including "Simple Gifts," is a vocal collection definitely worth exploring. Then, on an even grander scale, try Copland's moving **Lincoln Portrait.**

DEBUSSY

PRÉLUDE À L'APRÈS-MIDI D'UN FAUNE
(PRELUDE TO THE
AFTERNOON OF A FAUN)

When Claude Debussy (1862–1918) wrote his *Prelude to the Afternoon of a Faun,* he used the poetry of Stéphane Mallarmé (1842–98) as his inspiration. Debussy composed this symphonic jewel in 1894, eighteen years after Mallarmé had penned the final version of the poem *L'Après-midi d'un faune.* By that time Mallarmé was the most respected poet in France. However, it is safe to say the lasting fame of the poem was guaranteed not by his beautiful words, but by Debussy's gorgeous music.

Although Debussy called the work a "prelude" to the poem, it would be more accurate to describe it as a musical copy of the poem, as it, like the poem, tells the story of this faun and the dreams and desires consuming his thoughts in the course of an afternoon. It is probably not a coincidence that Mallarmé's poem contains 110 lines and the Debussy *Prelude* contains 110 measures of music!

In 1894, the year of the *Prelude's* composition and premiere in Paris, Czar Nicholas II assumed the throne of Russia, Rudyard Kipling wrote *The Jungle Book,* and George Bernard Shaw wrote *Arms and the Man.* In Berlin, a recording company created the first horizontal gramophone disc, setting in motion the series of inventions that would make cylinders of music extinct and ninety years later would lead to the creation of the compact disc!

Mallarmé's poetry and Debussy's music are late Romantic French bordering on the impressionist. The music especially constantly reminds the listener of calm, colorful, impressionist paintings, so many of which dealt with nature. The *Prelude* can be thought of as a descriptive musical painting, or as Debussy described it, "a very loose illustration . . . a series of images through which the faun's desires and dreams appear in the afternoon haze." Simply put, the poem, and in turn the music, describe the erotic daydreams of a faun who tries to recall if he really carried off two nymphs or only dreamt of doing so. Finally, exhausted, he falls asleep in the warm sun. The structure of the *Prelude* mimics the faun's progress: it begins lazily, grows more excited, then returns to the lethargy of the opening now combined with exhaustion. Debussy used an orchestra made up of three flutes, two oboes, English horn, two clarinets, two bassoons, four horns, two harps, strings, and near the very end of the piece, very quiet antique cymbals or, as they are sometimes called, tuned finger cymbals.

REFERENCE RECORDING:
DEUTSCHE GRAMMOPHON 429 728
BERNSTEIN/ORCHESTRA OF THE NATIONAL
ACADEMY OF SANTA CECILIA
TOTAL TIME: 11:37

A lazy, languorous flute solo unfolds sleepily as the faun's afternoon begins. A somewhat eerie chord (0:27) played by the oboes, clarinets, and horn introduces a slow glissando in the harp, possibly a musical impression of the faun stretching. The harp then plays another glissando (0:43) introducing the horns, who calmly call out. Though the horns are prominent, nothing in this opening section can be thought of as loud; it is slow and peaceful but with a clear indication the intensity will eventually build.

The flute reprises its opening solo (1:03), this time accompanied by shimmering strings. The oboe blends right into the end of the flute solo (1:25) adding a sense of longing to the sound. Then the wind instruments all join together while the strings continue shimmering (1:44) for the first quasi-loud section in the piece. As the sound swells, the violins join the wind instruments leading toward an abrupt pullback that leaves a lonely clarinet to finish the phrase.

Another flute solo, this one accompanied by the harp and sustained strings (2:14) is still languorous as before but also more playful. Eventually, the pace increases and the second flute joins the first and the strings (3:07), who now play a more significant role, although the flutes do dominate. After another relaxed moment, the clarinet with support from the horns (3:32) plays a playful, almost sexy melody while the harp adds an element of mystery. The next solo belongs to the oboe (4:03); the pace now becomes more animated. One should enjoy the luxurious richness of the sound especially when the violins join in. Gradually the intensity, the pace, and the volume increase as these ultralush moments lead to a sea of sonic rapture (4:37).

Following this explosion of sound, the pace slows and the passion diminishes leaving a calming clarinet solo (5:07) accompanied by the violins. This transports us to a series of sustained chords (5:33) that are truly the musical equivalent of painting's pastels or watercolors. Again there is a swelling of sound (6:06) as the horns take over with their rich grandeur riding over the rest of the orchestra's substantial sound. Quickly the violins reestablish the melody (6:14) while the wind instruments provide a steady pulse accenting the strings' melodic line. The overwhelming sonic passion of before returns, then retreats leaving the horns with a brief, expressive solo (7:12) that introduces an equally beautiful solo for the first violin (7:18).

With the harp repeating a short, flowing phrase, the solo flute reprises its opening melody (7:43). Interestingly, while the harp is more active than before, the flute now appears sleepier and more tired. The oboe changes the mood (8:04), providing a jolly twitter, like a slow bird commenting. This is only a momentary lapse, as the oboe then plays a solo filled with sexy yearning (8:20). But this mood is broken by the English horn gayly copying the oboe's twitter with even more playfulness (8:39). Calm is restored (8:58) as the two flutes join for a solo that truly stands out because of the charming antique cymbals quietly chiming. The flutes are soon joined by two solo violins softly and expressively adding a sinewy quality to the moment. While this section has a certain intensity, the overall mood remains sleepy. Another oboe solo (10:15) still filled with longing removes whatever strain and intensity remains. Beautiful, sustained chords in the strings provide a rich bed for slow, descending phrases in the harps (10:45) seeming to invoke the image of an animal slowly lowering itself to sleep. This section has a distinctly exhausted quality, especially when the muted horns (10:55) and violins play one final, short phrase. Finally, the flutes add their tired sound (11:07) as the antique cymbals quietly ring. Two lonely pizzicatos in the cellos and basses bring the faun's erotic fantasy to its sleepy end.

EUGENIA ZUKERMAN, RENOWNED FLUTIST, COMMENTATOR FOR *CBS SUNDAY MORNING*, AND NOVELIST:

"Inspired by the sensuous language of the poem to which it is set, Debussy's Prelude invokes a primeval and mythical world. A simple unaccompanied flute (as the faun) begins the piece, floating into the air, setting the mood of lust and loss. It is a piece to experience rather than to understand, to lose oneself in the misty, blurred harmonies, the cascades of harp notes, the shiver of tremolos from the strings, the warmth of sound. There are iridescent colors in these sounds, blurred impressions, and one listens as if to distant echoes, remembered loves."

COMPARATIVE RECORDINGS

BERNSTEIN/ORCHESTRA OF THE NATIONAL ACADEMY
    OF SANTA CECILIA
DEUTSCHE GRAMMOPHON 429 728   TOTAL TIME: 11:37

This recording pairs Bernstein with an orchestra he did not record much with, and one not necessarily known for its facility with French music. However, the result is one of the most languorous recordings of the work; it seems to tell the faun's story as clearly as the words of the poem.

JORDAN/ORCHESTRE DE LA SUISSE ROMANDE
ERATO 45605   TOTAL TIME: 9:40

This is a faster, somewhat excited reading making the work less languorous and more agitated. It is a valid, interesting interpretation, and the playing of the fine Swiss orchestra stands up well. In addition the sound is superb.

MARTINON/ORCHESTRE NATIONAL DE L'O.R.T.F.
EMI CLASSICS STUDIO 69587   TOTAL TIME: 10:27

Jean Martinon was one of this century's greatest interpreters of the music of Debussy and Ravel, and this delicate, sinewy, lush performance shows why. This was just one part of a collection of French-music recordings Martinon made, and each of them makes a wonderful addition to any collection. Though not a digital master, the sound is still superb.

IF YOU ENJOYED THIS PIECE . . .

There is a wealth of Debussy's music that is worth exploring, beginning with the famous symphonic work **La Mer.** For something a little more unusual there is a beautiful work for chorus, soloists, and orchestra called **La Demoiselle élue.** In the area of chamber music, Debussy's **String Quartet** is a cornerstone of that repertoire. Finally, Debussy's only opera, **Pelléas et Mélisande,** is an exquisite, emotion-packed experience that should be savored.

DVOŘÁK

SYMPHONY NO. 9 IN E MINOR
FROM THE NEW WORLD

When the Bohemian-born Antonín Dvořák (1841–1904) composed his Ninth Symphony, he was living in New York City and was the director of the National Conservatory of Music. The symphony titled *From the New World* is the perfect musical blend of Dvořák's Czech roots and the American spirit that surrounded him as he wrote the piece. The themes are derived from Czech folk tunes while the flavor is American and "folksy." In fact, Dvořák was intrigued by Longfellow's *Song of Hiawatha* and even included musical impressions of segments of the work in this symphony.

Dvořák began composing the *New World* Symphony in January of 1893 and completed it on May 24 of that year. The New York Philharmonic premiered the symphony at a Carnegie Hall concert on December 16, 1893; it was a huge success. The year 1893 also saw the composition of Tchaikovsky's last symphony (see chapter 39); Chicago was hosting the World Exposition; and Oscar Wilde wrote his play, *A Woman of No Importance*.

From the New World is a large, Romantic work and calls for big forces including flutes, piccolo, oboes, clarinets, bassoons, four horns, trumpets, three trombones, tuba, percussion, timpani, and strings. The music is infectious, each movement filled with melodies and rhythms that will at once remind you of American and Bohemian folk music, perfectly blended together. In culinary terms, one might think of it as Southern-fried chicken with a big helping of paprika. While this may not sound appetizing to some, the musical equivalent as Dvořák cooked it is a feast for the ears.

REFERENCE RECORDING:
DEUTSCHE GRAMMOPHON 415 509
VON KARAJAN/VIENNA PHILHARMONIC
TOTAL TIME: 42:07

FIRST MOVEMENT: Adagio–Allegro molto
(9:53)

The opening movement is a study in contrasts: moments of darkness followed by explosions of light; sections of calm broken by perky folk dances. It begins slowly as the violas, cellos, and basses set a thoughtful, melancholy mood. The clarinets and bassoons join (0:18) adding a haunted feeling continued by the horns, then passed on to the flutes and oboes. The calm is shattered as the strings lash out in anger (0:56) quickly supported by the timpani, followed by the flutes, oboes, clarinets, and horns. This is the first salvo in a series of mini-eruptions that start to move the music out of the melancholy. The anger is contrasted by the flutes and oboes (1:23) spiritedly dancing, like a flickering candle in a wind. The slow introduction is ended by a powerful timpani roll (1:55) that fades away as the main section of the movement begins.

The third and fourth horns start this faster section (2:02) (Allegro molto). Supported by shimmering violins and violas, the horns sound particularly regal and important, a quality assumed by the clarinets and bassoons as they take over the melodic line

(2:05). As the other sections of the orchestra join, the volume and intensity increase, leading to an explosion (2:38) led by the trumpets, whose sound cuts through the rest of the orchestra. Slowly, calm returns and the flute and oboe introduce a quiet new theme (3:11). Here is a true folk melody, and the rhythms will make you want to sway gently along with the melody.

The flute (4:17) plays a solo of the first melody, only now the energy seems to have been taken away, and a relaxed, listless version remains. But when the violins take over, they begin to reenergize the flow, and with this comes another eruption (4:44) with the brass instruments dominating, while the string instruments strain against one another. There is a clear horn call (5:04) like a new dawn, especially when the piccolo imitates it, twitting like a bird. Anger and intensity replace nature's calm; the trumpets (5:55) supply a particularly vulgar musical sneer that is evident even through the ferocity of the rest of the orchestra. But as quickly as it arrived, the anger disappears, replaced by a delightfully cheerful oboe solo (6:16). All of this, it turns out, is nothing more than a transition to the return of the regal horn passages that began the fast section of this movement (6:33).

In the midst of this bombast, the flute plays another jaunty, folksy melody (7:15); due to its simplicity, the contrast is great, making it seem even more delightful. Total calm takes over (8:15), the strings providing a lush bed of sound for the flute's solo. When the strings assume the melody, it is lazy and seems to drag a little. But then they get faster and faster; the horns return followed by the timpani and trumpets. The tension and anger return as the trumpets cry out (9:11), straining to be heard through the controlled chaos that develops. The movement ends with a series of angry, unison beats.

SECOND MOVEMENT: Largo   (12:21)

This is one of the most soulful movements in all music. Dvořák said it was inspired by the Indian burial in Longfellow's *Hiawatha*. The main feature of the movement is the haunting English horn solo presenting the melody.

A series of quiet chords, primarily in the brass, serves as the introduction. Then the muted strings create a tranquil base, leading to the entrance of the English horn (0:34). (Some may recognize the melody more easily by setting the words "Goin' home, goin' home, I'm agoin' home" to it. This music was used in a made-for-television movie about the life of Franklin Delano Roosevelt. In it, this prayerful, very human song was heard as the train bearing the president's corpse made its way through the American landscape en route to Washington.) It is a highly recognizable melody, filled with pathos and beauty. It unwinds slowly and has a way of sounding like a lullaby. As the English horn fades away (1:54), the clarinets quietly complete the phrase.

After a series of rich, yet quiet chords from the flutes, oboes, clarinets, and bassoons, and one sustained chord from the brass (2:37), the strings sneak back in with the first violins and cellos playing a prayerlike lullaby. Everything is at peace, and soon the English horn returns (3:29) resuming its plaintive melody, allowing the clarinets again to complete the phrase just before the horns copy it in their sleepy, distant rendition (4:10).

The flute and oboe start to rustle (4:33), moving somewhat faster, while the second violins and violas provide a shimmering, wintry accompaniment. Then, the shimmering dissipates and a sad but regal mood takes over (5:08). The funereal march, provided by the pizzicatos in the basses, sets the tone, heightened by the sad melody played by the clarinets, and later by the flutes and oboes. Again there is rustling, this time in the violins (6:02), as the pace picks up. This section is a series of swells and retreats as the flutes and oboes join the violins in a rhapsodic fantasy that flows onward. Ultimately the violins emerge soulfully playing the clarinets' melody from the earlier funereal march. It is passionate and sad.

Out of a quiet, sustained chord that is fading away, the oboe launches into a perky melody (8:06) that sounds like a bird happily flitting about, an image heightened when the flute, cheerfully trilling, takes over. Gradually the whole orchestra gets into this happiness, and the mood becomes almost raucous. Suddenly an explosion (8:33) cuts the celebration short, and the brass loudly reprise the first movement's angrier tone, complete with rumbling timpani. But calm is restored and once again the English horn is left to play its soulful melody (9:08), this time taken over by the muted violins and violas. The strings do not play the melody through, but rather chop it into sections, like a speaker carefully choosing each phrase before speaking. When all the energy seems to have been removed, a solo violin and solo cello join (10:10) for an exquisite duet rendition of the main theme. The first violins meander through an extended line, gradually slowing and disappearing, replaced by a series of prayerful chords played by the bassoons, horns, trombones, and tuba (11:20). A final chord in the flutes, oboes, violins, violas, and cellos starts quietly and fades away to nothing. The movement comes to rest with an almost inaudible chord in the basses.

THIRD MOVEMENT: Scherzo: Molto vivace
(8:32)

Here Dvořák was again inspired by *Hiawatha*, opting to paint a musical picture of the "festival in the forest" and Pau-Puk-Keewis's dance. Though American in inspiration, Dvořák's Czech roots are distinctly evident, and this could just as easily be thought of as a Bohemian peasant dance.

This fast movement is launched primarily by a ringing triangle, and powerful timpani beats supported by the flutes, oboes, clarinets, and bassoons. The strings then establish the pulse over which the flute, oboe, and clarinet start a bouncy, furtive dance-like melody. It is somewhat rough, especially when played by the strings (0:24), and then grows wild, like a pagan ritual, as the whole orchestra assumes the melody (0:30), now made even more exciting by the piercing attacks from the violins. The entire first section of the movement is repeated (0:45).

Following the repeat, the tension wanes as the pulse relaxes and the strings and bassoon introduce a more lyrical section with a new melody played initially by the flute, oboe, and bassoon (1:41). Gone are the creepy, machine-gun-like phrases of the opening section. In their place is a lovely, cheerful phrase that conjures up images of a gently rolling sea, or a sinuous dance.

When the cellos lend their rich tone and take the melody (2:15), it sounds gracious and genteel, and all the while a series of single triangle chimes are heard in the background.

When the phrase is completed, the violins take over (2:25) and quietly reintroduce the jagged figure heard earlier. Slowly the wildness creeps back and takes over. But it runs out of energy, and the graceful flow returns (3:29) with its delightful ringing triangle. The violins even create a more frivolous section (4:02), but the elegance still dominates. The graciousness eventually ends, replaced by a sudden return to the violins' angular phrases from the beginning (5:29). The fury and mystery start to rebuild quickly, getting louder and returning to a repeat of the entire movement from the opening.

A musical explosion (7:30) begins the final part of the movement. A scary tremolo in the strings (7:48) introduces powerful horn calls that contrast with the flute and oboe still chirping. Gradually the intensity of the horns increases leading to an outburst (8:10) that is like a sunny release of tension. With the energy released, the tension diminishes, and one by one the instruments sleepily drop out, leaving only the clarinets and violas. They, too, fade away, and there is a brief silence. One angry, final chord, led by the timpani and played by the whole orchestra, ends the movement.

FOURTH MOVEMENT: Allegro con fuoco (11:21)

An angry series of snarls in the strings that get faster and faster introduces a movement filled with ferocity. The first melody (0:15), dominated by the trumpets and horns, has an angry, militaristic sound, and when the strings take over (0:42), it becomes more determined.

The pace quickens (1:14) as the violins race ahead, and when the flutes, oboes, and clarinets interrupt (1:23), they fly through their passage like rushing wind. The first pullback (1:47) yields a more haunted, less confident sound heightened by an eerie, distant cymbal crash and an expansive clarinet solo. Though still tremulous, this section is calm and lyrical. But when the violins assume the melody, the intensity increases and a rumbling timpani roll (2:40) brings back some of the militaristic fervor alternating with the calm, mysterious moods.

Out of this hubbub, the flutes and clarinets join to reprise the main theme of the second movement (4:33), now blended with the anger of the final movement. It is almost as if the symphony were trying "to find itself" as it meanders through some undefined development. Then, after a gradual buildup, there is an explosion (5:08) bringing back the ferocity that started this movement, and when the trumpets and horns blare out their call (5:46), the anger is fully restored.

A sad peace replaces the "battle"; the oboe and horns (6:15) mournfully bringing everything to rest. The cellos try to cheer the mood, and with the help of the flute and oboe reminding us of the chirping birds, they manage to create a pastoral, calm atmosphere. (Listen especially for the flute and oboe contrasting with the bassoon [7:59].) A soft horn call (8:19) signals the beginning of the end of this reverie, as the horns get faster and faster, greatly excited, leading to an angry explosion (8:46). It is wild, controlled chaos. Eventually it becomes exhausted (9:46) and the ferocity disappears, replaced by a lonely clarinet joined sporadically by weak comments from different sections of the orchestra. Like taps at a funeral, the horns, accompanied by the quiet timpani (10:04), sadly recall the now lost power.

Out of this state of exhaustion, one last "rally" (10:17) is initiated by the violins and violas that leads to a drawn-out version of the movement's opening melody. It is loud as the trumpets, horns, and timpani are the main blocks in a wall of sound. Suddenly, as if energized by this final struggle, the pace quickens (10:53) and there is a furious race to the finish. The final unison chord is held only by the wind instruments; it slowly fades away.

FELIX CRAUS, SOLO ENGLISH HORN OF THE CLEVELAND ORCHESTRA:

"There is a sense of longing in much of Dvořák's music, but, for me, nowhere is it more affecting than in the English horn solo from the second movement of his final symphony. Though inspired by an

American spiritual, the theme of the motive 'Goin' Home' is univer-sal. With time, one comes to understand the real longing in Dvořák's music: one foot in the New World, the other in the Old."

COMPARATIVE RECORDINGS

VON KARAJAN/VIENNA PHILHARMONIC
DEUTSCHE GRAMMOPHON 415 509   TOTAL TIME: 42:07

Although some of Karajan's tempos are a little slow, espe-cially in the first movement, this is a good performance made better by the exquisite solo woodwind playing of the Vienna Philharmonic. The sound is excellent.

VON DOHNÁNYI/CLEVELAND ORCHESTRA
LONDON 414 421   TOTAL TIME: 40:43

A superb performance that is true to the composer's inten-tions and that allows the music to sound natural. There is some exceptional playing, especially in the second movement.

WALTER/COLUMBIA SYMPHONY ORCHESTRA
CBS MK-42039   TOTAL TIME: 42:04

A good recording by one of this century's legendary mae-stros. Though certainly not Walter's greatest recording, it stands the test of time and presents nothing unusual; just a very solid performance. The recorded sound is good.

IF YOU ENJOYED THIS PIECE . . .

Dvořák's symphonies are all excellent works, but the best to listen to on the heels of the *New World* are the **Sixth, Seventh,** and **Eighth.** Also of interest is his fabulous **Cello Concerto** and equally great **Violin Concerto.**

GERSHWIN

RHAPSODY IN BLUE

It was the roaring twenties when George Gershwin (1898–1937) was asked by bandleader Paul Whiteman to write a symphonic-style piece for his jazz band. Whiteman wanted to blur the lines separating the worlds of concert music and jazz, and so he wanted Gershwin to write something that would lead in the direction of symphonic jazz. The result was *Rhapsody in Blue*, a fifteen-minute fantasy for solo piano and a large jazz band. In fact the original program announced: "George Gershwin (Piano): A Rhapsody in Blue, accompanied by the orchestra." Gershwin composed the piece during a three-week period early in 1924, and it premiered at a concert in New York's Aeolian Hall on February 12 that same year. In 1924 Calvin Coolidge was elected president, Herbert Hoover was named director of the FBI, and D. W. Griffith brought *America* to the screen. In literature, E. M. Forster published *A Passage to India*, while in theater Sean O'Casey wrote *Juno and the Paycock* and George Bernard Shaw penned his *Saint Joan*.

After Gershwin completed the work, Ferde Grofé, the composer of the famous *Grand Canyon* Suite, who was the Whiteman

Band's orchestrator, reworked the *Rhapsody* for Whiteman's jazz orchestra. Following Gershwin's death in 1937, Grofé further expanded the orchestration so the *Rhapsody* could be played by full-size symphony orchestras. This is the version that most listeners are familiar with. This large-scale *Rhapsody* is scored for flutes, oboes, clarinets, bassoons, horns, trumpets, trombones, tuba, timpani, drums, saxophones, banjo, and strings. The solo piano often plays all alone, independent of the orchestra, yielding the freedom for an almost improvisational style. Interestingly, many different versions of the *Rhapsody* exist, and no two pianists seem to play the same thing. In the available recordings, the soloists delete different sections of the piece, each one putting his individual stamp on the work. But regardless of what occurs in the body of the work, the opening clarinet solo is one of the most recognizable phrases in all music. It was made even more famous when Woody Allen used it in his movie *Manhattan*. The *Rhapsody* is a fun piece that accomplishes what Whiteman wanted: to naturally blur the lines between jazz and classical music.

REFERENCE RECORDING:
DEUTSCHE GRAMMOPHON 431 048
BERNSTEIN/LOS ANGELES PHILHARMONIC
TOTAL TIME: 17:09

Slowly, and as sensuously as possible, the solo clarinet starts out with a seamless upward glide. This sinewy slide is one of the most difficult solos the clarinet has to play in any piece of music, and since it is played all alone, it is totally exposed. When it is played well, it seems to slip the listener right into the heart of the music and its jazzy overtones. Once the glide is completed, the clarinet introduces the opening theme. When the theme is finished, the horns, trombones, clarinets, and tenor saxophone start to speed the pace a little, sounding like a musical impression of a train slowly gaining speed (0:48). Then, a second, shorter clarinet glide (0:59) turns the melody over to the trumpet playing with a "wha-wha" mute. (The name of the mute is perfectly descriptive as the sound *wha-wha* emanating from the trumpet is unmistakable.)

The piano first sneaks in (1:11), blending quietly into the jazzy lines being played by the trumpet and supporting horns. This initial solo is brief, merely bridging to an explosive entrance by the full orchestra, complete with crashing cymbals (1:20). Compared to what has come before, this section is stiff, lacking the jazzy informality of the introduction. But when the orchestra stops, the piano returns for its first extended solo (1:34). Here is the classical equivalent of improvisational jazz. While the music is all written out for the pianist, Gershwin structured it so that the pianist could take liberties with phrasing, speeds, and even some of the rhythms. Be sure to note the piano copying the clarinet's opening glide midway through this solo (2:19).

Parts of the orchestra, led by the banjo, clarinets, second violins, violas, and cellos, add some texture to the piano's solo (2:31). But this is just a brief comment, as the piano launches into another extended solo (2:52), this one even jazzier and sexier than before. The pianist should be taking time throughout this solo to have fun with the music. This solo ends abruptly (3:56), interrupted by the full orchestra forcefully establishing a bit of stiffness into what has been totally loose and fluid. A more lyrical section features the strings alternating phrases with the piano (4:11) while the banjo and winds provide a steady pulse. But this too is short-lived, as the trombones lead a forceful attack (4:19) including a fluttering trumpet that seems to sneer, then starts a swinging, faster phrase highlighted by the drums (4:29). Here the propulsive jazz beats make it almost impossible to sit still!

Out of this rollicking hubbub the solo clarinet emerges (4:54) gradually slowing everything down, only to have the full orchestra regain control and launch into a steadier, lively version of the jazz lines (5:09). Once again it is the clarinet (5:34) that interrupts the festivities, only this time the trumpet again sporting its *wha-wha* mute and then the trombone, also with a *wha-wha*, copy the clarinet. Here (5:55) Bernstein makes the first cut in the music, choosing to go right into a lengthy piano solo leaving out a few bars of orchestral material that is repetitive of what has come before. In essence the cuts made in this recording make the solo more of a piece, eliminating the orchestral sections that break up the solo's natural flow. This solo should sound like total improvisation as the pianist has the chance to play with the melodies, stretching their shapes and making them sexier. During this solo the horns join to add occasional subtle accents (6:52). But then the piano continues all alone, jazzily meandering over the infectious melodies.

After all the percussive quality of the solo piano, the mood shifts drastically as we are introduced to a new lush and leisurely melody (10:37). The saxophones, strings, oboes, and clarinets provide a rich bed of sound for the horns, who dreamily move the pace ever so slightly. (For fans of television advertising this theme will be recognized as the music used in the commercials for United Airlines in the early 1990s.) A brief solo from the first violin and the oboe (11:31) is tender and seductive, conjuring up images of those black-and-white drawing-room-comedy movies filled with scenes of fancy parties in which illicit lovers glance longingly at each other across the room over full champagne glasses. The whole orchestra takes up this melody, increasing the lushness of the sound (11:47) and giving a lyrical contrast to the piano's jagged accents. The volume and richness steadily increase, until the piano joins the bells for a jaunty little section (12:37) introducing another lengthy piano solo.

The piano is joined by the horns, trombones, and tuba (14:53), these brass instruments providing a stodgy, heavy accompaniment to the fleeting piano line scampering all over the keyboard. As more instruments are added, this contrast quickly develops into something sounding like a big brass band with piano (15:06). The brass steadily increases the pace leading to a brief explosion of controlled cacophony (15:22) including a wild flutter in the horns and trumpets. Then it's off to the races as the piano quickens the speed, sounding agitated, an image that is heightened by the snare drum playing along.

After slowing down and coming to a complete stop (15:52), the whole orchestra launches into a pompous, steady series of beats that accompanies the solo piano now playing the *Rhapsody*'s main theme in a very square manner. This section ends with the piano all alone finishing the phrase. But then the music slows down even more, growing broader and more pompous (16:36), yet still filled with excitement highlighted by repeated, loud cymbal crashes. The power in this section comes primarily from the brass instruments although the whole orchestra is playing. The final moments of the work feature a long sustained chord played by the whole orchestra while the solo piano pounds out one last phrase to fill the void. One big unison chord brings the curtain down on *Rhapsody in Blue*.

MAESTRO MAURICE PERESS:

"With one fell swoop of a clarinet George Gershwin's Rhapsody in Blue *launched his concert career in earnest. In its original jazz-band format it stands as the most celebrated, if not the first, concert work inspired by the music of Afro-America. And the form! A seamless progression from infectious ragtime through a memorable grand tune in the remotest key possible and a dancing return home via the Caribbean. The* Rhapsody in Blue *is the veritable Rosetta stone of the Jazz Age."*

COMPARATIVE RECORDINGS

BERNSTEIN/LOS ANGELES PHILHARMONIC
DEUTSCHE GRAMMOPHON 431 048   TOTAL TIME: 17:09

Despite the edits that Bernstein makes, this is an exceptional performance with Bernstein serving as conductor and pianist. Clearly his skills as a composer aid him tremendously as he weaves through the piano part making it sound as if he were composing it on the spur of the moment.

DAVIS/PERESS/NEW PALAIS ROYALE ORCHESTRA
MUSICMASTERS 67082   TOTAL TIME: 16:18

Careful research by the conductor Maurice Peress went into the preparation of this recording as he sought to re-create the original Aeolian Hall concert of 1924. This fascinating recording is made even better by the excellent solo piano playing of Ivan Davis.

TILSON THOMAS/LOS ANGELES PHILHARMONIC
CBS MASTERWORKS MK-39699   TOTAL TIME: 15:45

An exceptional recording featuring Michael Tilson Thomas as soloist and conductor. He, too, makes cuts and some changes, but they do not diminish the piece in any way. His playing is jazzy and superb, as is the orchestra's.

If YOU ENJOYED THIS PIECE . . .

Few other composers had the ability to blend the classical and jazz styles the way Gershwin did, so to hear more of this sound it is necessary to listen to more Gershwin, especially the **Piano Concerto in F Major, An American in Paris,** and the **"I Got Rhythm" Variations for Piano and Orchestra.** Beyond these works, Gershwin's greatest compositions are the opera **Porgy and Bess** and many of his infectiously fun shows like **Girl Crazy** and **Strike Up the Band.**

GRIEG

*P*IANO CONCERTO
IN A MINOR, OP. 16

The Norwegian composer Edvard Grieg (1843–1907) has a secure place among the well-known composers of the past because of the incidental music he composed for the play *Peer Gynt* and for his ultraromantic Piano Concerto in A Minor. Of the two, the Piano Concerto has become an integral part of the standard repertoire, a favorite of pianists because it gives them a great opportunity to take and hold the spotlight. Simply put, this concerto is a series of fabulous piano solos with some pleasant orchestral accompaniment. However, the true greatness of the work lies in its rich melodies combining Scandinavian coolness with the hot passion of the Romantic era.

Grieg composed the Piano Concerto in 1868, the same year the German master Johannes Brahms composed his overpowering *German* Requiem, Renoir painted *The Skaters*, Dostoyevsky wrote *The Idiot*, and Louisa May Alcott created the immortal characters in her *Little Women*. In England, Disraeli became prime minister, while in the United States General Ulysses S.

Grant was elected president and the Cincinnati Red Stockings became the first professional baseball team.

Grieg's concerto premiered in Copenhagen on April 3, 1869, and was not well received by the critics. One German reviewer called it a "patchwork . . . an unfortunate and ungrateful piece." It is possible that Grieg was forging a style ahead of its time, the critics' ears not yet ready for it. However, now more than a century later, the work has not only survived but grown in popularity. Most of Grieg's other works were written for small ensembles, including many wonderful, intimate songs. But the concerto calls for a fairly large Romantic orchestra including flutes, oboes, clarinets, bassoons, four horns, trumpets, trombones, timpani, and strings.

REFERENCE RECORDING: RCA VICTOR 7834
CLIBURN/ORMANDY/PHILADELPHIA ORCHESTRA
TOTAL TIME: 29:39

FIRST MOVEMENT: Allegro molto moderato (13:00)

The very first thing to be aware of in this concerto is the way the orchestra and piano alternate; rarely do the two forces play together as equal partners. Rather, either the piano or the orchestra leads, and most often the orchestral sections are little more than melodic bridges linking the technically demanding piano solos. Another important element to note is the fluidity of the structure; frequently the pace speeds and slows, ebbing and flowing freely.

The beginning of the concerto is dramatic; a quiet timpani roll rapidly gets louder and erupts into one chord blasted by the entire orchestra and the piano. From within this explosion the piano emerges with its first solo, a thoughtful yet powerful introduction instantly establishing the romantic mood of the work.

The piano's final note is held as it fades away, leading to a momentary pause. The silence is filled as the strings provide a jerky accompaniment for the woodwinds, who quietly establish the melody (0:28); it is tentative and tinged with sorrow. The clarinet and bassoon continue the theme with a lyrical line (0:39) becoming more intense and passionate when echoed by the flutes, oboe, and first violins (0:50).

The piano then takes the melody (1:02) and plays it nobly and somewhat dreamily, qualities heightened when the strings add a lush background. Left alone, the piano speeds up, becoming animated (1:41) with a series of uneven, flitting passages. Listen for the way the oboe joins the piano (2:09), adding its soulful tone echoing the piano's melodic line. Then, after a gradual slowdown, the mood changes again, becoming ultraromantic as the cellos play a gorgeous solo (2:21) conjuring up images of candlelit elegance. (This is one of those distinctive themes frequently used to promote recordings of "classical excerpts," i.e., "your favorite melodies.") Following the pattern of alternation established early in the movement, the piano takes this new melody (2:47), turning it into a dreamy, thoughtful little phrase accompanied only by sustained, quiet notes in the strings; the dreaminess is heightened by the solo bassoon (3:08) adding its plaintive tone.

Slowly the speed increases, leading to another piano solo (3:47) ending as the orchestra takes over (4:01) excitedly. This, the first extended orchestra solo, is punctuated by dramatic trumpet calls (4:21) ringing through with militaristic fervor, tempered by a subdued horn solo (4:30) and fading into the return of the solo piano (4:36). This rhapsodic solo is accompanied by tender solos from the flute and horn. But the mood is shattered by a determined outburst (5:15) from the orchestra as the piano part turns even more rhapsodic and florid, gradually speeding up. The orchestra grows angrier with a series of blasts interrupted by the piano (5:36). Ultimately, as the strain eases, the orchestra fades, replaced by the solo piano reprising the movement's original melody (5:58).

The next sections are basically repeats of what has already been heard. As before, the piano becomes animated (6:36), speeding up, flitting gracefully over the keys. The ultraromantic cello solo returns (7:23) and re-creates the candlelit aura echoed by the dreamy piano solo (7:45) then heightened by a beautiful duet for the horn and piano (8:07). When the piano takes over (8:26) accompanied only by quiet bits in the orchestra, the intensity and passion increase, gradually leading to a determined outburst by the orchestra (9:00). Weighted down, the pace slows and leads to a dramatic timpani roll (9:11) followed by an abrupt full stop. Quickly filling the silence, the piano plays its cadenza (9:15), an extended rhapsodic interlude evoking romantic images as it ebbs and flows, a passionate, dramatic, technical tour de force for the soloist.

As the cadenza ends, the horn, timpani, and strings take over (12:10), leisurely at first. But when the solo oboe and bassoon play the melody (12:24) over an agitated string accompaniment, the speed picks up. The piano enters (12:35) reprising the movement's opening piano solo (12:40), then joining with the whole orchestra for a frantic race to the movement's final explosive chord and dramatic timpani roll.

SECOND MOVEMENT: Adagio   (5:59)

This extremely slow movement is mood music at its absolute best: pensive, lush, and passionate. It opens with just the muted strings led by the first violins carrying the melody. The bassoons and horns sneak in (0:40) adding a bittersweet quality to the sound, slowly swelling the volume until the horns soar dramatically over the strings (1:27). A lush, soulful cello solo (1:35) is echoed by the woodwinds before the horn brings this romantic introduction to a quiet close.

The piano makes its dreamy, meandering entrance (2:03) accompanied by quiet, sustained strings. After a brief burst of excitement by the piano, the strings play a short bridge (2:34) leading to the next piano solo, still wandering but with some swells in the sound and even a slight increase in speed. Seemingly spent, the piano pauses as the strings provide another bridge (3:12), reintroducing the piano with the flute and clarinet, then with the oboe and bassoon, and then with all four winds and the horn (3:32). Having gained strength through each of these phrases, the movement now seems energized, and there is a loud, determined outburst (3:37) using the piano, strings, clarinet, and bassoons; the richness in the sound is provided by the cellos' passionate line. The intensity wanes as the horn (4:07) plays a series of short bridges linking equally short piano solos. Throughout this section there are swells and pullbacks in the sound, like the sea rolling in and out over a sandy shore.

Quietly the woodwinds bridge to another short piano solo (5:12). As it dissipates, the horn and strings join (5:23), recalling the romance. Sleepily and quietly the piano and strings play the movement's final notes and fade into the silvery moonlit night.

THIRD MOVEMENT: Allegro marcato   (10:40)

There is virtually no pause before we are launched into the final movement, a propulsive piece in the style of a Norwegian leaping dance. The clarinets and bassoons establish the jerky, staccato pulse introducing the piano's forceful entrance that reaches its rhapsodic peak, pauses at the apex, and rolls back down to a single note from the orchestra. Then the piano launches into its version of the jerky dance with only occasional accents from the strings and lyrical but hard-to-hear support from the horn and bassoon. Listen for the wicked run up the keyboard the pianist has to negotiate leading to the orchestra taking over the melody with its full fury (0:41).

Accompanied initially only by the cellos and a bassoon, the piano returns (0:49) for more fast passages swirling about like a cyclone. The solo becomes less percussive, more singing (1:03), accented by jerky notes from the strings. Gradually the intensity grows, erupting when the trumpets add their biting sound (1:41); fiercer and angrier than before, there is a distinctly combative tone. But the piano interrupts (1:58) for one of its free-form solos culminating in a return to the jerky dance theme (2:17), now in a more tormented guise. The piano dominates this section but leaves its final phrase incomplete as the orchestra barges in (2:43) aggressively completing the phrase then quieting down and fading.

Tranquillity emerges with shimmering violins and violas accompanying a gorgeous flute solo (2:56) filled with hope. The luxurious sound swells (3:17) yet remains tender as the piano returns (3:31) calmly echoing the flute aided by the warm sound of sustained notes in the cellos. This section is pensive and slow, reminiscent of the second movement. The other strings join (4:15) followed by the flute and clarinet; the sound swells and recedes, becoming sexy. Then the pace slows, everything enters a state of dreamy calm, and gradually fades away.

Quietly at first, the oboes, bassoons, horns, and timpani reset the staccato pulse (5:51) joined by the strings. They are all replaced by the piano (5:57) reestablishing the jerky dance theme from the movement's beginning. (Much of what follows is a recapitulation of earlier material and will be familiar.) After a brief orchestral interlude, the piano takes over (6:35); here be sure to listen for the dramatic rushes of sound from the second violins and violas adding propulsion to the piano's already fast-moving part.

With each phrase the volume and intensity increase, leading to a broadening of the pace, as if this drive forward has suddenly become stuck, making motion more difficult. The strings alternate with the winds, each trying mightily to keep things moving while the piano plays between them, a wild flying over the keys. Mystery abounds as the strings tremble, the timpani rumble beneath sustained notes in the clarinets, bassoons, and horn. Something is brewing; the pace speeds up; the battle rages and then explodes in a sustained, fierce chord (8:07). The piano returns (8:11) for a brief, demonic solo leading to another explosive chord (8:21), this one between dissonance and jubilation.

The piano takes over (8:24) with a freestyle solo, pauses momentarily, then starts out anew on a jaunty, cheerful variation of the movement's original dance theme (8:44). (The change in the pulse will make the dance sound very different.) Hesitantly the orchestra chimes in, seemingly trying to fit into this new rhythmic pattern, gradually becoming more important as the pace increases, the dance getting wildly out of control, a feeling heightened by the trilling flutes (9:22).

Through the excitement the trumpets assert themselves (9:27) and manage to have a calming influence. The pace slows and the entire orchestra explodes into a much slower celebration (9:30) that sounds heavy in contrast to what has preceded it. Against this determined stiffness the piano races through some thrilling passages, the mood luxurious, as if the orchestra were wallowing in the bigness of the sound and the intensity of the passion. The sound swells, reaching explosive levels; the piano interrupts in midphrase for one last solo (10:06), before the orchestra joins the piano for an even slower, more effusive passage (10:14). A powerful timpani roll accompanies the four loud chords that end the concerto.

VAN CLIBURN:

"Once when I was doing a studio recording of the Grieg Concerto with Kiril Kondrashin and the Moscow Philharmonic, Maestro told me how the Russian people adored the works of the Norwegian composer. And years before that my mother told of how her teacher, Arthur Friedheim, related how his mentor, Franz Liszt, had the deepest respect for his younger colleague, and prophesied that his A Minor Piano Concerto would become standard repertoire for the piano. That work, in fact, had a personal stamp of great approval from Liszt, and it is one of my personal favorites as well."

COMPARATIVE RECORDINGS

CLIBURN/ORMANDY/PHILADELPHIA ORCHESTRA
RCA VICTOR 7834   TOTAL TIME: 29:39

An oldie but a goodie! This recording brings out all the romance, passion, and luxury that make this a wonderful piece of music. Cliburn's playing is astounding and the Philadelphia

Orchestra plays with great richness. The sound from the late 1960s stands up extremely well.

ZIMERMAN/VON KARAJAN/BERLIN PHILHARMONIC
    ORCHESTRA
DEUTSCHE GRAMMOPHON 410 021   TOTAL TIME: 30:56

The interpretation is a little bit on the dispassionate side, but the digital sound and the sound of the orchestra make this a recording worth hearing.

CURZON/FJELSTAD/LONDON SYMPHONY ORCHESTRA
LONDON 417 676   TOTAL TIME: 29:17

This is the oldest of the three recordings (1960) but Curzon's interpretation is a classic, bringing great romanticism and passion combined with technical clarity. The sound in the CD transfer holds up well.

IF YOU ENJOYED THIS PIECE . . .

Of Grieg's output the Piano Concerto stands on its own and is impossible to duplicate. However, his **Incidental Music to Peer Gynt** is delightful and evocative, if not quite as romantic. If you are drawn to the Romantic piano concerto, the usual companion work to the Grieg Concerto is the **A Minor Piano Concerto by Robert Schumann.** Another fabulously lush Romantic piano concerto is **Tchaikovsky's Concerto No. 1 in B-flat Minor.**

HANDEL

WATER MUSIC

The work known as *Water Music* by George Friedrich Handel (1685–1759) is actually an amalgam of movements written for ceremonial occasions in England between 1715 and 1717. The name *Water Music* comes from the fact that most of the movements were written for festive, royal boat trips on the Thames, the best-documented one occurring in July 1717. On that trip contemporary accounts reported about fifty musicians were positioned on a barge, entertaining for the entire length of the journey from Whitehall to Chelsea. This era was dominated by the great royal leaders: George I ruled in England, the regency of Louis XV replaced Louis XIV on the throne of France, while in Russia it was the reign of Peter the Great. In terms of the next generation, the future Empress Maria Theresa was born.

The movements of *Water Music* were assembled as suites, and it is evident from the orchestration that most of the movements were intended for the difficult acoustics of the outdoors, while others, the more intimate ones, were probably composed for indoor use. The orchestration is large for the baroque era, originally calling for twenty-four strings, flutes, piccolo, oboes, horns, bassoon, and harpsichord. While the strings are heard in

every movement, the winds used vary from movement to movement.

Through the years the work has gone through changes and
many interpretations, and different performing editions exist, so
the sequence of movements will vary from performance to performance. Regardless of movement sequences, the *Water Music* is
a thrilling work capturing the regal pomp of the English court.
The way it is written gives the listener a chance to hear how the
members of the orchestra can go from soloist to member of the
ensemble. Further, the structure of the work and its many repeats
allow performers some interpretive freedom, yielding even more
variety and allowing the listener to hear the same melodies in
different guises.

REFERENCE RECORDING: DG ARCHIV 410 525 PINNOCK/ENGLISH CONCERT
TOTAL TIME: 53:46

SUITE IN F MAJOR

I. OUVERTURE: Largo-Allegro   (3:19)

The slow but not heavy introduction features the oboes and
the strings, somewhat choppy and stately, filled with regal pomp.
The introductory section is played in its entirety two times
through. Then, the first violins begin a fast, bouncy section
(1:11) copied almost by the second violins. When the rest of the
orchestra joins in (1:25), the sudden richness of sound enhances
the images of courtly elegance. Out of this fullness emerges the
first solo from within the orchestra, as the oboe takes over the
dominant line (1:38) accompanied by one solo violin from each
of the two violin sections. The two solo violins take the next solo
as they do a bit of "dueling fiddles," alternating short phrases
(2:15). Linking the solo passages are busy, excited orchestral sections. One of these orchestral sections leads directly into the
movement's abrupt end.

II. Adagio e Staccato   (2:14)

Without pause a slow movement begins with four repeated notes followed by the oboe playing a plaintive solo (0:05). The mood remains brooding and heavy, especially when contrasted with the first movement's bouncy ending. The slow pace allows the oboist to ornament freely, giving the solo an improvisational quality. The violins take over the melody (1:02) until the oboe reemerges (1:15) with another soaring solo. The oboe plays by itself (1:52), like a brief cadenza, joined by the others for a unison, quiet ending.

III. (Allegro)—Andante—(Allegro da Capo)
(7:46)

A single chord played by the oboes, bassoon, and strings introduces the horns, who rousingly herald their arrival, like an awakening. In this initial series of calls the horns alternate with the rest of the orchestra. Then they are left to play a difficult solo (0:10) answered by the oboes. This pattern of announce and answer repeats several times in this movement, most evidently when the strings alternate with the winds (0:57) in a wonderful contrast of sounds.

The excitement grows steadily with the mood becoming exuberant, until an extended trill in all the instruments (2:29). The movement seems to end, then starts again with the Andante (2:34) as the oboes and bassoon play alone. The pace is slower, having gone from a romp to a stroll, and the joy of the earlier section is replaced by a distinct undercurrent of melancholy, made sadder by the entrance of the strings (2:53). Throughout this slow section listen for how the strings and winds interact, sometimes alternating and sometimes joining to create a rich sound. Out of one unison section, the oboe emerges with another solo (4:51) leading to a quiet ending. The peace is disrupted by a single chord (5:10) returning everyone to the movement's fast opening and the horn calls. The Allegro is repeated and the movement ends with the unison trill heard just before the Andante section.

IV. MENUET: Allegro   (3:12)

It is evident from the outset of this movement this is not a graceful, courtly minuet, but rather a fast romp supported by the strength of the horns and oboes adding a lusty, raucous quality. Listen for the horns blending with the other instruments at first, then emerging in a beautiful solo (0:12). After this solo, the first part of the movement is repeated. (Almost every part of this movement is repeated at least once, giving the listener the opportunity to note interpretational differences.) The repeat ends (0:39), and the movement continues with the orchestra playing in unison, leading to another horn solo (1:02), and a repeat of the second section.

The mood shifts after the second repeat, as the strings, now without the winds, play a more sullen melody (1:39). This is the only section of the movement not repeated. When it ends (2:18), we return to the beginning of the Menuet and a final repeat of the movement's first two sections.

V. AIR   (3:02)

This movement is calm and peaceful, but not sad. The first violins establish the melody and are immediately answered by the second violins. The winds do not play in this section, and as the violins play the melody, the cellos and bass provide a rich bed of sound. When the oboe, bassoon, and horn do enter (1:58), it is the oboe that joins the violins with the melody, while the bassoon adds its voice to the cellos and bass. The horn plays a long sustained note on its own before joining the melodic phrase. Be sure to notice how the addition of the horn makes the calm sound more regal. The movement draws to a close with the oboe, horn, and violins carrying the melody and the bassoon, viola, cello, and bass providing the accompaniment.

VI. MENUET   (3:24)

The first horn starts this stately movement, quickly joined by the second horn (0:04). They play the entire exposition alone, in one of the most regal-sounding sections of the entire work. Soon the rest of the orchestra joins (0:44), copying the melody established by the horns. A more intimate section follows (1:28) with the bassoon joining the strings in a different melody most easily heard in the first violins. However, try to pick out the viola and bassoon lines playing against the violins; the contrast is beautiful.

VII. BOURRÉE   (2:07)

This fast, bouncy movement has a most interesting structure. Initially the delicate melody is handled by the violins with the other strings adding support. When they have played the movement through in its entirety, the same sections are played by the oboes with accompaniment by the bassoon (0:41). This combination plays through the movement, and then all the instruments join together (1:22) and play through the movement a third time.

VIII. HORNPIPE   (2:36)

This is another jaunty dance movement, and its structure is identical to the bourrée. It is more stately, yet jovial, with a bouncy nature seeming to chuckle as it unfolds. As before, the strings play through the movement, followed by the oboes and bassoon (0:51). In the midst of the oboe section (1:22) the interplay of the two oboes yields a jerky, uneven feeling. The strings, oboes, and bassoon join together for the last time through the movement (1:41).

IX. ANDANTE   (3:06)

Beginning with the oboes and bassoon playing alone, this movement is filled with contrasts. While not fast, it moves at a good pace, and while not sad, it does have an undercurrent of tension. When the strings join in (0:21) with the first violins taking the melody, the oboes and bassoon play sustained notes that seem to stand out. Eventually the strings and winds alternate the melody (0:56), the winds emerging with one of the most beautiful solos in the entire work (1:01). As the intensity grows, the action becomes busier, with more interweaving of instruments, some playing the intricate melodic lines, others playing simple sustained notes. Suddenly the busy-ness stops (2:49), replaced by slow, sustained notes and a sad unison ending, similar to the one at the end of the suite's very first movement.

SUITE IN D MAJOR

X. OUVERTURE   (2:08)

The addition of two trumpets gives this suite an even more regal quality. A single chord played by the oboes, bassoon, and strings introduces the trumpets and their startling call, echoed by the horns (0:10). In this movement the orchestra is divided into two teams, one led by the trumpets accompanied by the oboes, violins, and violas, and the other led by the horns assisted by the bassoon, cellos, and bass. These two "teams" are actually divided into upper voices versus lower voices, creating a distinct tonal difference as they alternate passages. One particularly exciting response is provided by the horn team (1:12), as they traverse a difficult series of notes with wonderful support provided by the bassoon. After almost an entire movement of competing, the two teams join (1:21) and play in unison. Suddenly, the fast section ends (1:44), replaced by a slow series of notes in the strings, and a plaintive solo from the oboe and the movement's quiet ending.

XI. ALLA HORNPIPE   (4:13)

This is the most famous movement in the entire *Water Music*. At the outset, despite the absence of the trumpets and horns, there is a dramatic elegance and power. However, whatever strength the oboes, bassoon, and strings can muster is soon eclipsed when the two trumpets (0:16) and two horns (0:23) take the main theme. Once each instrument has completed its initial pass at the melody, the strings, oboes, and bassoon alternate with the trumpets and horns. To end the first part, the instruments join together (0:56) for a rousing section and a repeat of the movement's entire first part.

After the repeat, we are introduced to a new, intimate, fleeting section (2:07) with the feeling of creeping around. Gone are the pomp and grandeur of the first section along with the trumpets and horns. During this part, listen for the oboes and first violins. At the end of this more delicate section (3:05), there is a repeat of the movement's opening and its grand melody.

XII. MENUET   (2:52)

This graceful, peaceful movement introduces the flute, paralleling the first violins. None of the other wind instruments play in this movement. The melody is somewhat romantic, filled with longing. In this movement, each section is repeated at least once, providing another opportunity to listen for dynamic and ornamentation differences.

XIII. RIGAUDON   (2:43)

The oboes, bassoon, and strings are featured in this fast, bouncy movement. While other movements had the sections of the orchestra divided and playing against each other, this rigaudon has the instruments in unison. There is a distinct mood change (1:12) replacing the joviality with a more troubled quality. However, despite the mood change, the pace does not relent, and the movement ends with a return to the carefree bounciness in a repeat of the opening sections.

XIV. LENTEMENT   (2:01)

The tempo marking indicates that the pace should be leisurely, yet this does not mean it should drag; it should be stately, but not pompous. The trumpets and horns return, and right at the beginning the trumpets play the theme echoed by the horns. A second section (1:00), just as leisurely but somewhat sadder, is started by the oboes and copied by the strings. When this segment ends (1:26), the opening section of the movement is repeated.

XV. BOURRÉE   (1:20)

This is a cheerful romp played three times through using all the parts of the orchestra. The first time it is played by the trumpets and violins; the second (0:24) by the horns and the oboes, making a terrific sound; and finally (0:49) by the whole ensemble.

XVI. MENUET   (1:07)

Here is a minuet paced in the style of an elegant court dance. While not as fast as the dances in the other suite, this should not be thought of as slow because it does move. It is played by the strings alone and seems to have an undercurrent of melancholy.

XVII. ANDANTE   (1:39)

The piccolo (or baroque traverse flute) leads this movement with an interesting three-note phrase featuring a middle note that is always higher than the two notes around it, making it seem as if it is popping out. The piccolo is joined by the strings, and while the mood here is more cheerful than in the previous movement, there is still a distinctly pensive quality. The repeated three-note phrase continues for the entire first part of the movement and only changes in the second section (0:48). A descending phrase in the cellos and bass (1:11) leads to a repeat of the movement's opening section.

XVIII. COUNTRY DANCES I/II   (1:29)

A perky flute solo moves us from the court to the country-side. The flute, combining with the strings, makes this movement hop, creating the image of a totally carefree existence. When the bassoon replaces the flute (0:28), the sound becomes fuller, but the bouncy nature does not diminish. In fact, the main change is that now there is a sense of all-out abandon.

XIX. MENUET   (3:28)

For the final movement, we are definitely returned to the court, the melody now gracious, stately, and confident. It is another instance when we hear a movement three times through. First, as if to announce this final section, are the trumpets and the violins. The second time through (1:07) the horns and oboes join for an even more regal sound. Listen especially for the beautiful oboe solos (1:30 and 1:51). As is fitting, the entire orchestra plays the last time through the movement (2:13) in a joyous, elegant finale.

PRINCIPAL HORN OF THE ORCHESTRA OF ST. LUKE'S AND THE ORPHEUS CHAMBER ORCHESTRA, WILLIAM PURVIS:

"In a concert hall Handel's Water Music is a contradiction. You should try to imagine yourself on the Thames with this music coming at you in an exciting cacophony; particularly the horns and trumpets would be brilliantly blaring and wildly jubilant."

COMPARATIVE RECORDINGS

PINNOCK/ENGLISH CONCERT
DEUTSCHE GRAMMOPHON ARCHIV 410 525
TOTAL TIME: 53:46

Certainly among the best of the "original instrument" recordings, Pinnock's reading avoids the pitfalls that can make the repeats sound so boring. Especially good is the use of the harpsichord, which adds so much color to the sound.

MACKERRAS/ORCHESTRA OF ST. LUKE'S
TELARC 80279   TOTAL TIME: 54:19

While not the greatest performance of this work, there is some exquisite playing by the woodwinds of the St. Luke's Orchestra. The recorded sound is also quite good.

MARRINER/ACADEMY OF ST. MARTIN IN THE FIELDS
EMI CLASSICS CDC 49810   TOTAL TIME: 55:31

The Academy is one of the most distinguished interpreters of this and other baroque works. Under the guidance of Marriner they give an excellent account of the piece, especially for those who prefer their baroque music on rich-sounding modern instruments.

IF YOU ENJOYED THIS PIECE . . .

Handel's output is tremendous and there is a great deal of music to choose from, beginning with the **Suite for the Royal Fireworks.** There is also a wealth of **Concerti grossi,** especially the set known as **Opus 3,** each concerto showing the baroque orchestra at its absolute best.

HANDEL

*M*ESSIAH

ORATORIO IN THREE PARTS

There is a lot more to George Friedrich Handel's (1685–1759) *Messiah* than the "Hallelujah Chorus"! In fact, while the "Hallelujah Chorus" is exciting and uplifting, it is probably not even the best chorus in the oratorio. Simply put, *Messiah* is more than two hours and fifteen minutes of exquisite music.

Written in a period of just eighteen days during the autumn of 1741 while Handel was in London, *Messiah* received its world premiere in Dublin on April 13, 1742. It was an immediate success there but did not have a London performance until 1743. The year 1741 saw turmoil on the European continent: England had to mediate a dispute between Prussia and Austria; and Maria Theresa, who was to become important to the musical world some years later, accepted the Hungarian crown. Handel, though German by birth, was firmly in place in the British Isles, where he was considered the leading composer of his day. *Messiah* only enhanced his reputation.

Because of changes made by Handel after its premiere, there are several different performing editions of the oratorio extant.

The original orchestration was for strings, a harpsichord, an organ, and a solo trumpet used in only one number. For the London premiere Handel added oboes and bassoons to support the strings in the choruses. This is the orchestration that is most frequently used. There are four soloists (soprano, alto, tenor, and bass) and the chorus. The size of the forces depends entirely on the whim of the conductor, usually guided by the size of the performance space. Since many of the numbers are recitatives, the harpsichord and first cello are important.

The texts are drawn from the Holy Scripture and were selected by Charles Jennens. Since *Messiah* is in English, the story is easy to follow, and even though rather long, it never becomes dull because it is made up of many different-sounding short movements.

REFERENCE RECORDING: LONDON 414 396 SOLTI/SOLOISTS/CHICAGO SYMPHONY ORCHESTRA AND CHORUS
TOTAL TIME: 2:20:41

PART I

I. OVERTURE (ORCHESTRA ONLY)   (3:03)

The Sinfony, as it is called, is one of only two numbers in the entire work for the orchestra alone. It begins slowly; the mood is serious and filled with pomp. After the stodgy beginning the violins break into a fast section (1:18) and lead the other instruments who join and echo this more upbeat passage. It is this pace that continues until the end of the overture.

II. COMFORT YE MY PEOPLE   (3:04)

This is an accompanied recitative for the tenor supported by the strings and the harpsichord. It is stately and extremely peaceful, paralleling the call for the listeners to be comforted. The strings play a brief introduction, followed by the tenor's first entrance with the simple phrase "comfort ye" sung alone. As the recitative continues, the strings play their accompaniment while the tenor's melody often soars above them. When the tenor intones the words "the voice of him that crieth in the wilderness," the calm dissipates and he gets more excited, his words punctuated by single notes in the strings. This leads us to the end of the recitative, and an immediate attack on the next aria.

III. EV'RY VALLEY SHALL BE EXALTED   (3:37)

This tenor aria begins with a rousing orchestral introduction with great excitement increasing with each phrase. The tenor enters (0:21) and immediately picks up the original melody stated by the violins. The challenge for the tenor lies in the sections in which he sustains one syllable (such as *alt* from *exalted*) while having to sing an intricate extended passage, all while the strings are punctuating with occasional notes. A good performance of this aria will immediately give the listener a sense of excitement and anticipation for what is about to unfold. In typical baroque fashion, there is a brief orchestral postlude to end the number.

IV. AND THE GLORY OF THE LORD   (2:42)

This number brings in the chorus, the oboes, and the bassoons. After the orchestra introduces the bouncy melody, the altos enter (0:11) announcing, "The glory of the Lord," then echoed by the rest of the chorus. This is a joyful number. During it, each choral voice has a chance to sing alone, as the excitement builds. However, the most exciting moments come when all the voices sing together. The jaunty pace is maintained until a brief pause near the movement's end. Then all the voices join for the phrase "hath spoken it" (2:29) played broader and slower.

V. THUS SAITH THE LORD   (1:19)

In this accompanied recitative, the bass is introduced; his is a dark voice and usually delivers the angrier passages. Here a choppy, brief string introduction is followed by his angry announcement: "Thus saith the Lord, the Lord of Hosts." Though short, this is a demanding number because it is filled with passages requiring an agile voice. The end of the number has the bass singing virtually alone announcing what is to happen. It must be stentorian!

VI. BUT WHO MAY ABIDE THE DAY OF HIS COMING   (4:26)

The contrast between this number and the previous one is dramatic. This alto aria starts out sad and pensive; instead of announcing with confidence, the alto asks with timidity. The violins establish the plaintive melody taken by the solo alto when she enters (0:21). While this is an aria, the harpsichord and solo cello accompany the voice while the other strings play only when she is silent. This slow pace continues until a sudden shift (1:41) as the alto sings of "a refiner's fire." The rapid passages in the strings seem to portray the jumping flames of the fire. This pace is maintained until the energy wanes (2:34) and the aria returns to its original slow speed and pensive mood. Finally there is one more section of "fire" (3:15) as the speed returns, taking us to the end of the aria and the strings' fast postlude.

VII. AND HE SHALL PURIFY   (2:41)

This is one of the choruses that while not as exciting as the "Hallelujah!" is certainly as beautiful. The organ and lower strings cue the sopranos, who begin in an intimate fashion. It is jaunty and delicate with a strange undercurrent of mystery. The other choral voices join in one at a time, sometimes singing together and sometimes apart. The movement builds slowly, with each new entrance a little louder than the previous one. This continues until a unison (2:19) when the excitement seems to overflow. However, it quickly backs off, and the movement ends as it began: quietly.

VIII. BEHOLD A VIRGIN SHALL CONCEIVE (0:35)

This is a recitative for alto accompanied only by the harpsichord and cello. When it is sung properly, it evokes a sense of wonder about the story.

IX. O THOU THAT TELLEST GOOD TIDINGS TO ZION (5:26)

This number begins as an alto aria with the chorus joining in later. It is an exuberant piece, a mood established by the violins in the introduction. The alto entrance (0:25) immediately takes the melody. It is especially interesting to note that the voice and violins usually alternate and are rarely heard together; only the harpsichord and cello play while the alto sings. There are many repeats of phrases in the aria with variety supplied when the chorus and winds join (3:47) in a joyful explosion of sound. The orchestra ends the number with an upbeat postlude.

X. FOR BEHOLD, DARKNESS SHALL COVER THE EARTH (2:15)

Here the mood changes as the bass has a recitative accompanied by the strings. (It could actually be thought of as a short aria.) As its title indicates, it is somber. Yet, because of the movement of the phrases played by the strings, it is not slow. When the bass sings the words "but the Lord" (0:58), there is a distinct mood change; the darkness is lifted, replaced by a sense of hope.

XI. THE PEOPLE THAT WALKED IN DARKNESS
(3:30)

There should be virtually no pause before this bass aria begins. This is a slow, somber number with a distinct undercurrent of mystery. Throughout, the violins parallel the sung line, serving as an upper-voice contrast. Between sung phrases the orchestra often has short solos bridging between the bass's entrances. It ends with a short, serious orchestral postlude.

XII. FOR UNTO US A CHILD IS BORN   (4:19)

Here is one of the greatest choruses ever written. Its rather intimate beginning belies its power, developing gradually as each voice is added and the joy increases. Though not fast, its bouncy quality makes it seem to move rapidly. The full orchestra introduces the melody the sopranos then assume on their entrance (0:14). The tenors come in next, followed by the altos, and then the basses. Note how the vocal parts fit together, with each subsequent entrance adding a new dimension. As the movement progresses, it grows in volume with a series of mini-eruptions usually on the phrase "Wonderful, Counselor, the mighty God, the everlasting Father, the Prince of Peace." The final explosion (3:35) has the chorus singing in unison. It is followed by a delicate postlude and quiet ending.

XIII. PASTORAL SYMPHONY (PIFA)   (2:53)

Other than the Overture, this is the only nonvocal number in the oratorio. It is a slow, pensive piece for strings and harpsichord. Since the entire piece is played twice, it presents a good opportunity to listen for the ornamentation and the musical changes the conductor might make each time through.

XIV. (A) THERE WERE SHEPHERDS ABIDING IN THE FIELD (0:17)

This brief recitative is the first entrance of the solo soprano. It is the first of a sequence of short recitatives for the soprano narrating the story.

XIV. (B) AND LO, THE ANGEL OF THE LORD CAME UPON THEM (0:19)

Now the recitative is accompanied by the strings. It is somewhat flighty and excited.

XV. AND THE ANGEL SAID UNTO THEM (0:47)

Now we return to a slow recitative accompanied only by the harpsichord and cello.

XVI. AND SUDDENLY THERE WAS WITH THE ANGEL (0:18)

This recitative is introduced by fast notes in the violins creating an aura of expectant excitement, copied by the soprano. This serves as an introduction to the following chorus, which should be launched into as soon as the recitative ends.

XVII. GLORY TO GOD (2:03)

This is a thrilling number introducing the trumpets with the full orchestra. It begins immediately with the chorus announcing, "Glory to God," supported by the trumpets, while the violins play a fleeting passage. The excitement continues until there is a pullback (0:11) when the chorus sings "and peace on earth." This is the first of two sudden retreats. The excitement begins to rebuild when the basses enter singing, "Good will toward men" (0:42). Once again listen for how the vocal lines are pieced together. Despite the movement's power, it ends extremely quietly with the violins playing a delicate passage.

XVIII. REJOICE GREATLY, O DAUGHTER OF ZION   (4:21)

Following a brief introduction played by the violins, cellos, bass, and harpsichord, the soprano launches into a real showpiece with some hard-to-negotiate florid passages. As its title indicates, the aria is joyful. Listen for how the soprano and violins alternate passages, the strings echoing the vocal line.

There is a distinct mood change as the aria slows down and becomes more pensive (1:32), especially when the soprano sings "He shall speak peace" (1:43). This calm middle section precedes a return to the aria's bouncy opening (2:40) and the "rejoicing." This time, to add interest, the soprano's line is even more florid and demanding. The violins reassume the lead in the orchestral postlude ending the aria.

XIX. THEN SHALL THE EYES OF THE BLIND (0:36)

This brief recitative for the alto is an introduction to the following air.

XX. HE SHALL FEED HIS FLOCK LIKE A SHEPHERD   (4:54)

While this movement is slow, Handel's lyrical phrases seem to keep the pace moving. (It may remind you of the "Pastoral Symphony," movement XIII.) The strings establish the pace and the melody, soon taken by the alto. The overriding feeling is of absolute calm. Unlike many of the other solo numbers where the singer and strings alternate, here the strings continue playing while the soloist sings, yielding a rich texture. In an unusual twist, the alto is replaced by the soprano, who takes up the melody (2:02). Listen for the effect the higher vocal range has on the mood of the aria.

XXI. HIS YOKE IS EASY, AND HIS BURTHEN IS LIGHT   (2:29)

There is virtually no break before the chorus, led by the sopranos, launches into this fabulous chorus. Be sure to listen for how the addition of the oboes adds color. The movement starts quietly and builds with the addition of each section of the chorus. However, it never becomes heavy because Handel was careful to construct it so that the word *light* would dominate, and even when the whole chorus joins together (1:40), the movement does not lose its airy quality. Part I of the oratorio ends quietly, with the chorus holding the word *light* over sustained notes in the orchestra. Listen for the beautiful harmony provided by the oboes.

PART II

XXII. BEHOLD THE LAMB OF GOD   (2:38)

The choral number that begins Part II of the oratorio is very different from the one concluding Part I. This one begins slowly and mournfully; the altos enter after a stately orchestra introduction. The other voices join in, with the basses adding a particularly dark quality, a mood evident throughout. When the chorus finishes (2:17), there is a brief postlude that in essence is a string quartet, as the only instruments playing are the first and second violins, the violas, and the cellos.

XXIII. HE WAS DESPISED   (9:42)

This is the longest number in the entire oratorio. It begins with a regal yet sad string and harpsichord introduction leading to the alto entrance (0:39). This aria should be passionate and filled with a sense of disbelief, capturing the sentiment of the text telling how this "man of sorrow" could be "despised." A string interlude (3:41) ends the aria's first section and jumps immediately into the second section, filled with anger, depicted musically by the aggressive figure Handel gave to the strings; it gives the sense of forward propulsion. Over this the alto must depict anger with her tone. As quickly as the second section began, it ends, and we are returned to the stately orchestral introduction (5:21) that started the aria. The first section is then repeated in its entirety. Listen here for changes the alto makes, especially in the embellishments on any sustained notes.

XXIV. SURELY HE HATH BORNE OUR GRIEFS   (1:49)

From the choppy first phrase of this chorus, there is no doubt that the dominant mood is anger and defiance. After a short string introduction, the chorus enters in unison joined by the oboes creating an interesting harmony. Even in this short movement the mood does change briefly to sorrowful and peaceful (0:43), but it quickly reverts to the dominant anger.

XXV. AND WITH HIS STRIPES   (2:01)

There should be no pause between this chorus and the last. The sopranos launch right in, beginning a fugue. Their entrance is followed in turn by the altos, tenors, and basses. The different voices grow and decrease in importance, ultimately coming together for a peaceful unison ending.

XXVI. ALL WE LIKE SHEEP HAVE GONE ASTRAY
(3:56)

Again there should be no pause before the chorus and oboes begin this cheerful number. When the line becomes jaunty (0:24), the accompanying bassoons add a wonderful sound that heightens the upbeat mood. The movement builds steadily until there is a sudden change when the basses sing "And the Lord . . ." (2:50). From here on the movement is slow and pensive.

XXVII. ALL THEY THAT SEE HIM LAUGH HIM TO SCORN   (0:42)

This accompanied recitative for the tenor begins forcefully with the violins playing a choppy, repeated figure. The tenor's brief, angry recitative introduces the next chorus.

XXVIII. HE TRUSTED IN GOD   (2:12)

Now the anger boils over. The basses, cellos, double bass, and bassoon enter first, painting an immediately dark sonic image. The other voices enter in sequence again creating a fugue. However, unlike "And With His Stripes," this fugue is fast until the end, when the voices come together. Then the pace slows.

XXIX. THY REBUKE HATH BROKEN HIS HEART
(2:05)

The tenor has one of the simplest yet most moving and beautiful recitatives. His pensive lines are accompanied by sustained notes in the strings, and little filigreelike turns by the harpsichord.

XXX. BEHOLD, AND SEE IF THERE BE ANY SORROW   (1:15)

This tenor aria is filled with the sorrow reflected in the title. Most of the feeling must be delivered by the singer, since the orchestral accompaniment is really just a skeleton of color.

XXXI. HE WAS CUT OFF OUT OF THE LAND OF THE LIVING   (0:23)

Here the tenor and sustained strings deliver a thoughtful, slow recitative.

XXXII. BUT THOU DIDST NOT LEAVE HIS SOUL IN HELL   (2:15)

This tenor aria continues the thoughtfulness of the preceding recitative. Though similar in nature, the tempo moves, so this aria comes across as forgiving and almost thankful. Listen for how the violins alternate with the soloist.

XXXIII. LIFT UP YOUR HEADS, O YE GATES   (3:03)

Here is another chorus that is at least as great as the "Hallelujah," but not nearly as well known. After the long sequence of somber, pensive, and angry numbers that went before, this thrilling chorus stands out. The strings establish the melody, with the upper voices of the chorus, supported by the oboes, entering (0:10) after the melodic phrase has been played once through. In this number Handel divides the chorus into two distinct choirs so that they may question and answer. The first instance of this is when the tenors and basses ask, "Who is this King of Glory?" (0:22), a question they ask several times with increasing intensity. The answer comes from the rest of the chorus: "The Lord strong and mighty . . ." The effect of question and answer divided among two large groups of voices is overpowering. In fact, each time the sequence is repeated, the intensity and the volume increase, building to one final pronouncement: "He is the King of Glory" (2:51), as the pace broadens and all the voices join together.

XXXIV. UNTO WHICH OF THE ANGELS SAID HE AT ANY TIME   (0:23)

This is a recitative for tenor accompanied by the harpsichord and the cello.

XXXV. LET ALL THE ANGELS OF GOD WORSHIP HIM   (1:25)

With the entire chorus entering in unison, this is another joyful chorus that makes the listener want to stand up and cheer! As in the other big choral numbers, here the oboes add a wonderful texture. Listen for them, and for how the sopranos soar above the rest of the chorus and the orchestra.

XXXVI. THOU ART GONE UP ON HIGH   (3:21)

The violins play a lovely and bittersweet introduction to this aria. The alto's entrance (0:17) begins slowly, but soon requires the singer to be vocally agile. A nice orchestral interlude (1:02) precedes the second part of the aria followed by a recapitulation of the aria's first section and an orchestral postlude.

XXXVII. THE LORD GAVE THE WORD   (1:08)

The tenors and basses announce the opening of this chorus. But their stentorian beginning is quickly replaced by the full chorus, strings, oboes, and bassoon scurrying through rapid passages. This part comes to a sudden stop (0:24), and the sopranos and altos whisper the phrase the men sang initially; it, too, is replaced by the fast passages. When the chorus stops singing (1:00), the orchestra plays a fun postlude.

XXXVIII. HOW BEAUTIFUL ARE THE FEET (2:15)

This soprano aria returns us to the pensive mood. After the short exposition played by the violins, harpsichord, cellos, and bass, the soprano enters (0:21) and assumes the melody that the violins have established. In many ways this aria is reminiscent of the "Pifa" ("Pastoral Symphony," movement XIII), especially in the way it seems thoughtful and slow, but actually moves at a good pace.

XXXIX. THEIR SOUND IS GONE OUT   (1:25)

Here is another great chorus that is not well known. It features an important part for the oboes as accompanists to the sopranos. The other voices enter in descending sequence (i.e., altos, tenors, basses). While the number begins forcefully, there is a moment where it quiets down (0:28). But this is short-lived as the volume rebuilds, the movement growing toward its joyful conclusion.

XL. WHY DO THE NATIONS SO FURIOUSLY RAGE TOGETHER   (2:44)

The key to this exciting bass aria is the word *rage*. At the outset the strings launch into a furious attack, the anger and rage constant right through to the bass's final word. The challenge for the bass is to make the words sound clearly through the unrelenting orchestra, while negotiating the tricky passages written for him.

XLI. LET US BREAK THEIR BONDS ASUNDER (1:54)

Handel calls for an immediate attack in this choral number. As the voices enter, listen for how each vocal line fits into the overall puzzle. When the tenors launch into the phrase "and cast away" (0:15), the number seems to take on the quality of a happy, almost raucous drinking song. The orchestra's postlude is especially interesting, as it carries the number's jauntiness right to the end and highlights the "dueling" between sections of the orchestra.

XLII. HE THAT DWELLETH IN HEAVEN (0:14)

This is an angry tenor recitative that introduces the following aria.

XLIII. THOU SHALT BREAK THEM (1:56)

The opening violin phrase leaves no doubt that this is an angry number, and the continuing "stings" provided by the violins add to the tension. When done properly, this tenor aria should be venomous, right through the postlude.

XLIV. HALLELUJAH (3:39)

Here it is! Placed in context, it is quite a contrast to the preceding aria. One of the reasons this chorus is so overpowering is Handel's use of all his forces, including the trumpets and timpani, although it is the string instruments that establish the melody and introduce the chorus. The first major change from the theme everyone knows is when there is a sudden pullback (1:13) as the chorus sings, "The kingdom of this world . . ." But this section is short, and the explosives return and continue until the end, when the pace broadens for a loud, unison conclusion.

PART III

XLV. I KNOW THAT MY REDEEMER LIVETH
(5:47)

This is one of the most beautiful arias in the entire oratorio. Following the introduction played by the violins and cellos, the soprano enters and declares calmly, yet with conviction, that her "redeemer liveth." During this aria the same phrase is repeated several times. This is the perfect opportunity to listen for variations and embellishments the singer might make. The calm is maintained through the exquisite postlude.

XLVI. SINCE BY MAN CAME DEATH   (2:07)

This fascinating chorus begins with the voices singing alone, softly, almost whispering. Mystery prevails until the sound fades away and the bass and cellos play one note (0:35) followed immediately by the forceful entrance of the chorus, the violas, violins, and oboes. This section is exuberant. But it stops (0:58), and the a cappella chorus returns, followed again by a return to the fast section (1:34).

XLVII. BEHOLD, I TELL YOU A MYSTERY   (0:36)

With the strings playing sustained notes, this accompanied recitative introduces the next aria.

XLVIII. THE TRUMPET SHALL SOUND   (8:27)

While ostensibly an aria for the bass, this number should really be thought of as a duet for the bass and trumpet accompanied by strings and harpsichord. The trumpet speaks first, setting the regal, somewhat pompous tone. It is a rather long introduction, and when the bass does come in (0:39), the darkness of the low voice contrasts the soaring trumpet line. The bass sings virtually nonstop until a brief reprise of the trumpet's introduction (3:24) preceding a more intimate and personal section (3:51) for the bass, harpsichord, cello, and bassoon. But once that ends, the aria returns as the bass proclaims, "The trumpet shall sound!" (4:12) and a return to the aria's beginning. In this second time through, listen for embellishments by the bass and trumpet. The orchestra's postlude features the trumpet; it is a repeat of the aria's very beginning.

XLIX. THEN SHALL BE BROUGHT TO PASS
(0:26)

This recitative for the alto conveys a feeling of confidence.

L. O DEATH, WHERE IS THY STING?   (0:57)

This is one of the strangest numbers in the oratorio: a duet for the alto and tenor accompanied only by the harpsichord and one cello. The beauty of the duet lies in its simplicity, especially the way Handel weaves the two vocal lines together.

LI. BUT THANKS BE TO GOD   (2:04)

This chorus continues right out of the duet's final phrase. The voices convey a sense of being humble as they give thanks. Listen for how the sections of the chorus echo each other. While the chorus is segmented throughout the number, they come together (1:50) for a joyful, unison ending.

LII. IF GOD BE FOR US   (4:48)

The final aria of the oratorio copies the pattern of many of its predecessors; the violins provide a brief introduction followed by the soprano entrance (0:37). The mood is somewhat sad, yet there is a distinct undercurrent of hopefulness.

LIII. WORTHY IS THE LAMB THAT WAS SLAIN
(6:36)

The last movement of *Messiah* is moving, exciting, and uplifting as it brings all the forces together. It is a mixture of tempos, but the mood is consistently joyful. The opening is pompous and slow with everyone in unison. Then suddenly (0:28) the pace quickens and the excitement grows. This slow/fast pattern is repeated before the tenors and basses launch into a new, more forceful passage (1:22) echoed by the sopranos and altos (1:32). As they sing of "blessing and honor," the excitement intensifies, and when the trumpets and timpani join, the exuberance overflows. Then, a broadening (3:04) slows everything down. The excitement is replaced (3:17) by the basses quietly beginning a series of "Amen's," continued by the tenors, then the altos, and finally the sopranos. A brief orchestral interlude (3:59) leads to a sudden explosion (4:19) as the entire chorus loudly proclaims its "Amen's." The voices are layered one on the other, with each entrance increasing the volume. When the tempo broadens, it leads to a complete stop (6:12), followed by one final, unison "Amen" and a rumbling timpani roll that carries on to end the oratorio.

DAME KIRI TE KANAWA:
"*Each soprano aria in* Messiah *is at once delicate, dramatic, and simply beautiful. There is a tender passion that comes through; a rewarding piece to perform.*"

FOUNDER AND CONDUCTOR LAUREATE OF THE
CHICAGO SYMPHONY CHORUS, MARGARET HILLIS:
"*If you are hearing* Messiah *for the first time, you should first read the entire libretto. This will give you insight into the fact that it is*

essentially an opera that is not meant to be staged. There are scenes that hang together; for instance, the piece starts with an overture, followed by a tenor recitative and aria. Then the chorus continues the text that was set up in the recitative and aria. The structure from here on out is similar, and you will find to your surprise there is only a short section that refers to Christmas!"

COMPARATIVE RECORDINGS

SOLTI/TE KANAWA, GJEVANG, LEWIS, HOWELL/
    CHICAGO SYMPHONY ORCHESTRA AND CHORUS
LONDON 414 396   TOTAL TIME: 2:20:41

One does not associate Solti with Handel; however, his forces in this recording are superb. It is a driven, powerful performance filled with variety and interest. It has exceptional sound.

HOGWOOD/NELSON, KIRKBY, WATKINSON, ELLIOT/
    THOMAS/ACADEMY OF ANCIENT MUSIC/CHOIR
    OF CHRIST CHURCH CATHEDRAL, OXFORD
L'OISEAU-LYRE 411 858   TOTAL TIME: 2:15:25

If "authentic" performance, including the use of two sopranos, and "period" instruments are of interest, this is a good recording. The museum quality of the performance can render the work somewhat less than exciting, although parts are absolutely thrilling.

SHAW/ERICKSON, MCNAIR, HODGSON, HUMPHREY/
    STILWELL/ATLANTA SYMPHONY ORCHESTRA
    AND CHORUS
TELARC 80093   TOTAL TIME: 2:19:54

Shaw has specialized in the art of recording great choral works, and his ability to shape a work of this length, and to make a chorus sound superb and interesting, is what makes this recording a particularly good one.

IF YOU ENJOYED THIS PIECE . . .

There are numerous Handel oratorios similar in many ways to *Messiah*. Among the best are **Samson, Judas Maccabaeus,** and **Israel in Egypt**. If you are interested in hearing vocal music from Handel's Italian period, try the operas **Julius Caesar** and **Semele.**

HAYDN

♪YMPHONY NO. 94 IN G MAJOR

SURPRISE

Of Franz Joseph Haydn's (1732–1809) 104 symphonies, the *Surprise* Symphony is the best known thanks to its quirky second movement and the resulting catchy title. While certainly a good composition, Haydn's 94th Symphony pales in comparison to some of his other symphonies, such as the *Miracle*, No. 96, or the *Drum Roll*, No. 103. Nonetheless, the *Surprise* remains the most well-known symphony due to the "wake-up call" Haydn inserted in the second movement.

Haydn composed the symphony at the end of 1791, exactly during the last month of Mozart's life, when the younger composer's *Magic Flute* was being premiered. Haydn, though living in London, was writing against the backdrop of the French Revolution; it was in 1791 that the French king Louis XVI was captured while trying to escape. It was the year in which Thomas Paine penned his *Rights of Man* and Boswell wrote his *Life of Johnson*.

Haydn spent most of his career living within sixty miles of Vienna. It was not until 1791 that he moved to London where, for the first time in his career, he was not attached to any court, instead composing for concerts attended by the general public. The *Surprise* Symphony was the fourth symphony Haydn composed in 1791, and it premiered in London on March 22, 1792. It is scored for two flutes, two oboes, two bassoons, two horns, two trumpets, strings, and timpani. It is the timpani that plays the critical role in the *Surprise,* and in fact in German-speaking countries the symphony is known as *Mit dem Paukenschlag* (with the timpani stroke). In the quiet second movement listen for the "timpani stroke," which, as Haydn is reported to have said, "will make the ladies jump!"

REFERENCE RECORDING: CBS MYK 37761
SZELL/CLEVELAND ORCHESTRA
TOTAL TIME: 24:06

FIRST MOVEMENT: Adagio–Vivace assai (9:37)

For the most part, this movement is joyful, but occasionally the tone becomes a bit gloomy. The introduction is slow and opens with the oboes and bassoons supported by the horns, answered by the strings. The pattern repeats, this time with the flutes joining the oboes and bassoons. This brief introduction has an elegant quality with a somewhat sad undercurrent. A solo for the first violins (1:07) leads to a split-second pause followed immediately by the Vivace assai section started by the violins (1:15). Now the pace is fast yet graceful, and the mood happy. While the violins carry the melody a great deal of the time, listen for the flutes and oboes paralleling them when the whole orchestra joins in (1:20).

The first gloomy section occurs (2:17), but the happiness quickly returns. The strings have a calm interlude (2:48) joined by the flutes, oboes, bassoons, and horns. Then, as a contrast, the flutes and oboes play alone (3:09) with a distinct trill in the oboe sticking out. A series of repeated notes in the first violins (3:28) leads to a repeat starting where the Vivace assai section began.

Following the repeat, the mood changes (5:59), becoming more troubled, as if trying to work out a problem. Listen for the sustained notes in the wind instruments playing against the busier violin and viola parts. A series of repeated notes played by the first violins (6:54) brings us out of the turbulence and into a recapitulation of the movement's original ebullient melody played by the first violins and flutes. A later series of repeated notes (7:40) precedes a flowing violin solo echoed by the oboe (7:49).

A sudden silence (8:23), followed by a jerky series of notes, leads to quiet sustained notes from the horns, followed by the first violins restating the melody. Haydn then divides the orchestra: the flutes, oboes, and bassoons play alone (8:40), and the strings answer (8:49), before both groups join together (9:00) for an elegant phrase. This gentle section is replaced by a sudden burst (9:20) as the orchestra races to the movement's conclusion.

SECOND MOVEMENT: Andante   (6:24)

The melody of this movement is the one that is most often associated with Haydn. In fact, the words "Papa Haydn's dead and gone, but his music lingers on . . . " have jokingly been set to this melody and serve as a good way to remember the main theme as it goes through variations throughout the movement. Also, this movement is filled with repeats, so don't be surprised by the number of times you will hear each section.

The movement begins with the strings playing the quiet, jerky, yet steady melody. After the melody is heard a second time, there is a loud BANG (0:32) as the full orchestra, led by the timpani, gives its surprise wake-up call. Immediately after it, the strings take over again with a peaceful second theme, repeated by the flutes, oboes, and horns (0:50) adding support. The original theme returns played by the second violins and the violas (1:07), but this time the first violins and then the flutes add a fast-moving filigree. This is the first variation of the main theme.

Suddenly the mood changes (2:14), and while the theme is easily discernible, it is now in an angry guise. Then the tensions increase (2:46). The first and second violins alternate through a couple of fast exchanges, then join together, continuing the intensity. A solo for the first violins (3:13) serves as the bridge to a return of the cheerful melody of the movement's opening (3:22), this time dominated by the oboe. The next variation (3:39) is more contemplative: the violins play the melody while the flute and oboe add a sustained line. This variation is much like chamber music as the four intimate voices blend together. Later (4:12) the horns join the sustained line, which adds depth to the texture.

The mood turns raucous (4:12), like a carefree peasant dance. But it is short-lived as the strings and bassoon emerge with another variation on the theme. Another explosive surprise (5:20) breaks the quiet, and the mood turns celebratory. Listen especially for the trumpets (5:36). But all this exuberance ends (5:48) as everything grows quiet, as if Haydn simply decided to let the audience fall asleep after all.

THIRD MOVEMENT: Minuet and Trio   (4:15)

Do not expect an elegant, courtly minuet! This movement is more of a happy country dance, better suited to a grassy meadow than a stuffy ballroom. Again, it is filled with repeats giving ample opportunity to appreciate each section.

The opening uses the whole orchestra, quickly scaling back to a more intimate (0:08) ensemble featuring the flute, bassoon, and strings. After a repeat of the opening section, the bassoon and strings (0:34) take over, eventually scaling back to just the violins. When the full orchestra returns (0:43), there is a slight sense of trouble, perhaps a cloud on the horizon. But soon the movement's original cheerfulness returns.

The Trio section (2:09) is played primarily by the strings with significant contributions from the bassoon. The feeling is graceful, and calmer than the main portion of the movement, almost like a rest during the dance. Again each section is repeated, and when the Trio ends, the Minuet resumes with its happy dance.

FOURTH MOVEMENT: Allegro di molto (3:50)

The strings open the final movement at a comfortably fast pace, the delicate melody taken initially by the first violins. The flutes copy it (0:07), while the other wind instruments occasionally add their voices. The delicate quality diminishes as the pace quickens (0:32) with fast runs in the violins making it sound busy. There is a sudden, brief stop (1:02), and when the violins resume, they are accompanied by pizzicatos in the cellos and basses yielding an elegant, yet jazzy feeling.

A recapitulation of the main theme (2:03) precedes an angry version of the melody (2:09). This troubled section, featuring some demanding violin passages, evolves into a return to the initial theme (2:32), this time played by the violins and bassoon. Haydn injects one more sudden stop (2:55), then quickly restarts the elegant music. Eventually, the timpani breaks through with an angry, thunderlike roll (3:17). The pace quickens as the movement races to its conclusion, led by the horns and trumpets. Two surprisingly quiet woodwind chords (3:42), followed immediately by two chords from the full orchestra, end the movement. These final chords may sound like Haydn's last "Ha! Ha!"—his musical chuckle!

TIMPANIST CLOYD DUFF:

"As the timpanist of the Cleveland Orchestra for thirty-nine years, now retired, it was great fun to perform the 'Surprise' in this famous Haydn symphony. The timpani part is not difficult, as such; however, the clarity and openness of this writing requires great precision, intonation, and exactness in performance. The 'surprise' comes early in the second movement. After the exposition of the Andante theme, played softly, there is an enormous fortissimo chord in which the timpani has the most prominent part. With enthusiasm the timpanist can even overdo the accent! The novelty of Haydn's writing

proved effective in his day. Even today, when audiences are guilty of settling down to a snooze about this time, Haydn's enormous note still comes as a big 'surprise'!"

COMPARATIVE RECORDINGS

SZELL/CLEVELAND ORCHESTRA
CBS MYK 37761   TOTAL TIME: 24:06

One of the classic recordings of this symphony. Szell's traditional interpretation stands up well to the test of time. The woodwind playing is especially beautiful and the sound is excellent despite the recording's age, having been made in the 1960s.

FISCHER/AUSTRO-HUNGARIAN HAYDN ORCHESTRA
NIMBUS NI 5159   TOTAL TIME: 23:42

A lively, beautifully played recording made even more interesting by the fact that it was recorded in the Esterhazy Palace at Eisenstadt where Haydn spent most of his career. The sound is exceptional.

HARNONCOURT/ROYAL CONCERTGEBOUW ORCHESTRA
TELDEC 9031-73148   TOTAL TIME: 23:08

This is a beautiful recording led by a man who spent a good part of his career specializing in recordings of authentic period-instrument performances. Here he brings some of the classical performance practices and melds them with the sound of one of today's greatest orchestras.

IF YOU ENJOYED THIS PIECE . . .

There are over one hundred other Haydn symphonies that make excellent listening, especially the symphonies written after No. 85. Also, Haydn's **Sinfonia Concertante** for violin, cello, oboe, bassoon, and orchestra is a wonderful, unusual work. Finally, for more passion, be sure to listen to Haydn's stirring oratorio **The Creation**.

HOLST

*T*HE PLANETS, OP. 32

SUITE FOR LARGE ORCHESTRA

Long before John Williams composed the soundtrack scores for
the many outer space movies popular in the 1970s and 1980s,
Gustav Holst (1874–1934) wrote his seven-movement suite for
orchestra titled *The Planets*. As you listen to this massive creation, the similarities between it and its motion-picture descen-
dants will become apparent. Holst's fantastic use of the orchestra
creates an evocative musical picture of the heavens, giving each
planet its distinct characteristics.

Inspired by the study of astrology, Holst wrote this seven-
movement suite assigning astrological, not mythological, characteristics to each planet with pithy, brief descriptions to help
guide the listener through his solar system. English born, Holst
composed the Suite between 1914 and 1916 as the First World
War raged on the Continent. (It is probably not a coincidence
that the Suite begins with "Mars, the Bringer of War.") In 1916
the Russian monk Rasputin died as his country stood on the
brink of revolution, while in the United States Woodrow Wilson
won reelection to the presidency. In literature, James Joyce fin-

ished *Portrait of the Artist as a Young Man;* in art, Matisse painted *The Three Sisters;* in architecture, Frank Lloyd Wright designed the Imperial Hotel in Tokyo; while in the emerging field of motion pictures D. W. Griffith produced his epic *Intolerance.* *The Planets* received its world premiere in 1918 led by the legendary British conductor Sir Adrian Boult. Holst's orchestra is extremely large and includes, in addition to the more standard instruments, a bass flute, bass oboe, tenor tuba, celesta, xylophone, two harps, six French horns, organ, and a percussion section requiring three players to handle all the demands. Further, in the final movement, "Neptune," there is a heard but unseen chorus of female voices.

Due to its size there is too much going on within each movement to pick out all the interesting uses of the instruments or the shifts in mood. However, Holst's writing is so clever it will certainly conjure up terrific images of the heavens. As you listen, keep in mind the description of the planet illustrated by the music; it will guide you through the solar system. Finally, don't be surprised if parts of the Suite sound very much like the film scores composed more than half a century later; the similarities are hard to miss!

REFERENCE RECORDING:
TELDEC 2292-46316
MEHTA/NEW YORK PHILHARMONIC/NEW YORK CHORAL ARTISTS   TOTAL TIME: 53:12

I. MARS, THE BRINGER OF WAR: Allegro
(7:38)

In addition to composing a great work of music, Holst was clearly making a statement in this movement about the brutality and foolishness of war. Quietly at first, the strings and timpani begin a relentless hammering. Note how Holst accentuates this rhythmic pattern by having the string instruments play with the wooden sides of their bows, creating a prickly, angry sound. This is the basis for the horrific conflict about to erupt, and this pattern runs throughout the movement and contrasts with the sustained entrance by the lower wind instruments (0:05) including the bassoons, contrabassoon, and two of the horns sounding like the arrival of the first warships. Gradually the other wind instruments copy the sustained phrases, increasing the volume, foreshadowing the inevitable coming conflict.

There is a slight brightening of the mood (0:51) just before the first violins play the first passage using the hair portion of the bows (0:58); the phrase seems to soar over the continuous hammering in the background. There is a huge eruption (1:21) as the hammering climaxes, led by the pounding timpani as the wind instruments blast through; power and conflict abound.

For the first time the steady pounding in the background relents (1:56), replaced by a series of bursts highlighted by the swelling sound of the organ. A new pulse, a steady march established by the strings (2:18), accompanies a forceful solo by the tenor tuba joined by the trumpets. A strange quality here combines a macabre sense of humor with the horror of war. The solo sounds like an exaggerated melody for a pompous general swaggering with brutal confidence. When the violins take the melody (2:33), it becomes joyful and celebratory, but there remains a distinct undercurrent of tension.

A split-second pause (3:14) precedes a horrific outburst, like the explosion of a huge bomb; it fades away leaving nothing but a rumble. The distant snare drum (3:21) introduces the bassoons, contrabassoon, and strings brewing more conflict, an uneasy lull in the battle. Other instruments join in; it is clear the forces are reconvening as the movement moves inexorably toward another explosion (4:45) using the whole orchestra playing the original rhythmic pattern heard at the outset. Like fierce machine-gun fire, each round moves us closer to an angry outburst (4:51) featuring the brass instruments and sustained blasts before breaking into a wicked series of attacks and counterattacks.

As before, the rhythmic hammering stops (6:20), replaced by a series of huge sonic swells intensified by the organ. It seems impossible, but the volume and force continue increasing, culminating with the loudest eruption yet (6:37), this one dissonant and ugly, sustained by the powerful organ and the overwhelming percussion section. There is something very "twentieth century" about this moment: the conflict and strain, a musical evocation of the metallic horror of new-age conflagration.

Slowly the sound diminishes, some calm creeps in, and the strings (7:00), joined by the piccolo, flute, oboe, English horn, bass oboe, and clarinet, break into a fast passage accompanied by sustained chords in the horns. As it gains speed, it is interrupted (7:08) by a four-note blast: a fleeing soldier brought down by sudden gunfire. Each blast, loud, fierce, heavy, and dissonant, slows the pace a little bit. The movement ends with one final overpowering chord crashing down, exhausted by the conflict.

II. VENUS, THE BRINGER OF PEACE: Adagio
(8:06)

As diametrically opposed as war is to peace, so are the tone, mood, and pace of the two opening movements. "Venus" is slow and calm; a solo horn calls out from the silence, the atmosphere intensified by the ethereal sound of four flutes and three oboes (0:12). The cellos and basses lead into a magical section featuring the horns and harps with silvery chiming from the glockenspiel (0:53) and the celesta (1:01). Again the solo horn calls out (1:26), repeating its opening phrase, its shimmering calm taking us to a series of sustained chords (2:08) introducing a passionate violin solo (2:13). The violin's melody flows over a steady pulse provided by the oboe and English horn; it has a distinct sense of forgiveness.

The energy increases just a little (3:00) as the violins and violas play long flowing lines imbued with romanticism. Tired from this emotional display, the pace slows, leaving only a solo violin (3:18) accompanied by the flutes, sleepy and quiet, blending into an expressive oboe solo (3:42) in turn replaced by a dreamy clarinet solo (3:50). After a brief swell, a solo cello accompanied by the bassoons (4:30) returns to the slower pace of the movement's beginning, a calm, steady pulse in the horns.

The cool chiming of the celesta (6:40) intensifies the dreamy quality, a musical incarnation of bubbles floating aimlessly through space. There is a momentary stirring, threatening to change the total calm to something more intense. But as quickly as the swell occurred, it wanes, returning the steady calm (7:22) highlighted by the celesta and glockenspiel. The final moments are absolutely ethereal, the celesta gliding over the flutes and sustained strings, slowing down and fading away into space.

III. MERCURY, THE WINGED MESSENGER: Vivace   (3:55)

Despite the irony that the first sounds come from the orchestra's heaviest voices, this is an extremely fast, delicate movement. Quickly the piccolo, flutes, violins, and celesta (0:12) dance through a rapid, airy passage leading to a sustained, very high note (0:30) in the violins, accented only by the chiming celesta. The sustained note breaks into a jerky pulsing, sounding somewhat like Morse code, rebuilding the rapid pace and the quicksilver airiness accentuated by the ringing glockenspiel (0:45).

An unusual duet for solo violin and harp (1:03) adds a more intimate quality. Gradually the excitement builds as more instruments pick up the violin's melody, erupting (1:42) into a full-blast, joyful outburst. Quickly it calms, leaving only the flutes and bassoons (1:57) playing a haunting, slower theme. But the murmur of excitement returns and soon the fleet feet of Mercury return happily, scampering faster and faster to a sudden precipice (3:03) to be interrupted by a timpani solo. While the timpani rumble continues, the celesta chimes happily, and then the piccolo pipes in (3:17), followed by a solo violin (3:19). The bubbly spirit continues happily racing to the movement's final, delicate chord.

IV. JUPITER, THE BRINGER OF JOLLITY: Allegro giocoso   (8:09)

Bouncing, laughing violins begin this fast-paced movement joined by robust horns (0:05) calling out loudly. The first signs of jollity develop with the rapid addition of other instruments. This opening flight pauses for a split second (0:21), the void filled by an explosion of cymbals, the triangle, the timpani, and the rest of the orchestra. Quickly there is a retreat, leaving the shimmering strings and the horns excitedly announcing (0:29), filled with happiness and humor. Another sudden pause (1:02) precedes the strings and horns joyful, but somewhat heavier than the strings, as if sharing a good belly laugh. This changes into a slower, more stately section again featuring the horns and strings (1:41); British pomp comes to the fore, yet when some of the other instruments such as the tambourine get involved, it loosens up and takes on a more festive, free-flowing quality (2:01) that grows raucous. A sustained chord with a crash of the cymbals (2:34) and blasting brass instruments leads to a darkening of the happy picture, made more glum by the rumble in the violas and cellos (2:45).

Following another pause (3:05) a new section is dominated by the strings and the horns; it is soulful and proud with a slow, broad pace that seems to revel in the richness of its sonority. Gradually the volume increases, reaching its thrilling climax (4:40), the full force of the orchestra wallowing in the wealth of sound. The final note is sustained, fades away to blend into a return of the shimmering violins (5:08) and an English horn solo quietly announcing a return to the movement's original melody and jollity. A flurry of excitement leads to an explosion (5:30) of sound, like a loud laugh lengthening with each breath. The next sections are recapitulations of the movement's earlier passages with the wind instruments fleetingly exchanging laughs and giggles. Listen especially for the glockenspiel (6:53) adding its magical sound to the happy festivities, then leaving it to the tambourine (7:00) to keep the mood bright.

The sound grows and grows until a slow heaviness replaces the fast pace (7:32). It is dense, thanks to the brass trombone and bass tuba growling under the flutes, piccolos, clarinets, harps, violins, and violas, but retains great excitement. Suddenly, a huge burst (7:52) releases all the pent-up energy into a fast-moving, light, airy race highlighting the glockenspiel. The timpani continues to pound out its powerful machine-gun-fire beats, as the brass instruments sound off again and a single beat from the bass drum brings the movement to its thrilling conclusion.

V. SATURN, THE BRINGER OF OLD AGE: Adagio   (10:38)

Slowly and steadily the flutes, including the bass flute, and the harps intone a series of haunting, not quite dissonant chords; getting from one chord to the next is an effort, like the difficulty of moving in old age, yet there is a steadiness to the progression reminiscent of the endless ticking of a clock marking the passage of time. The rumble of the basses' entrance (0:14) only heightens the sadness and heaviness increased by a brief, mournful oboe solo (1:21). The flutes and harps continue their steady, quiet pulses as various instruments add their own somber interjection. Listen especially for the bass oboe (1:45) with its foghorn quality and the horns (2:07), who play the last of the mournful wails.

The flutes and harps stop as the cellos and basses play a steady marchlike pizzicato passage (2:20) introducing a solemn, funereal trio for tenor trombone, bass trombone, and tuba (2:29). When the trumpets join (2:52), the mood brightens slightly, growing peaceful despite the funeral-march quality. Gradually, as the strings grow in importance, there is an unmistakable happiness, as if a coming to terms with the passing of time. This grows to a state of comparative excitement (3:33) leading to a dramatic chord (3:59) that dissolves and returns to the flutes and harps. Only now the harps, joined by the timpani, quietly reinforce the flutes' steady, sullen march, each beat heavy and slow. Gradually other instruments join, increasing the strain and sadness; listen especially for the trumpets (5:15) with their more powerful sound.

Suddenly, as if unable to stay restrained within the confines of this horrific death march, there is an outburst (5:45); everything becomes animated and frantic as the bells toll loudly. This is just a passing frenzy as the heaviness of the march returns, now almost exultant, with the force of the trumpets (5:50). But this collapses in another frenetic outburst (6:00), the strings wildly keeping pace with the bells while the trumpets soar above the fray. The energy wanes, the bells chime steady and controlled as the frantic action turns calm and depressed, fading to a murmur. Like the sun breaking through thick clouds, the strings and harps emerge from the darkness ethereally lightening the mood (7:15). As if resigned yet able to accept old age, there is a new-found grace as the flutes and harps dance calmly over the sustained chords of the clarinets, bassoons, and horns (8:04). The bells return (8:34), their crazed chiming replaced by steady peals as the harps flow on sounding like gently falling rain. The organ (9:48) momentarily casts a shadow over this peaceful scene, but it quickly turns ethereal, sustaining its sound while the flutes play their airy pulses. There is an otherworldly quality that is absolutely haunting as the violins and violas sustain the final note and fade away.

VI. URANUS, THE MAGICIAN: Allegro   (5:48)

Four trumpets and three trombones forcefully begin followed by the tenor and bass tubas and four loud beats from the timpani. This is the invocation, and the first to answer its call are three bassoons (0:15) grunting their way into a jerky dance. They are quickly joined by some of the other wind instruments for this giddy dance that speeds up frantically with a distinctly macabre undertone heightened by the xylophone. A solo for the bassoon (0:54) with accompaniment from the piquant piccolos, flutes, and harps grows wild, erupting into a raucous dance made more energetic by the rattle of the tambourine (1:32).

A single, ugly, heavy blast (1:51) slows the pace briefly as the bass tuba further deflates the atmosphere (2:00) with its leaden tone. There is a definitely evil quality reminiscent of a witches' Sabbath, especially when the piccolo and flute flit scarily (2:14) like bats in the night air. Suddenly the powerful chords of the invocation (2:18) starts the timpani on its way, leading a resurgence of this wickedly wild dance. Out of nowhere the tenor and bass tubas seem to march in with a strong, determined melody (2:34). (Here the music may remind you of the scene at the witch's castle in *The Wizard of Oz* as the soldiers steadfastly march in double lines.) The snare drum adds its militaristic quality, and the power of the music is the dominant force, growing steadily into a ferocious explosion (4:07) bordering on the cacophonous.

The sound abates rapidly, revealing the strings sustaining a quiet, eerie chord; this is a complete transformation from wicked power to total calm, the harp's bell-like tones adding a magical quality. But not to be defeated, the bassoons restart their dance (4:51) joined by the tubas and the pounding timpani, leading to a violent eruption. When the organ blares through (5:08) conflicting with the brass instruments, the tone turns ugly, filled with terror; horror-movie music at its absolute best! The volume recedes leaving just the calm, sustained strings fading away slowly. The movement ends with the timpani and harp joining for two final beats, exhausted and weak.

VII. NEPTUNE, THE MYSTIC: Andante   (8:28)

This may be the strangest movement of all. In it Holst uses his forces sparingly, blending the more intimate sounds available into a fabulous sonic tapestry. The graciously paced, haunting melody is unveiled by the flutes; there is a feeling of great distance and of time standing still, conjuring up images of slow travel in deepest space. The plaintive English horn (0:53) adds a sense of longing, but the calmness stays constant, aided by the gently flowing plucked notes of the harps.

The first break in the pattern occurs when the trumpets and trombones play a sustained, quiet, almost dissonant chord (1:49) while the violins and violas quicken their pace shimmering under the brass. The celesta (2:05) chiming through augments the distant quality, peaceful and calm. There seems to be no sense of time; nothing is rushed, there are no outbursts, and everything remains fairly quiet. The bassoons and horns play sustained chords (3:29), an accompaniment to the endless flowing lines of the celesta and harps. The distant rumble of the organ (3:49) provides a haunting contrast to the bubbling celesta phrases.

This sonic layering, one instrument entering on top of another, serves as the background for the chorus of women who sneak in (4:42), inaudibly at first, with a sustained note; this is totally ethereal, like sirens calling from outer space. This effect is heightened because the chorus is placed in an adjoining room completely hidden from the audience's view. Only an opened door allows their sound to enter the concert hall. The chorus's sound complements the occasional slowly moving lines of the clarinets and horns. Not until the violins play a little bit of a melody (5:15) is there any sense of movement.

The chorus reenters (5:37), their voices a bit more apparently intertwined, accented by the repeated plucks of the harp, definite shapelessness as the phrases blend one into the next. The chorus stops suddenly (6:41) as a dissonant chord replaces this otherworldly mystery with a sense of foreboding. But the reemergence of the celesta (6:52) returns the magic of before. The chorus starts again (7:06) accompanied by the high, sustained line of the violins, the voices slowly fading into the darkness. When they are virtually inaudible, the door between their room and the concert hall is silently closed, ending *The Planets*.

PHILIP MYERS, PRINCIPAL HORN OF THE NEW YORK PHILHARMONIC:

"Holst wrote many works for brass band. Listen for the sections of this piece that sound more like band music than orchestra music. All you can hear is brass and winds and almost no strings at all."

COMPARATIVE RECORDINGS

MEHTA/NEW YORK PHILHARMONIC/NEW YORK
   CHORAL ARTISTS
TELDEC 2292-46316   TOTAL TIME: 53:12

A spectacular recording from every perspective. The performance shows the New York Philharmonic at its best; Mehta's interpretation is always exciting and passionate, and the sound is simply amazing.

> PREVIN/ROYAL PHILHARMONIC
> ORCHESTRA/BRIGHTON FESTIVAL WOMEN'S
> CHORUS
> TELARC CD 80133   TOTAL TIME: 50:28

Another excellent recording, this one featuring English forces. Previn, whose career has bridged the concert stage and the movie studio, brings tremendous clarity to this complex work. The sound is excellent.

> SOLTI/LONDON PHILHARMONIC ORCHESTRA/LONDON
> PHILHARMONIC CHOIR
> LONDON 414 567   TOTAL TIME: 49:45

Although recorded in the predigital era, this is a superb performance with a relentless visceral excitement. Solti's propulsive conducting brings out all the peaks of this out-of-this-world work.

❚F YOU ENJOYED THIS PIECE . . .

There is little in the classical repertoire to compare with *The Planets*. Another Holst work, though very different, is the **St. Paul's Suite,** a delightful composition lacking the power of his outer-space masterpiece. In the area of twentieth-century English music the next composer to explore is Ralph Vaughan Williams who was a contemporary of Holst's. Be sure to listen to the spectacular cantata **Dona Nobis Pacem,** a powerful plea for an end to war using religious texts as well as the poetry of Walt Whitman. If you still need more, try the soundtracks to the many outer-space movies of the 1970s and 1980s!

MAHLER

$\mathcal{S}$YMPHONY NO. 1 IN D MAJOR

TITAN

Gustav Mahler (1860–1911) began writing his First Symphony in 1885 and did not complete the first version of the work until 1888, the year that saw George Eastman perfect the Kodak box camera, J. B. Dunlop invent the pneumatic tire, and Benjamin Harrison's election to the presidency of the United States. It was also when Mahler became head of the Budapest Opera, and it was there he conducted the world premiere of his First Symphony in November of 1889. At that time the symphony contained five movements. After revising the symphony several times during the next few years, Mahler conducted the premiere of the four-movement version in Berlin in 1896.

The name *Titan* was chosen by the composer and first appeared in 1893 with the additional phrase "a symphonic poem in the form of a symphony." The inspiration for the title comes from the novel of the same name by Jean Paul Richter (1763–1825).

In 1899 the symphony was published in its four-movement version, which is the way the work is most frequently performed.

However, some recordings and performances do include the movement Mahler omitted, known as the "Blumine," which had originally been the second movement, positioned between the first and second movements in the four-movement version.

Mahler's First Symphony is what the title implies: Titanic. It is dramatic, sad, joyful, and in many ways overwhelming. The orchestra, which includes large wind and brass sections led by seven French horns, is used to the fullest to paint this large musical canvas. This music is clearly an outgrowth of the large-scale Romantic symphonies of Mahler's predecessors Brahms, Bruckner, and Schumann. But what Mahler did is develop the Romantic nature of the music and expand the boundaries, thus beginning the transition into the twentieth century, both chronologically and musically.

REFERENCE RECORDING:
CBS MASTERWORKS MK 42031
WALTER/COLUMBIA SYMPHONY ORCHESTRA
TOTAL TIME: 51:55

FIRST MOVEMENT: Langsam   (13:20)

It is important to keep in mind while listening to this symphony that Mahler intended to tell a story through his music. However, it is equally important for the listener to create his own story using the musical cues Mahler provides. In the first movement Mahler writes that it should be "like the sound of nature"; use that as your first clue and let the music conjure up images for you.

The symphony begins mysteriously. The sustained notes in the high ranges of the string instruments create an eerie calm broken by a soft outburst from the clarinets (0:35). Then distant trumpets seem to call for an awakening (1:15). This slow opening continues with more sections of the orchestra adding their interjections. The shroud of mystery is lifted when, led by the clarinets' imitation of a cuckoo, Mahler unveils a happy, lyrical melody initially played by the cellos (3:25). This bucolic section continues and swells, eventually involving the entire orchestra. It is soon replaced by a return to the sustained high strings (5:30) and a brief revisit to the opening mystery, now more sinister than before. The next section can be best described as a slow build, the tension increasing, moving toward some kind of resolution. That resolution is quietly heralded by the horns (8:08) leading the orchestra into a reprise of the lyrical melody (8:35). Throughout this next section it is particularly interesting to listen to how Mahler uses the harp. Calm prevails until the tension heard earlier returns (10:20) and grows while the trumpets valiantly sound an alarm (10:42). From here on, be sure to note the conflict of the strained strings against the lower wind instruments, especially the trombones. The building tension moves inexorably toward an explosion heightened by a cymbal crash (11:25) following the lead from the horns. Out of this chaos Mahler returns to the lyrical section now in an extremely energized guise, moving faster and faster, driving joyfully to an abrupt unison ending.

SECOND MOVEMENT: Kräftig bewegt   (6:50)

This movement is in the style of a Ländler, an Austrian dance popular at the beginning of the nineteenth century. The opening is strong and joyful and hints at raucousness. The strings start the festivities and the winds join in soon thereafter. The energy of the dance is passed around the orchestra with each instrument carrying the theme. When the horns have a quick solo (1:35), one gets the feeling that the excitement cannot keep growing, and moments later everything does calm down as the cellos take over and reestablish the base (1:50). The melody resumes and builds, leading to a joyful release of energy (2:21) led by the trumpets and the horns.

In the Trio section the rollicking is replaced by lyrical calm, best described as "Schmaltz." The melody is tender, the mood sweet, and it is sustained until a horn solo (5:28) leads everyone back to the dance, now more raucous than before. When the horns and trumpets pick up the melody (6:37), the speed of the dance accelerates and the movement comes to a loud, happy end.

THIRD MOVEMENT: Feierlich und gemessen
(11:23)

The opening of this movement is one of the oddest in all symphonic music. Eight measured timpani notes serve as the solemn introduction to a solo for double bass. While a double-bass solo is itself very rare, the fact that the melody it plays is a minor-key (very sad) adaptation of the French folk song "*Frère Jacques*" ("Brother John") makes this opening downright weird. The solo is written in a high range and is difficult for any double bass player, but Mahler adds to the challenge by leaving the bass totally alone and exposed except for the continuing timpani beats. This melody is then picked up by other instruments and it turns into a round (0:42), just as children might sing it. However, instead of the joy children might bring to it, in Mahler's hands this simple melody becomes a vehicle of depression.

The round continues until it is replaced by a mournful new melody played primarily by the oboes and trumpets (2:30). The music makes an attempt at becoming less sad as we hear a distorted militarylike march (3:02). But that attempt fails and the "*Frère Jacques*" melody returns as the relentless timpani beats are again prominent. This continues until, led by the harp and the violins (5:35), there is a new theme, dominated by a sad, resigned calm. Where the timpani had before been continuous, the harp now assumes that role until the timpani returns (7:53) bringing with it the return of the "*Frère Jacques*" theme.

To end the movement Mahler reintroduces the strange march with the cymbals (9:00), augmented by the clarinets sounding as if they belong in a circus (9:28). As the movement resolves, the timpani, now teamed with the harp, leads to a calm wind-down. The final seconds feature the repeated notes in the timpani and the tam-tam, all leading to a sad, uncomfortable peace.

FOURTH MOVEMENT: Stürmisch bewegt
(20:22)

The key to this final movement is the way calm alternates with absolute chaos; the image is that of a battle between the forces of good and evil. The opening leaves no doubt as to which side fires the first salvo: it is a ferocious, orchestra-wide crash followed immediately by frantic violins, wildly strong trumpets, and very angry brass instruments.

Out of this fury emerges a melody played at first by the oboes, clarinets, horns, and trombones (1:10). Still angry, this section gives the first inkling that a struggle between opposing forces is about to unfold. Throughout, the instruments war with each other, seemingly trying to establish some control in what feels like a whirlwind of chaos. Typically when the strings take over (2:48), they are confronted by blasts from the drums and the brass. Eventually the fierce energy wanes and the unrelenting battle breaks up, leaving only short gasps from a distant trumpet (3:20).

The initial battle over, the violins play a quiet melody filled with forgiveness featuring sustained phrases (3:36). Listen for the underscoring of the pizzicatos in the basses and cellos. The melody builds slowly to a swell (6:00) highlighted by a timpani roll followed by a beautiful, brief horn solo (6:25). Quietly the cellos lead and give the distinct feeling that this calm cannot last. Mystery abounds as the violins and violas add a tremolo. Three notes from the trombone and trumpet herald another explosion (7:20) and a return to the chaos of the opening.

Once again from the chaos Mahler reestablishes order as the oboes and clarinets play a phrase that seems to announce the arrival of the cavalry (8:00). When the trumpets take up the new theme, it is clear that, at least for now, the forces of good are winning. However, the storm resumes a few seconds later and chaos again reigns (8:40) until there is a joyous explosion led by the horns (9:40) with a lone triangle ringing support in the distance. This victory is sustained and leads to a quieting down, out of which appears the mysterious sound and melody from the beginning of the entire symphony (11:22). For the most part, calm prevails.

Short bursts from the violas (15:21) are the first clue that the peace will not hold and there will be another conflict. A series of trumpet calls confirms this (16:49). The surging continues until another huge explosion (17:33), featuring the trumpets and the horns. Through this new chaos cuts the trilling, shrill whistle of the piccolo. This time, however, the good forces win quickly as the horns sound a triumphant series of calls (17:47). The timpani becomes a driving force in what has turned into a propulsive march of victory. A series of joyful explosions (19:31) using the timpani, trumpets, trombones, tuba, and a constantly ringing triangle lead the symphony to its crashing, ebullient conclusion.

JOHN MCCLURE, PRODUCER OF THE BRUNO WALTER RECORDING:

"I was thrilled [by the recording sessions]. The first Mahler I had ever recorded and it was to be with Mahler's own pupil and assistant. During the session he [Walter] held back nothing and seemed like a virile man of sixty although he was well into his eighties. The music and the performance were revelations: the most vivid, natural recreation of a composer's score I had ever witnessed."

COMPARATIVE RECORDINGS

WALTER/COLUMBIA SYMPHONY ORCHESTRA
CBS MASTERWORKS MK 42031   TOTAL TIME: 51:55

Walter was a student of Mahler's and this is a classic interpretation. Though recorded in 1961 the sound holds up well, and the performance will hold your attention through repeated listenings.

DAVIS/SYMPHONIE-ORCHESTER DES BAYERISCHE
RUNDFUNKS
NOVALIS 150 033   TOTAL TIME: 56:30

An interesting performance that contains some exquisite
playing and excellent digital sound. However, the overall performance is just a little too placid, lacking Mahlerian fire.

BERNSTEIN/CONCERTGEBOUW ORCHESTRA OF
AMSTERDAM
DEUTSCHE GRAMMOPHON 427 303   TOTAL TIME: 56:05

This performance is part of the Mahler cycle that Bernstein
recorded using three different orchestras, and while this performance is filled with exaggerations and eccentricities, it is one
that is worth hearing because it helps explain why Bernstein
brought great popularity to Mahler's symphonies.

*I*F YOU ENJOYED THIS PIECE. . .

There are nine Mahler symphonies, the most popular being
the First, the **Second,** known as the **Resurrection,** the **Fourth,**
and the **Eighth,** known as the **Symphony of a Thousand.** Any of
these symphonies are a good next step. Once you have gotten
used to those, branch out to the remaining symphonies and some
of the song cycles such as the haunting **Das Lied von der Erde.**

MENDELSSOHN

*S*YMPHONY NO. 4 IN A MAJOR, OP. 90
ITALIAN

In 1830, the German composer Felix Mendelssohn (1809–47) took an extended journey through Italy. In addition to visiting the major urban centers, Rome, Naples, Bologna, and Venice, Mendelssohn toured through the Italian countryside. His Fourth Symphony, the *Italian*, became the musical manifestation of his observations, not only of the landscape, but also of the ceremonies he witnessed, including the coronation of the new pope, Gregory XVI.

Mendelssohn began work on the symphony during his Italian journey while still working on what would become his Third Symphony, the *Scottish*, completing the Fourth before the Third. The *Italian* had its world premiere in London in May of 1833 with the composer conducting. In some ways there was a distinct Italian accent in London in 1833 because, in addition to the premiere of Mendelssohn's *Italian* Symphony, that was the year that Turner's great Venetian paintings were first shown at the Royal Academy. The year 1833 also saw the abolition of slavery in the British Empire and the birth of Johannes Brahms.

The *Italian* Symphony is a hybrid, influenced by the symphonies of the classical era (Mozart and Haydn), yet filled with sounds and musical images that are very Romantic. The Symphony is in four movements and is scored for flutes, oboes, clarinets, bassoons, horns, trumpets, timpani, and strings. The first and last movements may sound familiar as they were used brilliantly in the movie *Breaking Away* to bring the spirit of the Italian bicycle racing team to the American heartland of Indiana.

REFERENCE RECORDING:
DEUTSCHE GRAMMOPHON 429 158
VON KARAJAN/BERLIN PHILHARMONIC
TOTAL TIME: 28:04

FIRST MOVEMENT: Allegro vivace   (8:02)

The symphony establishes itself immediately: a single plucked note in the string instruments launches a series of rapid repeated notes in the flutes, clarinets, bassoons, and horns, quickly followed by the soaring main melody played by the violins. The flutes and the horns take a small segment of the opening phrase and turn it into a subtle "wake-up call" (0:19), a brief phrase that is heard several times throughout the movement. There is an unbridled sense of happiness growing and then exploding into all-out joy with the full orchestra taking up the theme (0:42).

The movement ebbs and flows, then quiets down (2:12) just long enough to allow the clarinet a quick solo followed by the violins retaking the theme as they did at the movement's beginning. This time, however, the melody evolves into a mysterious-sounding version of itself (2:48). (Note how Mendelssohn uses only the string instruments to create this mysterious quality.) Eventually the intensity and volume increase, and out of the haze the wind instruments sound the wake-up call, a bit like rescuers coming in from the distance to save the day (3:26). All join together for a triumphant, almost militaristic version of the call (3:49), signaling the end of the conflict.

After a section of calming down, the oboe emerges with a sustained solo (4:30) played over the still-rumbling strings. In fact, several times in the subsequent section the wind instruments have fanciful solos with the strings serving as accompaniment. A repeat of the mysterious section, now played by the winds (6:03), is followed by the violins again, emerging with the original theme and the trumpets soaring with the call (6:43). A series of biting, repeated notes (7:48), especially evident in the horns, leads to three distinct chords ending the movement.

SECOND MOVEMENT: Andante con moto
(6:26)

In this movement Mendelssohn eliminates the trumpets and the timpani. The basic format of the movement is a march, but do not expect it to be a military-style march. Instead it should be viewed like a procession, part of a ceremony filled with pomp. The pace is regal, the overall tone serious, and something almost plaintive is evident in the opening phrase.

The theme first appears (0:12) in the oboe, bassoons, and violas, with the cellos and basses providing the solid pulse creating the processional effect. The pulse continues as the violins and flutes pick up the equally plaintive second phrase (0:43). However, where the first phrase was played by three instruments playing the same thing, here the flutes and violins play complementary but not identical passages. These two groups of forces alternate phrases while the bass pulse continues as a constant.

As in the first movement, Mendelssohn creates mystery through the strings (2:10), giving the sense of creeping around. This continues until the clarinets and horns come back (2:46) with a new open and airy phrase, a great contrast to what preceded it. However, the seriousness of the opening returns (3:30), now with more intensity. The airy melody returns briefly, but the creeping strings take over (5:20) and the bass-line pulse, running through most of the movement, continues right up to three soft plucked notes.

THIRD MOVEMENT: Con moto moderato   (7:59)

Mendelssohn brings back the trumpets and the timpani for this movement, which feels like a breath of fresh air after the mystery of the second movement. Here again the violins take the lead, and the strings play alone until the horns add support (0:13). The second phrase is a little more anxious than the first as the oboes join the strings (1:11), but the pastoral quality is maintained.

The Trio section (2:50) features a series of regal-sounding calls played by the horns and bassoons. These calls are picked up by the whole orchestra (3:53), and the controlled, regal quality continues as the timpani and strings lead the way.

The return to the movement's opening melody (4:55) is played by the strings with the cellos and basses introducing the violins, which play the theme as they did at the beginning. One last series of horn and bassoon calls (7:17) winds the movement down, and it ends with three short notes.

FOURTH MOVEMENT: Saltarello: Presto   (5:37)

The best way to describe this movement is: "We're off to the races." In fact, this movement was used as the bicycle-race theme in *Breaking Away.* The key to a good performance of this movement is that the tempo set has to be exciting and fast, but it cannot be allowed to run away, because then it will simply seem frantic and out of control. Another interesting element of this movement is the way the string instruments often play alone or with only one wind instrument. Although an entire orchestra is involved, this gives the sense that Mendelssohn was writing an enlarged form of chamber music.

The opening is five progressing, angry notes played in unison by the horns, trumpets, timpani, and strings, while the flutes, oboes, clarinets, and bassoons play a sustained trill. The initial melody is established by the flutes (0:07) over repeated notes in the violins setting the pace. This builds until every instrument joins in (0:36) driving the pulse forward. The energy does wane as the strings begin a brief fugue (1:30) with the flute joining in to play the original melody above them.

Throughout the next parts, Mendelssohn divides the orchestra with the strings serving as an accompaniment for the various wind instruments beginning with the clarinets (2:11). The strings then play by themselves in a jazzy section (2:33), and the winds even play alone with the timpani (3:15). The orchestra is put back together to play as a unit; this increases the intensity, and one can sense the steady tempo, set by the repeated timpani beats (4:05), straining to rush away. The movement calms down (5:00) as the winds play more sustained phrases while the strings interject the propulsive, rhythmic phrases. When the calm begins to erode and the pulse returns (5:19), followed by the timpani's entrance, the pace reestablishes itself for one last drive to another three-note ending.

ASSOCIATE CONCERTMASTER OF THE NEW YORK PHILHARMONIC, CHARLES REX:

"The most striking feature of Mendelssohn's Italian Symphony is the youthful enthusiasm which emanates from the music. It seems to be more than the enthusiastic reveling of a traveler's visit to Italy. In fact, I think that Mendelssohn expresses the sheer joy of being alive in this piece."

COMPARATIVE RECORDINGS

VON KARAJAN/BERLIN PHILHARMONIC
DEUTSCHE GRAMMOPHON 429 158   TOTAL TIME: 28:04

A big-sounding recording that is traditional in every way. The final movement is particularly exciting and allows the listener to hear the solo work within the orchestra.

MACKERRAS/ORCHESTRA OF THE AGE OF
    ENLIGHTENMENT
VIRGIN VC 7 90725   TOTAL TIME: 28:17

A fascinating, absolutely thrilling performance that continu-
ously bubbles with unbridled excitement. Here the detail is
equally evident, but there is an edge that propels the performance.

ABBADO/LONDON SYMPHONY
DEUTSCHE GRAMMOPHON 415 974   TOTAL TIME: 28:07

Abbado's extremely elegant reading of this symphony brings
out the inner voices in a fabulous way. There is less sheer excitement, but the middle movements especially benefit from this
slightly calmer approach. The sound is exceptionally clear.

*I*F YOU ENJOYED THIS PIECE ...

Although Mendelssohn composed five symphonies, the most
popular are the final three: the **Third,** known as the **Scottish,** the
Fourth, and the **Fifth,** known as the **Reformation** due to its use
of a Lutheran hymn. Also, listen to the early **String Symphonies**
and Mendelssohn's exquisite **trios for piano, violin, and cello**
and his less often heard **string quartets.**

MOZART

Quintet for Clarinet and Strings in A Major, K. 581

Few pieces of chamber music have the pure beauty and wide range of emotions that are integral parts of Wolfgang Amadeus Mozart's (1756–91) Quintet for Clarinet and Strings. Using just five instruments, Mozart paints a musical canvas that is at once elegant, simple, joyous, sad, romantic, and passionate.

What makes this Quintet even more astounding is that Mozart composed it when he was in dire financial condition; he was constantly writing to friends for assistance, always hopeful that his big break was just around the corner. Yet none of this trial and difficulty is evident in this exquisite composition. Written in September of 1789, just two years and three months before his death, the Clarinet Quintet is scored for clarinet and string quartet: two violins, a viola, and a cello. As you will hear, the clarinet is very much the lead instrument, first among equals. Mozart's writing highlights the clarinet's sweet tone, its flexibility, and its ability to take on different tonal characteristics.

One wonders if Mozart, who had to be consumed by his personal problems, was aware of what was going on in the rest of the world. After all, 1789 was the year of the first U.S. Congress in New York and George Washington's inauguration as president. In Europe the French Revolution raged on, and in England King George III recovered from his first attack of mental illness and was restored to power.

While most of Mozart's chamber compositions deserve to be included in any compilation of great works of music, the Clarinet Quintet stands out for two reasons. First, it is one of the very few works of any kind that give a lead role to the clarinet. Second, the piece gained popularity when it was used throughout the final two-and-a-half hour episode of the hit television series M*A*S*H. In that program, Maj. Charles Emerson Winchester encounters a group of Korean prisoners who play primitive instruments. Amid the chaos of war, Major Winchester finds solace in training these men to play the Mozart Clarinet Quintet, its haunting melodies becoming more recognizable as the show unfolds. Ultimately, the Koreans are killed, shattering Winchester's attempt at culture. It is a poignant scene, and the choice of the Clarinet Quintet to heighten the drama was ideal.

REFERENCE RECORDING: RCA 60723
STOLTZMAN/TOKYO STRING QUARTET
TOTAL TIME: 34:51

FIRST MOVEMENT: Allegro   (9:32)

The opening, played only by the strings, unfolds slowly. It is delicate and filled with a sentimental, bittersweet quality. The clarinet rises out of the strings (0:12) and plays a brief, fast solo that begins a pattern of the strings and clarinet alternating. After the clarinet's second solo, the two violins imitate the clarinet's line in a gorgeous harmony (0:33) that precedes these three instruments joining forces (0:37), although the clarinet maintains the lead. The cello then assumes the solo part (0:51) and gets its support from the second violin and viola.

A moment of silence (1:23) introduces the melody, now taken by the first violin while the cello plays some resonant pizzicatos. When the clarinet takes over this melody (1:41), it becomes sad, filled with sorrow and longing. As this solo unwinds, the mood gradually brightens and the movement's original tone returns. The violins sneak in a quiet reprise of their very first phrase (2:33) as the clarinet rattles off one more fast passage. Three unison chords lead to a repeat of the entire movement up to this point.

Following the repeat (5:27) the violins set a steady pulse that contrasts with a rhapsodic clarinet solo filled with mystery and passion. The atmosphere grows calm as the clarinet and cello contrast each other (5:35) with the theme from the movement's opening. There is a new richness to the sound here. The intensity wanes as the clarinet and first violin play sustained notes (6:36) leading to a reprise of the movement's opening, this time with the clarinet adding its voice to the string quartet (6:43).

The cello has a lovely little solo (7:11) accompanied by the viola and second violin. The clarinet rejoins (7:29) and alternates with the first violin until the clarinet ultimately takes over, racing toward another moment of silence (7:43). The pause introduces a calm, romantic section with pizzicatos in the cello providing the background for the first violin's solo. The strings then supply the pulse under another bittersweet clarinet solo (8:01) with a strange blend of mystery and sexiness. Once again the original melody emerges (9:18), introducing a final clarinet flourish and the movement's unison ending.

SECOND MOVEMENT: Larghetto   (7:19)

This movement is a musical evocation of moonlit romanticism. It is slow and luxurious. Think of it as an aria for the clarinet with a cozy accompaniment from the strings. At the outset a soulful, loving solo flows seamlessly from the clarinet, while the strings provide a steady background. The first violin gets a solo (1:35) that turns into an extended, dreamy duet with the clarinet while the other strings provide the base.

The clarinet reestablishes its preeminence (3:14) as the first violin blends back in with the strings. The strings stop (3:53), leaving the clarinet to unfold a lovely little cadenza that fades and becomes the beginning of the aria again (4:10) with the strings returning to provide the background. As before, the first violin joins the clarinet for a reprise of their extended duet (5:48). The viola and cello quietly take the lead (6:53) as the movement winds down to its sleepy ending.

THIRD MOVEMENT: Menuetto   (7:10)

Since this is a typical classical minuet, each section of the movement is repeated at least once, giving many opportunities to listen for what each instrument does in every section.

The mood is cheerful as all five instruments start out together, the melodic material distributed evenly among them. The elegance and grace are unmistakable in this introductory section, which is repeated (0:10). Following the repeat, the strings initially play alone with the first violin dominating before handing off to the clarinet (0:30). The movement's first melody returns (0:40) and leads to a repeat of the second section (0:51).

After this repeat, the Trio section of the minuet begins. Here the clarinet does not play at all, leaving us with a standard string quartet. (This section is reminiscent of many of the tender moments of any of Mozart's late string quartets.) The first violin again dominates, playing against the other strings; there is a poignant, almost resigned calm here. The first part of the Trio is repeated (1:46), and when it continues on to the next section (2:10), there is still no clarinet, but now there is more of a strain between the first violin and the other strings. This second section is also repeated (2:45), and when it ends, we return to the beginning of the entire movement (3:22), which is played through without repeats.

After the reprise of the two opening sections there is another Trio which features a somewhat quirky solo for the clarinet played over a meager string accompaniment (4:04). Like the other Trio, this one has sections that are repeated. When the first-section repeat ends (4:40), the first violin takes on a more important role, playing a duet with the clarinet while the other strings play an elegant pizzicato accompaniment. Soon the clarinet solo returns (5:11) over the strings' simple accompaniment. Another repeat (5:33) returns us to the violin/clarinet duet and the string pizzicatos. At the end of the second Trio there is one last return to the beginning of the movement (6:29), and the opening sections are played through one more time without any repeats.

FOURTH MOVEMENT: Allegretto con variazioni (9:48)

The final movement is a theme followed by a series of variations that show Mozart at his creative best. Each variation has a distinct sound and style, and yet in each one the original theme remains evident. The violins start the simple, cheerful theme and are quickly joined by the other instruments. The second phrase of the theme (0:29) is played initially by the first violin with an echo from the viola.

The first variation (0:58) has the violins playing exactly as they did in the movement's opening, only now the clarinet weaves a rhapsodic variation above them. A repeat of this first passage ends (1:28) with the clarinet moving on, adding phrases that almost seem like an improvised jazz solo. This second section is repeated as well (1:43).

The second variation (2:00) begins without the clarinet; the first violin takes the lead while the other strings play a fast but steady accompaniment. The clarinet does sneak in (2:07) just before the first repeat (2:15). Following the repeat (2:30), the first violin leads until the clarinet joins (2:37). The last section is repeated (2:44).

The third variation (3:01) features the viola, which leads as the clarinet stays silent. The viola's tone heightens a sadness that permeates this variation, and when the clarinet does join (3:10), its tone adds another color to the musical palette. After the first repeat (3:38) the first violin assumes the solo before turning it back over to the viola (3:47).

The fourth variation is a dramatic contrast to its predecessor (4:15) as it returns to the movement's cheerful roots. The violins reprise the original melody while the clarinet seems to flit about, musically giggling. Not to be outdone, the first violin takes the fast line (4:22), while the clarinet observes silently. Coming out of the repeat of this opening section (4:43), the violin continues the fast, flighty passage, but now the clarinet adds a series of soaring comments until it takes the fast part (4:50). Following the final repeat (5:11) there is a brief additional section that features short flourishes from the clarinet. Then the first violin and in turn the clarinet slow everything down to end the variation, seeming to leave it incomplete.

This leads to an Adagio (5:25) that is suddenly sleepy, slow, and quiet. The first violin starts out, moving slowly. When the clarinet joins (5:40), we are returned to the dreamy quality of the second movement; this solo is calm and subdued. After a repeat of the Adagio's beginning (6:45), the movement continues with the clarinet soaring from a low note up to a high one and then sustaining the lyrical line it has developed. Here the clarinet and cello are dominant, but the first violin eventually takes over (7:04) before this entire section is repeated (7:27). At the end of the repeat (8:10) the Adagio continues with the clarinet and first violin sleepily paralleling each other. There is absolute calm as the pace slows, leading to an expansive clarinet cadenza.

The mood is shattered (8:54) as we return to the fast (Allegro) part of this variation, the energetic section that was left hanging when the Adagio began. Now the violins and clarinet playing fast again and with energy seem almost raucous in comparison to the dreamy interlude we have just come through. It is this cheerful, bouncy mood that carries all the way to the movement's end.

CLARINETIST RICHARD STOLTZMAN:

"This work is the most perfect chamber music ever written for clarinet. To record perfection and yet give the re-creation of the warmth and humanity which Mozart lavished on this masterpiece— that is the challenge. The great flutist Marcel Moyse stopped in the middle of coaching me in the larghetto to say softly, 'This is the music they will play in heaven.' The difficulty then is to play the Mozart Clarinet Quintet with complete honesty and humility while realizing each note you sound is perhaps the most important of your life."

COMPARATIVE RECORDINGS

STOLTZMAN/TOKYO STRING QUARTET
RCA 60723   TOTAL TIME: 34:51

An elegant, superb performance that brings out all the moods without having to exaggerate in any way. It is a natural, fun-loving performance with excellent digital sound.

DE PEYER/AMADEUS QUARTET
DEUTSCHE GRAMMOPHON 429 819   TOTAL TIME: 32:52

A classic recording that features a string quartet noted for their interpretation of the Mozart string quartets. It is clear that they have brought that tradition to this recording, and they blend beautifully with de Peyer's sound.

NEIDICH/MENDELSSOHN QUARTET
MUSICAL HERITAGE SOCIETY MHS 512258
                                             TOTAL TIME: 32:07

This recording is fascinating because it uses Mr. Neidich's reconstruction of Mozart's original version of the Quintet for basset clarinet. An excellent second recording of the work that will bring out different elements of Mozart's writing.

IF YOU ENJOYED THIS PIECE ...

The ideal next piece is Mozart's exquisite **Clarinet Concerto, K. 622,** written during his final year of life. It has all the beauty of the Quintet with the added richness of a full orchestra. Then move on to Mozart's **late String Quartets,** especially the six he dedicated to Haydn. Finally, staying in the chamber-music arena, try the **Oboe Quartet, K. 370,** and the **Quintet for Piano and Wind Instruments, K. 452.**

MOZART

₽IANO CONCERTO NO. 21
IN C MAJOR, K. 467
ELVIRA MADIGAN

The first thing to know about this superb piano concerto is that Wolfgang Amadeus Mozart (1756–91) did not give it the name *Elvira Madigan,* nor was it so named during his lifetime. Mozart's Twenty-first Piano Concerto became his most well-known concerto when the film director Bo Widerberg used the concerto's second movement as a recurring theme in his 1967 movie *Elvira Madigan.* The beauty of Mozart's melody and the film's exquisite impressionist cinematography are by far the best parts of this rather boring movie.

Mozart wrote six of his "mature" piano concertos in 1784, then began 1785 by composing the Twentieth Piano Concerto in D Minor. By March 9, 1785, he had completed the C Major Piano Concerto, and three days later it premiered at a performance in Vienna with Mozart playing the solo part and conducting. While the Austrian capital was filled with Mozart's music and playing, across the Atlantic the still very young United

States was dealing with issues like James Madison's Religious Freedom Act abolishing religious tests in Virginia.

The year 1785 also saw Mozart complete the fifth and sixth String Quartets, which were part of the glorious set of quartets he dedicated to Haydn. Ironically, at this time Mozart was better known as a pianist than as a composer. The piano concertos he wrote and performed are technically demanding for the soloist, and there is little doubt Mozart wrote them to show off his brilliance at the keyboard. But we should not ignore the brilliance of the music, especially in the Twenty-first Piano Concerto. Most important is to hear the way the solo piano and orchestra are equal partners, their parts interweaving; sometimes the piano plays with the strings, sometimes with the winds, and sometimes with the whole orchestra.

The orchestra for this concerto is made up of one flute, two oboes, two bassoons, two horns, two trumpets, timpani, and strings.

REFERENCE RECORDING:
CBS MASTERWORKS MK 34562
PERAHIA/ENGLISH CHAMBER ORCHESTRA
TOTAL TIME: 27:30

FIRST MOVEMENT: Allegro   (13:58)

The strings begin with a quiet, marchlike introduction. The first violins step away from the unison opening (0:07), and then the wind instruments answer (0:11) with a regal-sounding passage. When the orchestra does play as one unit (0:20), "sunny" is the dominant feeling; however, sections of strain occasionally cloud the mood.

A series of short solos by the winds, the oboe (2:02), the bassoon (2:05), and the flute (2:09) introduces the solo piano's (2:13) series of start-and-stop passages, the last one leading to a pause (2:22) and the soloist's first cadenza. This solo ends with a trill that continues as the violins return with a repeat of the movement's initial melody (2:31). The piano takes over the melody (2:39) playing most of the next section alone, save for intermittent accompaniment primarily from the strings. After one such orchestral interjection, the solo returns (3:21), but now the melody is filled with strain and a distinctly sorrowful quality. One of the hallmarks of this movement is the way the piano interacts with other instruments in the orchestra, often in a one-on-one format. This transforms the concerto into chamber music and is especially effective when the solo winds get to play with the piano. First we hear the flute, oboe, and bassoon (4:11). Then the flute soars over the piano (4:33) and is replaced by the sustained oboe lines, all while the strings set the pulse—great examples of the interweaving of voices that Mozart brought to his concertos.

A demanding series of runs up and down the keyboard leads to another piano trill (5:50); the piano stops and the orchestra takes over. During this orchestral interlude, there is a distinct sense of strain, intensified by occasional timpani beats. This mood is continued and heightened by the return of the piano (6:43), its melodic lines now filled with sorrow and longing. In the midst of this, the piano has some fast, tricky passages, accompanied by the strings and winds playing sustained notes (7:34). It is here we begin to hear the first sign that the gloom might lift. A few more moments of uneasiness lead to the reemergence of the original theme, with all its sunny qualities, played by the orchestra alone (8:16).

The piano returns (8:57) picking up the melody and playing initially with the flute. The oboes join in, and finally the strings get to play a little chamber music with the piano. Much of what is heard in the next sections is a recapitulation of the movement's earlier parts. When the piano plays an ascending run (11:16), it is joined in sequence by the bassoons, the oboes, and then the flute, paralleling the piano's upward pattern. This leads to another trill (11:30), and the piano stops while the orchestra takes over for a brief symphonic interlude, ending with a chord that seems as if everything were suddenly put on hold (11:56). It is here the pianist gets to show off with another cadenza. The "hold" is removed when the piano plays an extended trill (13:11) leading to the orchestra's return. The orchestra plays alone bringing us to the movement's end.

SECOND MOVEMENT: Andante   (6:56)

This movement, which does not use the timpani and trumpets, has the ultraromantic melody used over and over again in the movie *Elvira Madigan*. Part of what gives this movement its feeling of pensive intimacy is that the strings are muted, yielding a somewhat introspective quality.

The second violins and violas, accompanied by pizzicatos in the cellos and basses, set the steady pulse from the movement's outset. Over this, the first violins play the languorous melody. It is important the pace not be slow, even though its calm nature might indicate that. When the wind instruments join in with sustained notes (0:28), their voices seem like a gentle breeze blowing across a field. The sound becomes bittersweet (0:44) as the winds, especially the bassoons, play against the strings.

The wind instruments take over the steady pulse (1:27), joined by the piano, while all the strings now play the pizzicatos. The piano then takes the main melody. The effect of the steady pulse, combined with the plucked strings, all played against the melody in the piano, yields a jazzlike section. The bittersweet quality returns (2:22) with a strained passage in the first violins. The piano takes over, playing with the strings, continuing the sadness yet maintaining the elegance. When the winds add their voices (3:00), the strain intensifies, but never overwhelms. An important section dominated by the winds (3:38) continues the effort to return to the untainted romanticism of the opening, but the mood stays bittersweet and elegant.

Finally, after a brief transition featuring the piano with the flute, oboe, and bassoons, the gloom lifts and the original melody returns (4:49). With the distinct pizzicatos in the strings, and the melody in the piano, this section seems particularly jazzy. During the movement's final moments, there is a wonderful duet between the piano and the oboe (5:48), followed by the flute and bassoon adding their voices (5:59). When the steady pulse is again played by the winds (6:34), everything winds down, seeming to run out of energy. The movement ends quietly, in total calm.

THIRD MOVEMENT: Allegro vivace assai (6:36)

Along with the timpani and trumpets, the energy returns for this final movement. The opening theme, played by the violins, is brisk and lively; it seems to bounce around, yet is unmistakably elegant. After the quick introduction, a chord is followed by a trill in the piano (0:20), and the opportunity for the pianist to play a mini-cadenza. Then the piano takes up the fast-moving melody (0:29) accompanied by the strings.

The piano's solo is brief, and the orchestra regains control. Listen for the fabulous interplay among the woodwind instruments (0:44). The piano returns (0:56) joined initially only by the horns, but when the piano pauses, the violins recapture the melody (1:08) and pass it on to the winds. This, too, is short-lived, as the melody passes back to the piano; here contrast the perky piano line with the sustained notes in the strings.

Chamber music returns in the form of a quirky little passage played by the flute, oboes, and bassoons over sustained notes in the horns (1:35). The piano joins in and the strings soon replace the winds (1:41), with everyone playing together soon after. Lots of fast interplay leads to the next "hold" (2:25) and another mini-cadenza, followed by a return to the main theme in the piano (2:34).

The orchestra takes over (3:00) and leads to a series of stops and starts (3:07) as the mood changes to somewhat gloomy. But when the piano returns (3:20) with the sprightly melody, there is no longer any doubt that cheerfulness will win out. But again the tone becomes uncertain (3:40), growing angry, and then seeming like an argument, especially in the nasty-sounding comments provided by the oboe and bassoon (3:50). But cooler heads prevail, and we again return to the original cheerful melody (4:11). Following a short orchestral interlude (4:20), listen for the demanding solo passages that the pianist must navigate.

One more symphonic interlude (5:33) precedes the final cadenza (5:38), and again an extended trill brings the orchestra back in (6:16). Now the piano and orchestra play together, the soloist fitting an incredibly large number of notes within the orchestra's lines. Flittingly, they move toward the concerto's close, and its three unison chords.

PIANIST MURRAY PERAHIA:

"The most exquisite thing about Mozart's C Major Piano Concerto is the poetic, seamless flow of the second movement; it flows from phrase to phrase and is the perfect center section between the lively first and third movements."

COMPARATIVE RECORDINGS

PERAHIA/ENGLISH CHAMBER ORCHESTRA
CBS MASTERWORKS MYK 34562   TOTAL TIME: 27:30

Perahia, following the tradition Mozart set, plays and conducts this splendid recording. The tempos are just right, the interweaving is detailed, and the elegance and romance are omnipresent.

RUBINSTEIN/WALLENSTEIN/RCA VICTOR SYMPHONY
   ORCHESTRA
RCA GOLD SEAL 7967   TOTAL TIME: 28:06

If elegance is your thing, then this 1961 recording featuring Artur Rubinstein is the recording for you. Every phrase is perfect and can transport the listener into another realm. The sound on this transfer is first-rate.

DE LARROCHA/DAVIS/ENGLISH CHAMBER ORCHESTRA
RCA 60825   TOTAL TIME: 29:23

This 1991 recording combines the talents of two excellent Mozart interpreters, and the recording is a delight from first note to last. In addition it has a big, lush, ambient sound that lets the piano's tone resonate.

IF YOU ENJOYED THIS PIECE ...

Each of Mozart's mature piano concertos is a gem, but the place to begin listening is with the **Twenty-third in A Major.** Then try the two great "minor-key" concertos, the **Twentieth in D Minor** and the **Twenty-fourth in C Minor.** After getting to know these great works, fill in the missing concertos from number fifteen to number twenty-seven. They are all magnificent.

MOZART

SYMPHONY NO. 41 IN C MAJOR, K. 551

JUPITER

Wolfgang Amadeus Mozart (1756–91) wrote his last three symphonies in the span of three months during the summer of 1788. The last of these, the Symphony No. 41 in C Major, K. 551, known as the *Jupiter,* was written in the amazingly short period of two weeks and has come to be one of the most performed works in the symphonic literature. Mozart did not give the symphony its name; it only became known as the *Jupiter* after his death. Exactly when the subtitle was appended or who first used the name is not known. However, the otherworldly name is certainly evocative and appropriately descriptive and must have been coined to try to give a sense of the symphony's almost supernatural, noble majesty.

In Europe, 1788 was a year of upheaval. Austria, Mozart's homeland, declared war on Turkey. France, on the eve of revolution, experienced violent bread riots, while in England King George III suffered his first attack of mental illness. Across the Atlantic the very young United States was still in its formative stage, the Constitution taking effect when New Hampshire became the ninth state to ratify it.

The *Jupiter* Symphony, in four movements, is scored for flute, oboes, bassoons, horns, trumpets, timpani, and strings. Note that Mozart did not use any clarinets. You will be struck by the big sound this relatively small ensemble can muster, strengthened especially by the trumpets, horns, and timpani. This symphony, the culmination of Mozart's symphonic output, is at once powerful and gentle, angry and tender, elegant and romantic. It is truly one of the greatest symphonies in the entire repertoire and will reveal new wonders with each hearing no matter how many times it is enjoyed. Of all the works in the repertoire this may be the one most difficult to describe using the vocabulary available; perhaps it is enough of a description to simply say Mozart's Forty-first Symphony is the *Jupiter*.

REFERENCE RECORDING:
TELDEC 9031-74858
HARNONCOURT/CHAMBER ORCHESTRA
OF EUROPE
                         TOTAL TIME: 40:52

FIRST MOVEMENT: Allegro vivace   (12:31)

The very first thing to listen for is how Mozart immediately establishes an incredibly majestic feeling; the powerful opening statement is filled with exuberance. Immediately after this outburst the strings alone play a tender response. This pattern repeats before the movement really gets going (0:18), building vivaciously with a great sense of confidence. A brief pause slows the progression (0:44); the flute, oboe, and horns gently resume, timidly introducing a more lyrical phrase. When the strings take over (1:03), they lead to a resumption of the earlier, powerful section totally reenergized, driven by the steady pulse of the horns, trumpets, and timpani (1:07).

Just when the propulsion seems to be unstoppable, there is another halt (1:37) followed by the strings tenderly playing the more gentle phrases, weaving amongst themselves with only occasional interjections from the flute and bassoon. Gradually the strings' sound diminishes, fading away just before another total stoppage (2:21). A sudden explosion shatters the silence (2:23), the trumpets, horns, and timpani majestically leading the charge; this is joyful, excited music! But, as quickly as it came, the surge disappears, leaving just the first violins to play the final, quiet phrase (2:56). The strings timidly restart the graceful theme, and as the other instruments join the sound, it becomes bigger and more animated, never losing any of its elegance (3:15). (Note: In most performances, including this one, the opening section of the movement is repeated [3:32].)

Following the repeat (7:01) the flute, oboes, and bassoons start out alone bridging to the strings' entrance as they resume the delicate, elegant theme, joined occasionally by the oboe and bassoon. But this elegance disappears (7:24); the flowing ease so dominant thus far is gone, replaced by strain, making it seem as if getting through the passages requires much more work, the sections of the orchestra seeming to bicker among themselves. Gradually this bit of dark clouds starts to break up (8:00) leaving just the flute, oboes, and bassoons. When the strings replace them (8:04), the problem has been resolved and they gently return to the movement's original theme (8:10), played more quietly with a soulful bassoon line added.

The unease creeps back (8:17) as the flute, oboes, and bassoons start to show signs of the strain while the strings murmur quietly in the background. Apparently unable to resolve this conflict, the orchestra explodes in a fit of anger (8:27) as the strings, now in the foreground, snipe nastily. But the ire wanes, the strings growing timid, seeming to back away from the conflict, gently leading to a recapitulation of the movement's opening (8:57). As before, there is a brief pause (9:38) followed immediately by a quieter, more mysterious section as the winds and strings weave together brewing a bit more unease. Instead the sound becomes powerful and majestic, then relaxes, turning tender as the violins gently resume elegantly (10:30).

Another pause (11:11) precedes a powerful explosion, excited and driven by the trumpets, horns, and timpani. The first violins complete the phrase (11:47), once more becoming graceful as the wind instruments add some fabulous sonic colors. A final burst of excitement (12:05) sets the entire ensemble off on a jaunty, unison journey to the movement's end.

SECOND MOVEMENT: Andante cantabile
(11:11)

This movement is silky and soulful using neither the timpani nor the trumpets. The muted strings begin tentatively, undecidedly inching their way. The violins gently take the lead (0:20) and start a flowing melody that seems to glisten in the moonlight, growing brighter when the flute and bassoon join (0:39). When the cellos and basses play the melody (0:50), it takes on a new profundity and richness, a distinct contrast to the airy flow of the violins (0:55).

A brief bridge from the oboe and bassoon leads to a new section; gone is the gentle ease, replaced by a newfound sorrow (1:23) as the violins cry out over the steady, propulsive pulses in the lower strings. Listen especially for the richness and passion the sustained chords in the winds add. Gradually calm is restored by the first violins and the oboe (1:59) and with it the movement's original romantic mood returns (2:22); it seems more tired, somewhat resigned, slowly winding down, leading to a repeat of the opening minutes of this movement (3:21). (Note: It is not unusual for this repeat to be eliminated.)

The first violins lead out of the repeat (6:45), the sound swelling as the winds join and the sense of sorrow returns (6:55). A pause in the struggle (7:36) allows the calm to gradually return highlighted by a lilting duet between the flute and oboe with string accompaniment (7:45) that takes us straight into a recapitulation of the movement's opening (7:56). The easy flow is energized by powerful pulses from the horns (8:26) building to hint at the strain and sorrow (8:51), then receding and returning to the silky elegance of the moonlit romance.

Toward the movement's end the violins accompany an exquisite solo for the bassoons (9:56) that is echoed by the horns. Just when it seems the movement is going to wind down, the first violins restart the original theme (10:19), but leave the phrase incomplete, allowing the flute and bassoon to take the flowing line. This is totally relaxed, almost lethargic, until the first violins and oboe retake the lead (10:34) completing the phrase they began. The horns' quiet yet still propulsive pulses (10:53) gradually slow down and lead to the sleepy final phrase.

THIRD MOVEMENT: Menuetto: Allegretto (5:48)

The trumpets and timpani return for this airy, elegant movement that makes you want to get up and dance. Gracefully the violins ease into the melody, becoming more powerful when the full ensemble joins (0:10) exuberantly leading to a repeat of this brief opening section (0:19). After the repeat (0:37) the oboes and violins start a more flowing passage propelled steadily by the pulsing of the horns. The gentle flow is halted by a firm interruption from the strings and horns (0:46) echoed by the other winds, trumpets, and timpani. But this is temporary, as the flow resumes (0:50) now more energized and excited. The woodwinds blend their sounds for a beautiful, intimate ensemble (1:09), bridging to the return of the full orchestra (1:18) and a repeat of this second section (1:27).

Following this repeat (2:17) the Trio section of the Minuet begins quietly as the flute, bassoons, and horn seem to stretch until the first violins and oboe enter, tentative and delicate. These phrases are repeated (2:28). Then a somewhat angry outburst (2:38) forcefully imposes a rigidity to the flow of the dance, disrupting the courtly elegance. This short digression introduces the first violins accompanied by steady pulses in the other strings calmly winding down, as if they have grown tired and lethargic, before returning to the beginning of the angry section for another repeat (3:05). A brief pause (3:31) and we are back at the beginning of the entire Minuet, the opening sections of which are heard again up until the start of the Trio.

FOURTH MOVEMENT: Finale: Molto allegro
(11:02)

The key to the final movement is the four-note theme established by the first violins in the opening phrase. Be sure to listen for its reappearance throughout as it makes its way into each section of the orchestra taking on several guises.

Right from the violins' first statement the pace is fast, moving stealthily, fleeting gently from note to note, leading to an excited outburst (0:07) as the full orchestra gets involved it becomes reminiscent of the regal splendor of the symphony's first movement. Amid this sonic brilliance try to pick out the four-note theme boldly played initially by the violins. The strings scurry to a split-second pause (0:29) just long enough to catch one's breath before the second violins embark on their own taking the four-note theme. This is the first entrance in a fugue as the first violins (0:32) jump in, followed by the violas (0:35) and the cellos (0:37), each instrument weaving delicately with the others, blending together for an exuberant outburst (0:43).

Tenderness returns (1:00) led primarily by the strings, but with some particularly beautiful interjections from the oboe and flute. There is an unmistakable bubbliness as the pace moves rapidly and happily until a tiny bit of strain (1:45) creeps into the sound. It resolves quickly, bringing back the ebullience, leading to a delicate oboe solo (2:04) and a repeat of the opening section of the movement (2:10).

After the repeat (4:20), the violins and violas play the four-note theme with occasional interjections from the wind instruments, only now there is a distinctly mysterious quality as this once confident, noble melody becomes unsettled. An outburst (4:33) shatters the mood, launching a series of angry volleys, the sections of the orchestra seeming to fire attacks back and forth against each other. A fabulous blending of sounds of the various wind instruments (5:00) begins to quell the fury, removing the anger, leading to a recapitulation of the opening theme (5:18). This time, though, the melody grows angry sooner (5:25) and races forward, becoming more excited until a pause halts the progress (5:57).

As if reconsidering the anger, the brief void is filled by a new tender section led by the strings with occasional interjections from the flute, building excitedly, flying to a joyful explosion of noble sounds (6:50). A brief pullback, gentle and sweet (7:03), leads to a repeat of the movement's second section (7:08). (Note: This repeat, included in this recording, is not always observed.)

Following the repeat (9:56) there is great strength provided by the trumpets, horns, timpani, and strings. This is just a brief outburst, the power disappearing almost instantly as the violins quietly restart the four-note theme (10:00), only now in a slightly different guise, making it sound unlike any of the earlier versions. As other instruments follow the violins, the sound and energy are slow to rebuild; something new is mysteriously developing, waiting only for someone to take the lead and pull the rest in some definite direction. It is the violas who firmly play the first note (10:10) introducing the bassoons, horns, and cellos boldly taking the four-note theme, now proud and exhilarating. As the other instruments echo, note how the four-note theme gets passed around the orchestra, making a forceful sound as the full ensemble propels joyfully in unison to the symphony's thrilling conclusion.

MAESTRO NIKOLAUS HARNONCOURT:

"Mozart's last three symphonies [numbers 39, 40, and 41] seem to be related in many ways. They are linked in terms of motif and also by a kind of continuing tempo from a dramaturgical point of view. Although each is very long when played with all the repeats, I wanted to present them all together, uncut, in the full majesty of their impact—almost like a self-contained work."

COMPARATIVE RECORDINGS

HARNONCOURT/CHAMBER ORCHESTRA OF EUROPE
TELDEC 9031-74858   TOTAL TIME: 40:52

Harnoncourt made his reputation as an interpreter of baroque music performed on period instruments. Here he gives a thrilling performance of this classical masterpiece, tinged with a fantastic crispness and clarity allowing the listener to hear the inner voices without sacrificing any of the overall lushness in this symphony.

REINER/CHICAGO SYMPHONY ORCHESTRA
RCA 6376   TOTAL TIME: 25:37

A superfast performance without repeats that is an absolute classic. The Chicago Symphony under Reiner was machinelike in its precision yet could play tenderly, qualities used to the fullest in this recording.

KLEMPERER/PHILHARMONIA ORCHESTRA
EMI CLASSICS CDMD-63272   TOTAL TIME: 29:55

In this collection of ten Mozart symphonies the *Jupiter* stands out as one of the absolute best recordings ever made of this masterpiece. Every tempo is ideal and the playing is exquisite. Klemperer was at his absolute best.

IF YOU ENJOYED THIS PIECE . . .

Mozart's output was amazingly consistent, and one can listen to any of the middle through the late symphonies and hear great music. To track his development it is interesting to start with the **Twenty-fifth Symphony** and work your way through to the *Jupiter*. However, be certain to listen to the penultimate symphony: the incredible **Fortieth in G Minor.** Be sure also to spend some time with Mozart's operas, especially **The Marriage of Figaro** and **Don Giovanni.**

MOZART

REQUIEM

Surrounded by fantastic stories, some true and some fiction, and filled with heartbreaking melodies and passion, Wolfgang Amadeus Mozart's (1756–91) Requiem is one of the most astounding choral works ever written. The most incredible part of the story is that as Mozart began work on the Requiem, he had a premonition he was composing this mass for the dead for his own death. The premonition came true, and Mozart died in December 1791, leaving the work to be completed from his sketches by his pupil Franz Süssmayer.

The other part of the story is the work was commissioned anonymously by a wealthy count who wanted to claim he had composed the Requiem as a tribute to his late wife. Always in need of money, Mozart accepted the terms of secrecy and began composing the work in July of 1791. With each passing month, he grew weaker and sicker, ultimately dictating passages of the music to his pupil. But Mozart succumbed in December, leaving his widow to ask Süssmayer to complete the piece. Since Mozart had dictated some sections of the work, there is no precise delineation as to where Mozart actually stopped composing and Süssmayer began. All the mystery surrounding the Requiem yielded the dramatic focus of the final scenes of the movie *Amadeus*. However, the creators of *Amadeus* took great liberties by having Mozart dictate parts of the Requiem to his rival, the composer Antonio Salieri. This certainly never occurred, but it does make a great story, and the use of the music from the Requiem in the movie is fabulous.

Despite Mozart's ever-worsening condition in 1791, he used his final months to compose some of his greatest works, including the Twenty-seventh Piano Concerto, the Clarinet Concerto, and two operas, *La Clemenza di Tito* and *The Magic Flute*. It was also the year in which Haydn, who was old enough to be Mozart's father, composed his *Surprise* Symphony (see chapter 18), a mere ten symphonies and eighteen years before *he* died!

Mozart's Requiem conforms to the structure of the Latin mass for the dead, containing a total of fourteen sections. It is written for soprano, alto, tenor, and bass solo voices, chorus, and an unconventional orchestra made up of basset horns, bassoons, trumpets, three trombones, timpani, strings, and organ. It is particularly interesting to listen for the way the basset horns and bassoons play off each other, and for the rich sonority of the trombones. While it is interesting for musicologists to debate where Mozart actually stopped composing and where Süssmayer began, the fact remains that the entire work is a masterpiece and deserves its place in the standard repertoire. And, though Mozart's music certainly stands on its own, the Requiem will take on an almost otherworldly quality if the listener keeps in mind that Mozart composed it convinced he was writing it for his own death, and this horrifying premonition came true.

REFERENCE RECORDING:
EMI CLASSICS 47342
BARENBOIM/SOLOISTS/CHORUS AND
ORCHESTRA OF PARIS
TOTAL TIME: 55:41

I. INTROITUS: REQUIEM AETERNAM: Adagio
(5:31)

At the outset the pace is slow, the mood somber. Mozart accomplishes this simply, as the strings set the pulse with short notes, while the bassoon plays a plaintive, sustained melody. The bassoon is joined by the basset horns (0:11) playing the sad melody in a higher range. Simply put, this section is nothing more than the four voices of the basset horns and the bassoons interweaving, as the strings provide a steady, funereal pulse.

When the bassoons and basset horns stop, the strings' pulses suddenly get louder, longer, and angrier (0:47), a sound intensified by three distinct notes played by the trumpets and the timpani. It is these notes that introduce the basses in the chorus, who intone the first phrase: *"Requiem aeternam ... "* (Eternal rest ...) (0:54). In ascending order, the tenors, altos, and sopranos copy the basses' opening, each voice category increasing the tension and intensifying the sense of struggle and strain. This opening section is a plea to the Lord to grant the dead eternal rest. As the text changes to a request that "perpetual light may shine upon them" (*et lux perpetua ...*) (1:40), the strain diminishes, as the violins' passage goes from stressful to graceful.

Now, the basset horns emerge with a calm, yet sad, solo (2:10) taken over by the bassoons and leading to the solo soprano's first entrance (2:21) quietly singing: *"Te decet hymnus, Deus, in Sion"* (A hymn, O God, becometh thee in Zion), accompanied only by the strings. A loud response from the chorus (2:55) calling, *"Exaudi orationem meam"* (Hear my prayer), reenergizes the movement before another basset horn/bassoon line plaintively emerges (3:32), leading to a return of the strain in the strings (3:44) and a recapitulation of the basses' opening

"*Requiem aeternam* ... " This continues through the "*lux per-petua*" section. The opening movement ends quietly with the chorus and strings in unison.

II. KYRIE ELEISON: Allegro   (2:46)

This movement repeatedly implores, "Lord, have mercy, Christ have mercy." It is powerful, beseeching with tremendous energy and a fast, steady pace. Each section of the chorus enters strong, then backs off to blend into the whole, a pattern heard many times. Further, each section of the chorus is teamed with a specific group of instruments, in effect dividing the forces into four teams, with the organ adding its voice to each team as needed.

The basses, joined by a bassoon, the cellos, and the double basses, launch the Kyrie. The altos and one of the basset horns and the second violins (0:03) enter next, followed by the sopranos (0:10) teamed with the other basset horn and the second violins, and finally the tenors (0:13), teamed with the other bassoon and the violas. Throughout this movement, try to follow each team as it enters with strength and then blends into the overall sound.

With each entrance the volume and intensity increase, like surging surf that pounds more of a beach with each ensuing rush. This is especially evident when the trumpets and timpani add their powerful sounds to the basses' team (1:46). While the teams have been vying for dominance throughout the movement, they ultimately join together (2:15) on the word *eleison* with the trumpets and timpani blasting forceful support. Everything stops (2:21), then resumes with one more, very slow, unison "Kyrie eleison," an almost desperate final plea, strengthened by relentless timpani beats.

III. SEQUENZ: DIES IRAE: Allegro assai (1:46)

Mozart's musical vision of the "Day of wrath" (*Dies irae*) is one of the scariest hundred seconds of music ever composed. It is a possessed, relentless vision, driven and furiously paced. The full chorus launches into the movement with tremendous force. After the initial "Dies irae" listen for the additional power generated by the timpani and trumpets. When the chorus pauses (0:27), the brief interlude is provided by the furiously flying violins leading to another angry "Dies irae" (0:31).

Though quieter, the mood becomes even scarier when the text changes to "*Quantus tremor* . . . " (How great a terror. . .) (0:45), almost as if this will be a punishment beyond belief. The basses intone: "*Quantus tremor* . . . " (0:59), only to have the rest of the terrified chorus respond with a reminder that this is "*Dies irae*," the Day of Wrath, until finally they all loudly cry out about the impending terror (1:14). From here on the chorus sings nonstop until they halt all at once (1:35), and the scurrying violins, supported by the basset horns and bassoons, but especially by the trumpets and timpani, race to the movement's end.

IV. TUBA MIRUM: Andante (4:15)

Although this section is about how the trumpet will be heard through the tombs of all lands calling all before the throne, Mozart begins with an unusual solo for the trombone. It is stately and regal, dramatically different from the anger and fury of the preceding movements. The solo bass echoes the trombone's opening phrase (0:07) and is then joined in a strange duet by the trombone, as the strings provide a steady accompaniment.

The tenor solo takes over (1:10) accompanied only by the strings. This is more passionate than the movement's opening, as the tenor's first word is "*Mors* . . . " (Death). When calm returns (1:33), the tenor is joined by the trombone playing quietly at first, but then becoming an equal partner in a duet. As the tenor sustains the last note of his solo (2:11), the alto takes over. The transition from one voice to the other should be seamless, a technique repeated when the alto holds her last note (2:35) and the soprano solo takes over.

The four soloists finally sing together (3:19): *"Cum vix justus sit securus?"* (When even the just will need mercy?). This is the most peaceful moment thus far in the work. When the soloists stop (4:01), the strings, basset horns, and the bassoons calmly play to the end and quietly fade away.

V. REX TREMENDAE   (2:29)

The strings begin this solemn, angry movement and are answered by a distant, yet somehow powerful chord intoned by the winds. The chorus enters (0:14), four times calling out *"Rex!"* (King!). Following the fourth call, they continue pleading to this "King of dreadful majesty" to save them, the supporting timpani adding urgency to their cry. When the line is complete, each section of the chorus moves on its own, creating a layering of voices that adds to the tortured quality. Momentarily they join together (1:03) for one cry of *"Rex tremendae majestatis"* before splitting up into distinct sections.

Again the voices unite (1:29) for an extended, powerful plea. The strings, playing alone, calm everything and introduce the women of the chorus, who quietly, almost prayerfully sing *"Salva me"* (Save me) (1:40), a plea echoed by the men (1:51). Then they all beg softly in unison for salvation (1:58) accompanied by the strings. They end together, leaving the last two resigned, sad notes of the movement to the strings.

VI. RECORDARE   (6:16)

This movement, which asks Jesus to recall the reason for his journey, begins with a beautiful solo for the basset horns and the cellos. The pace moves, but should not feel rushed; the mood is peaceful and almost cheerful. After the introduction, the other strings assume the flowing melodic line (0:16). The first voice heard is the solo alto (0:35) followed immediately by the solo bass. The soprano then takes over (0:51) and is joined by the tenor, before the four solo voices sing in unison asking for remembrance.

The mood becomes slightly more agitated (1:43) with the bass and tenor alternating passages with the soprano and alto. Calm returns (2:04) as the teams change; now the alto and bass alternate with the soprano and tenor for what sounds like a slow-motion game of Ping-Pong, ending when the four soloists sing in unison (2:16). The next sections are a series of contemplative solos for the voices, some overlapping and some alone.

The four voices come together (3:19) with the strings, basset horns, and bassoons for the "*Ingemisco*" (I groan as one guilty). This section is steadily paced with occasional swells of passion and intensity. But the relative calm is broken by an angry string passage (4:54), and louder solo voices responding. Before the movement's end, calm is restored, the solo voices end together (5:56), and the strings, led by the violins, play the final, graceful passage.

VII. CONFUTATIS: Andante   (2:45)

This is the movement that, in the movie *Amadeus*, Mozart dictates from his deathbed to Salieri. The dissection and explanation of the music in that scene was superb. Yet somehow, when taken apart, the glory of the music is dissipated, for this is a powerful movement dealing with the condemnation of the damned to the flames of hell!

From the very first note the strings dominate. Though not fast, they play a lot of notes, making it sound busy, angry, and spiteful. The basses and tenors enter almost immediately, alternating cries of "*Confutatis, maledictis*" (When the wicked are confounded), all sung over the relentless strings and aided by the trombones and timpani. Suddenly (0:18), there is a pause as the basset horns and bassoons play a brief bridge and we hear the women of the chorus tremulously singing "*Voca me . . .* " (Call me with the blessed). With only the violins as accompaniment, they sound like heavenly angels. But their prayer is interrupted by the angry men (0:35) and the furious strings.

When the voices stop, the strings establish a steady pulse (1:31) and the basset horns, bassoons, and trombones play sustained chords. Quietly the chorus enters (1:35), now in a solemn prayer continuing to the movement's end.

VIII. LACRIMOSA   (3:14)

A day of weeping and sorrow is the day the guilty man shall rise again from the ashes to be judged. This is the thrust of the Lacrimosa, and Mozart captures this dramatic depression in the strain of the violins and a heavy pulse in the violas. When the chorus enters in unison with the plaintive basset horns and bassoons (0:19), the feeling of sorrow is overwhelming. Slowly the intensity builds, growing in volume and sorrow with each passing phrase. When the swells are particularly powerful, listen for the strong accents provided by the timpani, trombones, and trumpets.

Briefly the chorus stops (1:56) and a lovely basset-horn duet emerges bridging to a return of the strain in the violins (2:09) and the chorus's reentrance (2:14) now pleading for eternal rest. The pain is heightened by the steady timpani beats struggling to get from one beat to the next. The movement ends with a sustained "Amen," sung in unison by the chorus and supported by a timpani roll (2:53).

IX. OFFERTORIUM: DOMINE JESU:
Andante con moto   (4:02)

A great change occurs here: suddenly we have a movement that is relatively cheerful and bouncy. The chorus begins quietly, supported by the strings and the organ, and then jubilantly explodes on the words "Rex gloriae."

When the strings and bassoon launch into a flurry of activity (0:59), the mood becomes less joyous. With the addition in sequence of the tenors, altos, sopranos, and basses, a fugue erupts like an angry, yet controlled fight. The next fugal section is started by the solo soprano (1:32), followed by the solo alto, tenor, and bass. Ultimately this resolves into a vocal quartet with the four soloists ending together. The return of the chorus (2:05) brings back the warring factions: the anger in each voice finds its place in a complex, ever-evolving puzzle. As it develops, the pieces move closer and closer together, quieting down (3:07) to a less jagged sound. There is one more return to controlled anger and chaos (3:24) prior to a clear broadening of the pace (3:36) and a sustained unison resolution.

X. HOSTIAS ET PRECIS: Andante   (5:11)

Calm is the predominant quality as the strings establish a steady, stately pace. The chorus enters together with the basset horns and bassoons, singing humbly of the sacrifices and offerings they give to the Lord. Under the melodic line in the chorus, try to listen for the important support provided by the violins, and for the lovely transition they play (1:11) leading to the chorus's return, louder and with more strain. The next moments are a series of alternating loud and soft passages, with the strings playing throughout, and the basset horns and bassoons joining the chorus only in the loud phrases. This section of the movement ends quietly, resigned.

This sad peace is shattered by the basses (3:14), strongly supported by the trombones, angrily singing "*Quam olim Abrahae . . .* "— their reminder to God that he promised Abraham he would pass the dead to life. The bass entrance is the first part of another fugal section, with the rest of the chorus entering in ascending order; tenors, altos, and sopranos. As in the earlier fugues, each entrance is initially prominent and then blends into the overall sound. Ultimately, the ferocity diminishes (4:15) and the lines become more sustained. But it is a brief respite, as the basses restart the angry battle among the voices (4:34). This time, though, they join together and sing in unison, supported by wonderful wind lines, to the movement's sustained conclusion.

XI. SANCTUS: Adagio   (1:43)

An outburst of the word *"Sanctus!"* (Holy!) accented by a series of timpani beats launches this slow, steadily paced movement. The repeatedly sung *"Sanctus"* from the full chorus is uplifting, like a strong ray of sun piercing through after many days of dark clouds. Each subsequent outburst seems to intensify the joy and relief, and despite the slowness of the pace, it never sounds heavy.

There is a sudden change of gears (1:01) as the basses launch another fast section singing, *"Hosanna in excelsis!"* (Hosanna in the highest!). The tenors, altos, and sopranos enter sequentially creating another fugue, yet, unlike most of the others that have occurred in the Requiem, this one leads to a joyful explosion (1:29) and a unison ending.

XII. BENEDICTUS: Andante   (6:07)

This movement begins with a brief orchestral section featuring the first violins and the basset horns, with support provided by the bassoons, trombones, and the other string instruments. The pace is steady but not slow; the melody is peaceful and forgiving as it introduces the solo alto entrance (0:17) and the words "Blessed is he that cometh in the name of the Lord." As the alto sings, note the importance of the first violins paralleling the solo voice. When the solo alto completes the first phrase, the line is taken over by the solo soprano (0:34), while the important accompaniment in the orchestra shifts to the basset horn.

The solo tenor and bass join the solo soprano and alto in a series of short comments (0:55), with each voice entering for one part of a phrase. Now, when all the parts are put together, the pieces come together to create a sustained line. Through this section the voices weave in and out, the soprano line occasionally soaring over the others. But finally the four voices come together on the word *"Domini"* and then fall silent (1:48).

Now the orchestra takes over: the wind instruments intone rich, heavy chords. The sound gives the feeling of summoning, as if the heavens are calling forth. After a basset-horn solo, the solo bass resumes the Benedictus (2:14) immediately answered by the three other solo voices. Again, the solo voices weave in and out, sometimes singing one at a time, sometimes in pairs, and sometimes all together. As they complete the word *"Domini,"* they are immediately replaced by the summoning chords in the winds (5:06), now more intense and filled with a sense of ceremonial pomp. This stately section is interrupted and replaced as the tenors in the chorus launch into a fast *"Hosanna in excelsis"* (5:32). In rapid succession the other sections of the chorus follow, entering in ascending order creating another fugue, just as busy and intense as the ones heard earlier. Ultimately, all four choral lines join together (5:58) for a joyful ending.

XIII. AGNUS DEI (3:15)

A single note in the basset horns, bassoons, trumpets, and timpani introduces the sad, nervous line played by the violins. If the end of the Benedictus made you forget that this is a mass for the dead, the beginning of the *"Agnus Dei"* (O Lamb of God) will remind you. While the violins continue to play their fleeting passages, the chorus enters (0:04) with sustained, beseeching phrases. On the line *"Dona eis requiem"* (Grant them rest) (0:30), the basses begin, dark and mysterious, while the rest of the chorus accompanied by the strings answers with a lighter, more prayerful passage. A beautiful, short bridge played by the basset horns and the bassoons (0:44) returns us to a repeat of the movement's opening phrases.

This time, the sopranos begin the *"Dona eis"* (1:22), their voices creating a light, forgiving sound. The other voices join for a soft, prayerlike ensemble. The strings provide the next bridge (1:47) leading to another series of *"Agnus Dei"* much like the movement's opening, each entrance increasing the intensity. They all come together (2:44) for a sustained, quiet, yet intense plea for eternal rest, and the voices fade away.

XIV. COMMUNIO: LUX AETERNA: Adagio
(6:17)

If this music sounds familiar, it should, because here Süss-mayer used Mozart's themes from the first movement, making some changes to accommodate the different text. Starting with the plaintive introduction played by the basset horns and the bassoons and continuing with the solo soprano entrance (0:13), this is a copy of the second section of the opening movement. The calm is disturbed by a jerky passage in the violins (0:43) as the altos, tenors, basses, and then sopranos loudly proclaim: "*Lux aeterna*" (Light everlasting).

The basses, sounding more grim than before (1:36), intone: "*Requiem*," introducing the rest of the chorus pleading for eternal rest. Listen for the violins as the strain increases, unceasingly continuing a series of two-note interjections. When the sopranos emerge (2:30) with the phrase "*et lux perpetua*," the rest of the chorus accompanied by the strings echoes their plea. This force-ful section contrasts with the final plea sung in unison by all the voices. As they fade away, listen for the sustained trumpet chords, and the timpani beats.

Out of this silence, the bassoon and basses launch into the work's final section: "*Cum sanctis tuis in aeternum . . .*" (With thy saints forever . . .) (3:24). Again, this will sound familiar because it is a copy of the music Mozart composed for the Kyrie. To remind you, it is a fugue with each voice entering prominently and then blending into the overall fabric, the intensity increas-ing with each subsequent entrance. The pace is fast, but not fran-tic. Ultimately (5:41), the voices all come together, forcefully and loud, seeming to strain, yet held together by the solidifying force of the timpani beats. There is a complete stop (5:50), fol-lowed by one slow, final phrase: "*quia pius es*" (for Thou art mer-ciful). All forces are together now for a sustained note dominated by the thundering timpani, a final moment seeming to sum up the tragic sadness of the Requiem, and the supernatural story of its composition.

ARTISTIC DIRECTOR OF THE ORCHESTRA OF ST. LUKE'S, MICHAEL FELDMAN:

"The first time I heard Mozart's Requiem I was struck by the bleak wind orchestration, totally unlike anything else of Mozart's. There are no flutes, oboes, or French horns—just basset horns, bassoons, trumpets, and trombones. Only later did I realize what many have written since: perhaps Mozart never had time to finish the orchestration."

COMPARATIVE RECORDINGS

BARENBOIM/BATTLE, MURRAY, RENDALL, SALMINEN/CHORUS AND ORCHESTRA OF PARIS
EMI CLASSICS 47342   TOTAL TIME: 55:41

Barenboim leads a first-rate quartet of soloists in a consistently exciting performance that combines tremendous power with appropriate compassion. The Dies Irae is particularly hair-raising.

VON KARAJAN/TOMOWA-SINTOW, MOLINARI, COLE, BURCHULADZE/VIENNA SINGVEREIN AND VIENNA PHILHARMONIC
DEUTSCHE GRAMMOPHON 419 610   TOTAL TIME: 52:09

Recorded late in Karajan's career, this is a good performance highlighted by the fabulous chorus and orchestra, although the singers are not universally good and the reading does lack some passion and fire.

MARRINER/MCNAIR,WATKINSON,ARAIZA, LLOYD/ACADEMY AND CHORUS OF ST. MARTIN IN THE FIELDS
PHILIPS 432 087   TOTAL TIME: 50:01

Marriner worked on the movie of *Amadeus*, and therefore this recording holds a certain interest. It is a good performance with some good solo singing. But the orchestra pales in comparison with the Vienna, and the overall reading is somewhat bland and reserved, lacking the tragedy and drama that should dominate.

IF YOU ENJOYED THIS PIECE . . .

While there is only one Requiem, there are many other works by Mozart capturing some of the elements that are prevalent here. For choral music, there is the beautiful **Mass in C Minor, K. 427.** The opera **The Magic Flute** was composed at about the same time as the Requiem and has some wonderful choral and solo sections. Finally, the **Twentieth Piano Concerto in D Minor** foreshadows the sound of tragedy that so dominates Mozart's final masterpiece.

MUSSORGSKY

*P*ICTURES AT AN EXHIBITION

While reading about Modest Mussorgsky's (1839–81) *Pictures at an Exhibition*, keep in mind that you are further removed from the original source of the music than usual. Here we have an orchestrated version of the original music itself inspired by an exhibit of watercolors and architectural designs. The story goes like this: In 1874, Mussorgsky wrote a suite of solo piano pieces inspired by an exhibit of paintings by his late friend Victor Hartmann. Then, in 1929, Maurice Ravel, who was born in 1875 and was one of the first "impressionist" composers, orchestrated Mussorgsky's piano work, the result the now popular version of *Pictures at an Exhibition* that is a cornerstone of the symphonic literature.

To bring the coincidences full circle, in 1874, the year Mussorgsky wrote his original version, the first impressionist exhibition was held in Paris, the name of the movement derived from Monet's painting *Impression Sunrise*. Clearly this was an era of transition: in 1874, Disraeli became prime minister, and Thomas Hardy wrote *Far from the Madding Crowd*. But more significantly, it was a year that saw the births of an extraordinary number of people who would influence the shape of the twentieth century,

including Herbert Hoover, Winston Churchill, Chaim Weizmann, Robert Frost, W. Somerset Maugham, Gertrude Stein,
Gustav Holst, Arnold Schoenberg, and Guglielmo Marconi.

The adaptations of *Pictures at an Exhibition* did not end with
Ravel, for the work's broadest popularity occurred in the early
1970s when the rock group Emerson, Lake & Palmer arranged
the entire suite for their unusual combination of electronic keyboards, guitar, and drums. To this day it remains an interesting
version of a great classical work. Further, it represents one of the
very first efforts at blurring the barriers between genres of music.
Emerson, Lake & Palmer's version, including some lyrics used to
popularize the arrangement, does not hold a candle to the Ravel
orchestration and the unmatchable power of a large orchestra
and its ability to musically depict the many colors and moods of
Hartmann's original paintings.

Ravel's orchestra includes flute, piccolo, oboes, English horn,
clarinets, bassoons, contrabassoon, four horns, three trumpets,
three trombones, tuba, saxophone, celesta, timpani, percussion,
harps, and strings. While listening to *Pictures at an Exhibition*,
remember that this music was written to tell a series of stories,
and be certain to focus on what images the music conjures up in
your mind. Then, compare those impressions to what the inter-
national "creative team" intended and see how successfully they
conveyed what this "picturesque" music was supposed to depict.

REFERENCE RECORDING:
SONY CLASSICAL SK 45935
GIULINI/BERLIN PHILHARMONIC
TOTAL TIME: 36:25

I. PROMENADE: Allegro giusto, nel modo russico, senza allegrezza, ma poco sostenuto
(1:51)

A stately stroll into the gallery, played by a solo trumpet, is
the initial image. This opening theme will be heard in several

guises throughout the suite, usually serving as the bridge between musical pictures. Once the trumpet's pronouncement is complete, the other trumpets, horns, and tuba respond (0:10) in an equally regal manner, the richness of the brass instruments blending to create an impressive wall of sound. This pattern of announce and respond is repeated several times as the movement unfolds.

When the strings join (0:36), they add a tremendous elegance, building gradually to an expansive outburst (0:53), then pulling back as the excitement wanes. But it quickly rebuilds, heightened by glorious horn calls (1:16) in the midst of the orchestra's huge sound. A fabulous chorus featuring the brass instruments alone (1:35) literally rumbles, preceding one final phrase played by the entire orchestra before the movement's abrupt end.

II. GNOMUS: Vivo   (2:47)

This portrait of a limping dwarf and his grotesque movements begins with the clarinets, bass clarinet, bassoons, contrabassoon, violas, cellos, and basses in unison loudly blurting out an angry statement, followed immediately by the horns reacting and quickly fading away. The music seems to have trouble developing a flow; like the dwarf, its "movement" is jerky, starting and stopping, then coming to a complete halt (0:23).

A new theme, more steady but still jerky, begins (0:24) featuring the flutes, oboes, and a hollow-sounding xylophone. It is haunting and creeps along deliberately, abruptly stopped by two nasty comments from the bass clarinet, bassoons, contrabassoon, horns, cellos, and basses. Mysterious sounds created by the celesta, clarinet, harp, first violins, and the violas and cellos sliding up and down their strings (0:34) quietly mimic the new theme.

Slow and heavy are the key qualities (1:00) as the wind instruments plod through each note, accentuated by the pounding of the bass drum, like the resounding steps of Bigfoot. The somewhat discordant sound of the winds only underlines the ugliness of this section. With each passing phrase the volume and intensity increase, eventually leading to a gripping eruption (1:52), straining to become wild. A loud clap, played by the wood block (2:20), stops everything until the bass clarinet quietly trills, restarting the mysterious theme with the xylophone. Two brassy, harsh blares (2:36) from the horns, trumpets, trombones, and tuba launch a wicked race to the finish.

III. PROMENADE: Moderato commodo e con delicatezza   (1:05)

It is time to stroll to another painting, and Mussorgsky returns to the first movement's melody played initially by the horn, this time less powerful, more delicate and pensive. The oboe, clarinets, bassoon, and the flutes carry the melody for most of the movement joined only at the very end (0:50) by the violins.

IV. IL VECCHIO CASTELLO (THE OLD CASTLE): Andante   (4:42)

Muted cellos introduce a sorrowful solo for the bassoons. The saxophone (0:18) assumes the melody, its hollow tone eerier than the bassoons, languorous but not lethargic as it moves steadily, pushed by repeated notes in the cellos. The violins, also muted, stir the stillness (1:15) before the oboe and saxophones share a strange, short duet (1:32).

The pace seems to slow down as the intensity diminishes until the flutes and clarinet take the lead (3:01) and steadily restore the intensity. But this, too, fades away, leaving the bassoon quietly playing what had been the steady beat of the cellos (3:43) introducing the muted violins. One last, sensuous saxophone solo (4:05) shrouded in haze restates this movement's main theme and fades away. The void is broken by a final cry from the saxophone (4:31), like a last gasp, that slowly dissipates.

V. PROMENADE: Moderato non tanto, pesante
(0:38)

The trumpet calls us to stroll to the next work joined by the lowest voices in the orchestra, cellos, basses, bass clarinet, bassoons, and contrabassoon, making this walk ponderous. When the upper strings and wind instruments are added (0:11), the mood brightens. The promenade stops suddenly and ends with a delicate three-note call.

VI. LES TUILERIES: Allegretto non troppo, capriccioso (1:13)

This delicate movement is a depiction of children and their governesses at play in The Tuileries, the famous Paris park. An octet of woodwinds starts out capriciously, the mood happy and light, especially in the passages given to the flutes and oboes. The violins change the melody (0:30) and slow the pace. This section is fluid and a little quirky; an image of children playing a game of hide-and-seek is suggested. A single chime from the triangle (1:04) restarts the woodwind octet and a repeat of the initial happy melody, followed by another abrupt ending.

VII. BYDLO: Sempre moderato pesante (2:45)

If you have ever wondered how a composer might portray an ox wagon with huge wheels, here's your chance! Weight is the key, and the lower voices including the bassoons, contrabassoon, cellos, and basses accompany a tuba solo. While the tuba surprises with its melodic ability, the other instruments plod along relentlessly. When the violins, violas, and harp join (0:53), the mood lightens somewhat, but still has its restrained quality suggestive of prisoners marching, hopeful but most probably doomed. This steady march grows as more instruments are added, and when the snare drum joins (1:35), the feeling that this is a desperate death march becomes overwhelming.

Soon the march seems to move on, the sound growing softer, and the tuba resumes its sad melody (1:58), again plodding. One weak reprise by the muted, distant horn (2:24) is heard, just before the movement ends, exhausted.

VIII. PROMENADE: Tranquillo   (0:46)

Three flutes and two clarinets begin this tranquil reprise of the stroll music. They are replaced by the oboes and bassoons continuing this atmosphere of total calm. But there is a sudden mood swing, and the calm changes to strain and darkness (0:20). The melody stops (0:40), and this promenade ends with a short, giddy, final comment.

IX. BALLET DES POUSSINS DANS LES COQUES: Scherzino: Vivo leggiero   (1:13)

Mussorgsky's inspiration for this movement was a drawing of a scene from the ballet *Trilby*, oddly titled "Ballet of the Chickens in Their Shells." The pace is fast as it scurries about, light and delicate, especially in the flutes and oboes. A sustained chord (0:14), sounding strangely like cartoon music, leads to a repeat of the movement's first few seconds.

After the repeat (0:32) the flutes and bassoons play a strange duet while the violins trill relentlessly, like chirping birds. Briefly the violins take the lead (0:49), but the unstoppable, annoying flutes reprise the movement's opening, and the flutes, oboes, and piccolo chirpingly bring this "pecking" to an end.

X. SAMUEL GOLDENBERG UND SCHMUYLE: Andante   (2:30)

There is no promenade before we encounter this depiction of a conversation between two Jewish men, one rich and one poor.

The introduction is heavy, with a distinctly Slavic/Gypsy tone created by the strings, the English horn, clarinets, and bassoons, although it is the rich string sound that is predominant. A rapid-fire, sniping solo trumpet (0:51) accompanied only by the oboes and clarinets contrasts with the somber opening. Sneering, the trumpet seems to be hurling insults (1:24) while the horns add to the tension.

Angrily, the strings, clarinets, bassoons, and contrabassoon answer the trumpet (1:32). Now the weighty first theme and the sniping, rude second theme are heard together as the argument grows louder and continues until it is abruptly cut off (2:02). A new theme played by the oboes and first violins fills the silence; it is sullen and plaintive. Reminders of the argument crop up occasionally as this movement grinds to its conclusion.

XI. LIMOGES—LE MARCHÉ: Allegretto vivo sempre scherzando (1:32)

Another argument, this one among women in a market, is the theme of this fast movement; from the outset the horns establish one voice, and the violins answer with another. (The violins may remind you of the "Pick a Little, Peck a Little" number from the show *The Music Man*.) The music is busy and flighty and seems to bounce around out of control. A sudden stop (1:19) silences everyone, then the music resumes even more frantically, a truly wild scene filled with hysteria. A final race brings the argument to a screeching halt, and we are thrust directly into the next movement.

XII. CATACOMBAE SEPULCHRUM ROMANUM: Largo (2:37)

A startling change occurs as the flighty fight in the market is replaced by the ponderous reality of mortality and the catacombs. The source of this movement was a drawing of Hartmann himself exploring the Paris catacombs by the light of a lantern. The heavier instruments, primarily the trombones, tuba, and horns, solemnly announce our arrival at this hallowed burial area. The chords are sustained, swelling and receding like the music for a gothic horror movie. The only trace of light is provided by the solo trumpet (1:30) and its forgiving melody slicing through the somber brass. But angrily the other brass instruments (1:46) bring back the "horror movie" music. This attack quiets, and one final blast (2:16), leading to an eerie rumble from the tam-tam, ends the visit to the catacombs.

XIII. CUM MORTUIS IN LINGUA MORTUA:
Andante non troppo, con lamento   (2:16)

This movement bears the creepy heading "Speaking to the Dead in a Dead Language," an image Mussorgsky conjured up by himself inspired by Hartmann's creative spirit leading the composer to the skulls in the catacombs. He speaks to them and they slowly become illuminated from within, an interesting premise for a musical composition.

Extremely quiet, muted violins play a sustained chord introducing the oboes and English horn, who play a slowed-down variation of the original promenade theme (0:06). The violins, now joined by the violas, tremble while the bass clarinet, bassoons, contrabassoon, cellos, and basses take the melody from the oboes (0:19). The low, slow-moving voices combined with the shaky upper strings yield a creepy sound reminiscent of a graveyard scene in a horror movie.

Emerging from the haze, the oboe and clarinet begin to brighten the mood (1:09). The creepiness diminishes, replaced by tranquillity as the harp lightens the tone. One can almost see the dense fog rising, allowing the sun to shine through. Calm prevails, the movement ending softly with a sustained chord that just fades away.

XIV. LA CABANE DE BABA-YAGA SUR DES PATTES DE POULE: Allegro con brio, feroce (4:01)

There is no pause as we are catapulted into a ferocious attack highlighted by the timpani and bass drum. The Hartmann painting inspiring this movement was of a clock in the shape of the legendary Russian witch Baba-Yaga. The beginning starts and stops, seeming to build up energy, the strings, English horn, clarinets, and bassoons snapping out a series of gruff comments. Once the engine gets going, it sounds driven as if possessed, developing relentlessly until the trumpets cut through (0:27) like the cavalry trying to gain control of a wild situation. But the other brass instruments angrily blare out sustained retorts and the orgiastic excitement continues unabated, eventually growing slower and heavier (1:09). Instruments drop out one by one until there is only a solo trumpet left (1:16) playing a series of eight notes.

The flutes change the mood and begin a free-flowing, gossamerlike solo (1:20) accompanied only by occasional comments from the bassoons and basses. Mystery abounds, especially when the tuba (2:00) heavily burps its notes and the response is led by the celesta, xylophone, and harp. (This section may remind you of the music played during the witch's-castle scene in the movie *The Wizard of Oz*.) As this creepy music fades away, an angular outburst from the flutes, piccolo, oboes, clarinets, xylophone, and violins abruptly snaps everything to attention (2:35). But the trembling cellos and basses, and an eerie single tam-tam crash, sap any remaining energy to reach a dead stop.

The silence is shattered by an angry interjection (2:47); this is just the first volley in a series of outbursts that reprise the section of the engine getting going. Steadily, with its vulgar blasts, the pace and intensity increase, and as before the trumpets try to cut through the wildness (3:06), but are overwhelmed by the witch's power. The violins, screeching demonically (3:41), seem to fly up and down over their strings, ending the movement abruptly on a high note.

XV. LA GRANDE PORTE DE KIEV: Allegro alla breve. Maestoso. Con grandezza   (6:29)

Without a pause between movements, the final impression begins; this time Mussorgsky drew his inspiration from an architectural design for a large gate in Kiev. The majestic melody, played loudly by the bassoons, contrabassoon, horns, trumpets, trombones, tuba, timpani, and bass drum, is reminiscent of the Promenade theme that began the work. Now, it is broad and overpowering, and when the rest of the orchestra joins in, led by the crashing cymbal, the sound is even bigger, a fitting musical portrait of the massive Russian structure it depicts.

A sudden quiet takes hold (1:05) as the clarinets and bassoons play a prayerlike interlude, a tremendous contrast to the power preceding it and the explosion that follows it (1:40). Here the brass instruments dominate, while the flutes, oboes, harps, violins, and violas excitedly race through exhilarating passages. Another midphrase interruption silences this most recent eruption (2:19), replacing it with a reprise of the prayerlike calm provided by the clarinets and bassoons, with the flutes adding an angelic quality. As the interlude ends, a heavy plodding starts (2:53), the lower voices steadly alternating pulses as the second violins and violas rustle (3:02), quickening the pace, like a reawakening. The contrast of the flowing string phrases against the heavy plodding creates a bit of tension that begins to resolve when the flutes, piccolo, oboes, and clarinet sneak in (3:18). All of this leads to the reemergence of the melody (3:26), now more splendid, shining like the sun slowly coming out from behind clouds, growing brighter and brighter by the second.

As if what has already been heard was not powerful enough, there is yet another explosion with the full orchestra reprising the main theme (4:01), broader and more majestic than ever. The pace slows dramatically giving plenty of time to bask in the powerful radiance of the sound. One final quieting (4:42) starts the final push to the end; gradually the sonic power rebuilds, instruments chiming in one by one until a huge explosion featuring the brass instruments (5:18) takes hold. Unbelievably, the sound grows larger still (5:39) in another eruption, as the tam-

tam, drums, cymbals, and triangle, along with the rest of the orchestra, joyfully reach the final musical image of this stroll through the art gallery.

PRINCIPAL TRUMPET OF THE NEW YORK PHILHARMONIC, PHILIP SMITH:

"This is 'program music' at its best! Imagine walking down a long hallway at a great art museum with paintings lining both walls. As you 'promenade' you are drawn to stop and examine works that capture your imagination.

"Listen to the saxophone and strings as they paint a mysterious castle; the woodwinds as they portray a ballet of chirping chicks, straining their necks in search of food; the tuba as he plods along with the ox cart on a mud road; the brass declaiming with ringing bells the grandeur of the Great Gate of Kiev. This is truly a museum of painted sound and colors.

"Every artist and photographer knows that a little red in the picture makes the picture come alive—be sure to watch the trumpet player's face get bright red in 'Samuel Goldenberg and Schmuyle' and in 'The Great Gate.' "

COMPARATIVE RECORDINGS

GIULINI/BERLIN PHILHARMONIC ORCHESTRA
SONY CLASSICAL SK 45935   TOTAL TIME: 36:25

This is a fabulous performance, elegantly interpreted, beautifully played, and exquisitely recorded. Giulini brings the requisite power without sacrificing any of the impressionistic delicacy so necessary.

ASHKENAZY/PHILHARMONIA ORCHESTRA
LONDON 414 386   TOTAL TIME: 34:05

This recording is made particularly interesting not by Ashkenazy's conducting skills, but by the first-rate piano version he plays here. The orchestral version is good, but to be able to hear the two versions in sequence is fabulous.

DUTOIT/MONTREAL SYMPHONY ORCHESTRA
LONDON 417 299   TOTAL TIME: 32:47

This is a brisk, efficient recording that is long on technique and glittering sound and somewhat short on pathos. As a sonic spectacular this may be the performance to beat: brilliant and riveting.

IF YOU ENJOYED THIS PIECE . . .

First of all, be certain to listen to the original piano version of *Pictures* and contrast it with the orchestral. Then, if you want more Mussorgsky, his opera **Boris Godunov** is three hours of majesty and pathos requiring massive forces and great singers.

ORFF

CARMINA BURANA

Carl Orff (1895–1982) is one composer whose fame and reputation was secured by a single staggering work of music: *Carmina Burana*—*Cantiones profanae* (*Songs from Benedict-Beuern*). Though firmly a work of the twentieth century, *Carmina Burana* has its roots in a group of secular thirteenth-century songs discovered in a monastery at Benediktbeuern during the 1800s. The main subjects of these texts are Fortune, the coming of Spring, Drinking, and Love. Overall this massive work has the image and sound of a pagan ritual.

Carmina Burana was completed in 1936, the year that Hitler and Mussolini proclaimed the Berlin-Rome Axis. It was the year of the famous Berlin Olympics hosted by Hitler during which Jesse Owens won four gold medals; Dale Carnegie wrote *How to Win Friends and Influence People;* Margaret Mitchell won the Pulitzer Prize for *Gone with the Wind;* and Charlie Chaplin set the world on its ear with his astounding film *Modern Times.* In essence, 1936 was a year the world was on the brink of chaos, a mood well captured in the powerful music that Orff composed in *Carmina Burana.*

Carmina Burana received its world premiere in Frankfurt in 1937 and was first heard in the United States in San Francisco in January of 1954. It has been a cornerstone of the repertoire ever since, despite the fact that it requires large vocal and instrumental forces. The vocalists include a solo soprano, tenor, and baritone, a large chorus with a smaller choir within it, and a children's chorus. In addition to substantial string, wind, and brass sections, the huge orchestra features two pianos, a celesta, and a spectacular array of percussion instruments including three glockenspiels, xylophone, castanets, ratchet, sleigh bells, triangle, finger cymbals, large cymbals, tam-tam, bells, tambourine, two snare drums, and a bass drum. The wealth of sounds created by this unusual instrumentation gives Carmina Burana much of its controlled cacophony and a distinctly jazzy quality in sections.

There is a tremendous amount to absorb in Carmina Burana. One hearing will not reveal all the wonders of the piece, even though much of the music is repeated at least twice to accommodate the multiple verses of the lyrics. Each subsequent hearing will bring out new melodies, intricacies, and favorite parts. In any event, be certain to read the texts before listening to each of the twenty-five sections. The words will draw you right in and will illuminate Orff's brilliance as a composer and orchestrator.

REFERENCE RECORDING: LONDON 430 509
BLOMSTEDT/SOLOISTS/SAN FRANCISCO
SYMPHONY/CHORUS
TOTAL TIME: 59:07

FORTUNA IMPERATRIX MUNDI
(FORTUNE, EMPRESS OF THE WORLD)

I. O FORTUNA (O FORTUNE)   (2:32)

The opening moments of Carmina Burana set the tone for the work: dramatic, powerful, and exciting. The full orchestra and chorus, led by the steady beat of the timpani, explode in an attenuated "*O Fortuna.*" After the initial volley of sound, every-thing grows quieter and more mysterious as the voices, supported by a pulse in the bassoons and pianos, almost whisper (0:22). A sudden explosion (1:32) breaks the spell, the phrase the same, only now much louder with the winds and timpani augmenting the pianos. The volume increases steadily, unable to be held back, driving inexorably toward the final sustained choral note (2:11) as the glockenspiel and trumpets add brilliance while speeding up toward the movement's exuberant end.

II. FORTUNE PLANGO VULNERA
(I BEMOAN THE WOUNDS OF FORTUNE)
(2:41)

The first thing to note here is the unusual instrumentation; lower voices are the key. At first, the only instruments used are the two pianos, bassoons, contrabassoon, cellos, basses, and bass drum. This rumbling assortment provides sustained chords to accompany the male voices of the chorus as they chant the text. The pace picks up on the words "*Verum est*" (0:13), remaining quiet, but becoming bouncy. On the next pass at the words "*Verum est*" (0:29) the volume increases with the addition of the women in the chorus and the violins. Then, almost like a series of nasty sneers, the trumpets punctuate the end of each phrase with snappy, four-note interjections. When the chorus stops (0:43), the orchestral forces speed up and race ahead, led by the trumpets and horns, who cut through the other instruments. With the percussion instruments adding to the fury, the move-ment's first verse comes to an end.

This is one of the movements that has three verses, allowing the music to be heard three times. The second verse begins immediately following the riotous end of the first (0:52), and the final verse also follows with no pause after the second (1:46).

PRIMO VERE
(SPRINGTIME)

III. VERIS LETA FACIES
(THE MERRY FACE OF SPRING)   (3:25)

The opening of this movement seems to be tinged with a bit of the Orient, a mood created by the piano, flutes, oboes, and xylophone ringing three times, like dainty wind chimes. When the last of these has faded away (0:11), solemn chords played by the horns, trumpets, trombones, and pianos serve as the introduction and base for a prayerlike chant sung by the altos and basses of the small chorus.

The upper voices, led by the piccolo, flutes, and celesta, take over (0:42) providing an airy support for the tenors and sopranos of the small chorus, who also chant, only theirs is much less solemn and more ethereal. There is a sustained "Ah" sung by the sopranos and tenors accompanied by the flutes, celesta, and triangle (0:59) that slows down and brings the phrase to a restful end. Then the lower voices return for a reprise of the movement's beginning. After the final, sustained "Ah," two quiet chords (3:14) played by one horn, one trumpet, one trombone, the timpani, and the pianos end the movement.

IV. OMNIA SOL TEMPERAT
(THE SUN WARMS EVERYTHING)   (2:03)

The glockenspiel and piccolo play four even notes to introduce this solo for the baritone, who sings his lyrical chant over sustained chords provided by the violas and basses. His first phrase complete, the baritone pauses to allow the piccolo and glockenspiel to again intone their four notes (0:32), followed by more of the baritone's solo. This pattern is repeated twice more during the movement, and after the final time the piccolo and glockenspiel play their four notes (1:45), one horn, one bass, and one piano growl a very low chord that fades away.

V. ECCE GRATUM
(BEHOLD, THE PLEASANT SPRING)   (2:43)

This cheery choral number begins with the tenors slowly intoning the words *"Ecce gratum"* with support from the glockenspiel, pianos, and the chime. After the initial phrase (0:08) the pace increases, remaining steady and graceful. Even when the rest of the chorus joins in with the flutes, clarinets, violins, and cymbals (0:16), the music retains its airiness. A calm, lyrical phrase (0:24) replaces the steady pulse that has been the trademark of this movement. Then the pace quickens (0:32) as the tenors, singing the words *"Iam iam cedant tristia!"* are joined by the oboes, horns, and timpani. The whole chorus picks up this new speed (0:37), and the excitement increases to an almost feverish pitch until a sustained "Ah" with a shaking tambourine dominating the sound (0:47) brings the festivities to a sudden halt.

The tenors again intone (0:54), this time on the words *"Iam liquescit."* This is the beginning of the second verse. The final verse also begins with the tenors, this time singing *"Gloriantur"* (1:44), and the movement ends with the sustained "Ah" and the shaking tambourine.

UF DEM ANGER
(ON THE GREEN)

VI. TANZ (DANCE)   (1:47)

This is the only movement in the entire cantata without voices. It is a charming dance number for the orchestra filled with catchy melodies and infectious rhythms that make it hard to sit still. Don't be deceived by the deliberate introduction; the wild explosion featuring the timpani, bass drum, and snare drum (0:05) launch us directly into a highly excited, rhythmically jerky dance pattern given a peasantlike quality by the repeated strumming by the second violins, violas, and cellos.

The pace never slackens, even when two violins take over (0:17) and solo with a slightly quieter string accompaniment, replaced by the big sound of the full orchestra (0:26). The next soloists are the flute and timpani (0:37), who slow the pace a bit, but do keep the rhythms catchy. This brief peace is shattered as the horns lead the timpani and strings into another very excited section of the dance, now a bit raucous (1:09). Not to be outdone, the trumpets and cymbals launch the final salvo in this wild dance (1:29) without strings, racing right to the movement's exuberant, brusque end.

VII. FLORET SILVA
(THE NOBLE WOODS ARE IN BLOOM)   (2:50)

The jubilant chorus leaps right into the *"Floret silva,"* supported by the winds and strings with repeated accents from the tambourine. Soon everything calms down almost to a whisper, as the women of the small chorus accompanied by the strings sing a peaceful, lullabylike passage (0:27) beginning on the words *"Ubi est antiquus."* Rough, jerky string phrases (0:50) shift the mood again as a timpani solo accompanies the tenors of the small chorus singing the text: *"hinc, hinc, hinc,"* a section that fades away replaced by calm as the women sing. An ethereal *"Ah"* (1:20) sustains and then gradually disappears. The second verse begins with a recapitulation of the *"Floret silva"* as in the opening (1:25). The movement concludes with the sustained *"Ah"* sung by the women (2:45).

VIII. CHRAMER, GIP DIE VARVE MIR
(SHOPKEEPER, GIVE ME COLOR)   (3:28)

Fast, cheerful sleigh bells ring in the start of this movement, gaining momentum as the airy flute and oboe solo accompany the women of the small chorus, exquisitely delicate. Then the full chorus answers with a peaceful, sustained humming (0:18) that serves as a base for the solo flute. The women of the small chorus continue with "*Seht mich an*" accompanied by three muted trumpets and three solo violins (0:43), remaining delicate and returning to the humming and solo flute (1:00). The sleigh bells are back signifying the beginning of the second (1:07) and third (2:17) verses. A final hum (3:19) ends the movement suspended on the chorus's breath.

IX. REIE (ROUND DANCE)   (4:04)

There is no pause as this movement emerges from the suspended hum of the previous number. The orchestra starts alone, muted and calm; it seems to stroll deliberately but steadily, like a walk at sunset. Listen for the muted strings and the subtle timpani adding a steady pulse. A quiet cymbal clash (0:23) introduces the horns soaring into the sky. A distant ringing triangle ends the interruption, and the strings return to their gracious stroll, until stopped again as the trumpets mimic the horns (0:52). Another triangle ring reintroduces the strings, who resume their stroll, now with a somewhat quickened pace. One final interruption from both the horns and trumpets—all muted (1:18)—brings the stroll to an end.

Wildly strummed violins launch the section known as "*Swaz hie gat umbe*" (Those Who Go Round) (1:39) and introduce the bassoons, who interject rather nastily and grotesquely. The men of the chorus loudly proclaim the initial "*Swaz hie gat umbe*" (1:45), echoed by the women with controlled anger as the voices join together for a series of "*Ah's*" (2:01), the orchestra growing louder, more frantic, and wilder.

Without a break the next section, "*Chume, chum Geselle min*" (Come, Come, My Love), begins (2:09) again with strumming that starts forcefully but quickly quiets down to allow the altos of the small chorus to sing the lyrical phrase "*Chume, chum Geselle min*" (2:15). The men of the small chorus take over the melody (2:27) accompanied by four solo violins casting a sleepy spell, a mood enhanced by a lovely flute solo (2:39). The altos resume their song with the word "*Suzer*" (2:51), repeating musically what they did before. A reprise of the peaceful flute solo

(3:18) ends and continues right into a repeat of the wild strumming (3:31) as the full chorus again forcefully announces, "*Swaz hie gat umbe.*" The final moments are fabulously wild, heightened by the shaking tambourine.

X. WERE DIU WERLT ALLE MIN (IF ALL THE WORLD WERE MINE)   (0:53)

This is a fast, riveting movement begun by the weird combination of three trumpets and three trombones playing in unison. They are quickly replaced by four horns and the violins and violas (0:06). The chorus joins, celebrating joyfully, aided by the crash of the cymbals and the beat of the timpani (0:12). There is a brief, slightly calmer section (0:19) quickly supplanted by a broadening of the pace, as if the celebrants want to savor the moment (0:26). An eruption (0:38) leads to a wildly thrilling reprise of the opening with the trumpets and trombones, snare drum, and bass drum. A final comment from the horns, timpani, and strings leads to a single, shouted "*Hei!*" in the chorus ending the movement.

IN TABERNA (IN THE TAVERN)

XI. ESTUANS INTERIUS (BURNING INSIDE)   (2:18)

After a sustained sneer in the wind instruments heightened by the tambourine, the strings launch into a fast, jerky, propulsive beat quickly copied by the solo baritone, who almost speaks his words. When the strings and winds shift to a more sustained line (0:12), the propulsive beat is taken by the timpani.

The horns and strings loudly announce a more bravado entrance by the baritone on the words "*Feror ego veluti*" (0:33). This solo becomes a series of bravado pronouncements alternated with broader, more lyrical passages, leading to the brass and percussion instruments racing excitedly (2:09) to a curt, two-note ending.

XII. OLIM LACUS COLUERAM (ONCE I LIVED ON LAKES) (3:35)

This is possibly the weirdest movement in the whole cantata. The pace is slow and tortured beginning with a high-pitched, strained bassoon solo. Perhaps the fact that the "I" in the song's title is a swan roasting on a spit explains the strain and tortured quality of this movement's music. The tenor begins his eerie solo (0:29), which, like the bassoon's introduction, lies very high in his range, forcing the singer to strain for the notes. Between the tenor's phrases the xylophone adds creepy sounds that make vivid the image of the bird burning on the spit.

The basses of the chorus loudly and forcefully chant, "*Miser, miser!*" (1:10) supported by the trombones and timpani. The men stop singing (1:20) and the xylophone, upper winds, and trumpets play a repeated rhythmic figure that gradually slows, leaving a solo horn to fade away on a sustained note. This leads to the second (1:28) and third (2:30) verses, the movement ending with the horn fading into the distance.

XIII. EGO SUM ABBAS (I AM THE ABBOT) (1:36)

The solo baritone begins all by himself, declaring angrily and forcefully stopping to be replaced by organized cacophony from the orchestra (0:15). He then resumes his declaration (0:20), now almost speaking, interrupted again by the wild orchestra (0:54). Quickly he shouts, "*Wafna*" (0:57), violently echoed by the men of the chorus. A wicked series of "*Wafna's*" loudly shouted by the chorus precedes a single, sustained tuba note (1:25). The men shout, "*Ha ha!*" and the movement ends.

XIV. IN TABERNA QUANDO SUMUS
(WHEN WE ARE IN THE TAVERN)   (3:58)

The bassoons, violas, cellos, and basses start the steady pulse introducing the chorus men, who quietly chant copying the instruments' rhythmic pattern. It sounds like some kind of eerie mystical incantation with periodic swells in volume that always retreat. The pattern is broken (0:43) when the pulse becomes drawn out as the men sing, "*Primo pro nummata vini*," each phrase punctuated by jagged interjections spread throughout the orchestra. The pace increases even though the men have returned to chanting (0:54), the bassoons and clarinets adding spice with occasional interjections from the trumpets. Then the tone becomes ponderous (1:10) as the text changes to "*Octies pro fratribus perversis*" and the winds drop out, save for the occasional trumpet accent. The speed returns to the fast chant (1:19) and develops into a raucous celebration spearheaded by the bass drum's beats, while the trombones give the feeling of an out-of-control circus band.

The chorus men rapidly fire off the phrase "*Bibit hera*" as they join the bassoons and horns in a funny, fast section (1:42) that grows steadily, finally exploding (2:07) wildly with cymbal crashes, blasting brass instruments, and exotic percussive sounds as the men sing "*Parum sexcente nummate*." Suddenly, in mid-phrase everything stops (2:39) then explodes again on the words "*Io, io*" accentuated by the xylophone. Another sudden silence is replaced by the horns and trombones starting softly, then getting steadily louder, until they can no longer be contained and all erupts into a final, loud "*Io!*"

COURS D'AMOURS
(THE COURT OF LOVE)

XV. AMOR VOLAT UNDIQUE
(CUPID FLIES EVERYWHERE)   (3:07)

Calm prevails; a slow, luxurious opening featuring the flutes, oboes, English horn, triangle, glockenspiel, and piano casts a magical spell. Then two rich chords seem to resolve all the conflict that has come before. With the flutes dominating (0:21) the tone becomes otherworldly, and the angelic voices of the children singing alone (0:42) heighten the ethereal quality.

Repeated notes in the celesta and violins (1:34) introduce a mystery-filled flute solo with a distinctly Middle Eastern sound. The solo soprano makes her first entrance (1:43) echoed by the piccolo; peaceful and sexy are the qualities of her solo. A quiet, sustained note sung by the soprano (2:23) accompanies the flutes, who reprise their Middle Eastern melody. One final section sung by the children (2:43) leads to the clarinets and violas ending this romance-filled movement.

XVI. DIES, NOX ET OMNIA
(DAY, NIGHT, AND EVERYTHING)   (2:34)

A sustained cello note supports a steady, yet slightly jerky pulse played by the violins as an introduction to a moderately paced baritone solo. The pulse is broken by a single exquisite chord (0:17) created by the blending of sounds from the piccolos, oboes, horns, strings, and celesta, as the baritone sings at the high end of his range. The steady pulse returns (0:39) and is followed by another beautiful chord (0:56). This pattern of pulse followed by a chord is repeated until the end of the movement.

XVII. STETIT PUELLA (A GIRL STOOD)   (1:39)

Quietly, the violins reestablish the steady pulse and lead into a piquant soprano solo that alternates between short, choppy phrases and long, held notes. The flutes, clarinets, and one horn join the soprano for a more lyrical phrase (0:33) reminiscent of a romantic vocalise. Accompanied by a hidden steady pulse in the flute (1:27), the soprano reprises the lyrical line. The final note of the movement is a gentle chord played by the piccolo, glockenspiel, and celesta.

XVIII. CIRCA MEA PECTORA (IN MY HEART)   (2:01)

Ominous beats played by the lower instruments including the bassoons, contrabassoon, cellos, basses, horns, piano, and timpani introduce a forceful baritone solo. He grows more excited with each phrase, and there is a wonderful contrast between his long phrases and the choppy lines played by the flutes, oboe, and piano (0:10). While he holds a sustained "Ah," the men of the chorus copy his initial phrase (0:16); the sound is filled with mystery, like rituals in a cult meeting. The pace grows faster and more animated when the chorus's women interrupt (0:25) repeatedly singing, "Mandeliet," seeming to peck annoyingly at the men. The snare drum, xylophone, and two pianos heighten the angular nature of this passage.

The lower voices with the baritone solo return to begin the second (0:42) and the final (1:22) verse. The baritone's forcefulness is at its peak in the final verse; it is intense until it all comes to an unexpected, sudden stop.

XIX. SI PUER CUM PUELLULA (IF A BOY WITH A GIRL)   (0:56)

No instruments are used in this entire movement. It is an angry series of exchanges between the tenors and the baritones and basses of the chorus. Occasionally, a soloist may step out from among the choristers to intone one of the lines. The tenors have the final word ending the movement.

XX. VENI, VENI, VENIAS
(COME, COME, O COME) (0:58)

There should be no pause before this movement. It is another strange piece, using both pianos and most of the percussion instruments as accompaniment for the chorus, now split into two distinct choruses with different parts. This movement is jazzy and requires exceptional pianists to establish and maintain a steady, fast pace. The addition of the triangle, cymbals, tambourine, snare drum, and bass drum (0:17) keeps everything jagged and energized. Gradually the mood turns raucous, but through all that is going on, try to stay somewhat tuned into the fascinating and jazzy piano parts. The movement ends abruptly, as if cut off in midnote.

XXI. IN TRUTINA (IN THE BALANCE) (2:32)

Slow, muted strings instantly create an atmosphere of calm as the soprano solo enters (0:11) with a forgiving, prayerlike melody, the flutes and horn continuing over her final sustained note (0:59) slowing the pace. The strings set a new pulse and the soprano starts again (1:22), softer than before, but this time at the end of her phrase (2:11) the flutes and horn are joined by the timpani and the sustained, hushed strings, the last note fading away to nothing.

XXII. TEMPUS EST IOCUNDUM
(THIS IS THE JOYFUL TIME) (2:25)

A wild explosion led by the percussion, pianos, and chorus shatters the sleepy calm. This movement is a series of choral outbursts interspersed with solo turns, the first of which goes to the baritone (0:14), who, accompanied by the second piano and percussion, especially the castanets, almost speaks his way through what sounds like a carousing, drinking song, beginning with the sounds "O, O, O"! The chorus then takes over (0:25), shouting before the soprano takes the next solo joined by the children's chorus (0:41), again with the percussion playing a critical part. The chorus is next (0:53) followed again by the baritone (1:09), who is steady and strong, a contrast to the joyful voices of the soprano and the children (1:37). The chorus's final passage (1:49) sets off the baritone, children, and the chorus in the wildest series of "O, O, O" yet (2:05), but the frivolity comes to a sudden stop.

XXIII. DULCISSIME (SWEETEST ONE)   (0:37)

This brief interruption is a delightful soprano solo sung over a muted, sustained chord played by the violas, cellos, and basses. It is like a sinewy love call that ends with a delicate chord played by the glockenspiel, celesta, piano, and strings.

BLANZIFLOR ET HELENA
(BLANCHEFLEUR AND HELEN)

XXIV. AVE FORMOSISSIMA
(HAIL MOST BEAUTIFUL ONE)   (1:46)

Like chiming crystal, the three glockenspiels set the tone for this exquisite choral movement that begins with the full orchestra and chorus in a stately series of declarations. Dividing the declarations are steady, fairly ponderous punctuations from the violins and violas under the chorus's sustained notes. There is a steady buildup throughout the movement leading to a huge explosion (1:16) on the word "Blanziflor" as the cymbal crashes, the tambourine jangles through, and the bass drum makes its presence felt.

XXV. O FORTUNA
(FORTUNE, EMPRESS OF THE WORLD)   (2:38)

The preceding movement never really ends, but rather leads directly into an explosion that is the return of the very first movement of the cantata. The distinctive crash of the tam-tam starts a reprise of the chorus's forceful "O Fortuna," bringing the work full circle. Even the mysterious section from the opening movement returns (0:22), rebuilding to another overpowering explosion led by the timpani (1:33). While the chorus holds the final note (2:11), the full orchestra cavorts wildly, controlled cacophony, until it too sustains its final note, growing ever louder and ending in a fabulous unison climax.

MAESTRO HERBERT BLOMSTEDT:

"The basic challenge in this work is balance. With some three hundred and fifty singers and players onstage, everyone has to know exactly how to hold back or come forward.

"The next challenge is expression and color. This wonderful score builds very much on repetition of small motifs or phrases. For maximum effect these have to be executed with much variation and great imagination.

"The final challenge is to mold the twenty-five separate movements into a convincing whole. Since there is no dramatic story binding them together, the means must be purely musical."

COMPARATIVE RECORDINGS

BLOMSTEDT/DAWSON, DANIECKI, MCMILLAN/SAN
FRANCISCO SYMPHONY AND CHORUS
LONDON 430 509   TOTAL TIME: 59:07

A spectacular recording that illuminates the great cross rhythms and melodies that make this a superb piece of music. The sound is excellent.

MUTI/AUGER, SUMMERS, VAN KESTEREN/
    PHILHARMONIA ORCHESTRA AND CHORUS
EMI CLASSICS 47100   TOTAL TIME: 59:11

Although recorded in 1980, this performance holds up well. Muti's Italianate style works in this work of many cultures. The soloists are good.

CHAILLY/GREENBERG, BOWMAN, ROBERTS/BERLIN
    RADIO SYMPHONY ORCHESTRA AND CHORUS
LONDON 411 702   TOTAL TIME: 59:06

One of the interesting elements of this recording is its use of a countertenor. Further, Chailly does some exciting things with the dynamics and pacing that seem to differ from the norm. This is probably a good second recording.

IF YOU ENJOYED THIS PIECE . . .

Carmina Burana is certainly in a class by itself, but the first thing to turn to after this would be the other two works that Orff put with this cantata to form his trilogy called Trionfi. The other pieces are **Catulli Carmina** and **Trionfo di Afrodite.** If twentieth-century choral music interests you, start with the wonderful **Gloria** by Poulenc, or Ralph Vaughan Williams's **Dona Nobis Pacem.**

RACHMANINOFF

*R*HAPSODY ON A THEME OF
PAGANINI, OP. 43

Sergei Rachmaninoff (1873–1943) was a composer whose music is flavored by two quirks of timing and locale. Rachmaninoff was born into the nineteenth-century world of czarist Russia and ended his career and life in the very twentieth-century world of Beverly Hills, California. This duality of eras and nationalities is evident in Rachmaninoff's *Rhapsody on a Theme of Paganini*.

Based on the last of Niccolò Paganini's (1782–1840) Twenty-four Caprices for Solo Violin, Rachmaninoff composed his Rhapsody for Piano and Orchestra in a period of slightly more than a month during the summer of 1934. The world picture at that time featured the events that would develop into World War II, especially the German plebiscite vote for Hitler as führer, and the admission of the USSR into the League of Nations. F. Scott Fitzgerald wrote *Tender Is the Night*, the movies *It Happened One Night* and *The Thin Man* premiered, as did Cole Porter's "Anything Goes" and Virgil Thomson and Gertrude Stein's strange opera *Four Saints in Three Acts*.

Rachmaninoff was regarded as one of the premier pianists of his day, and he was the soloist when the *Rhapsody* received its world premiere in November 1934 with Leopold Stokowski conducting the Philadelphia Orchestra. The recording of that collaboration is an accomplishment against which all other recordings are judged, and it is fortunate that Rachmaninoff was so much a man of the twentieth century that he became one of the leading recording artists of his day. The romantic lushness so evident in the *Rhapsody* will conjure up images of candelabra on a large, shiny black piano, the perfect meshing of Rachmaninoff's heritage and the movie images of his American adopted homeland.

The structure of the *Rhapsody* is a brief exposition followed by twenty-four short variations, not coincidentally the same number as the Paganini Caprice that served as Rachmaninoff's inspiration. The orchestra is big, including trombones, trumpets, bells, and a large contingent of percussion instruments.

REFERENCE RECORDING: CBS MYK 36722 GRAFFMAN/BERNSTEIN/NEW YORK PHILHARMONIC

TOTAL TIME: 23:00

The introduction (Allegro vivace) is an orchestral buildup with occasional accents from the piano that leads to the first variation (0:09). Initially the piano is silent while the orchestra connects scattered fragments of sound; like pieces of a musical jigsaw, they are mysteriously fitted together. The percussion instruments and the trumpets dominate. Then the piano joins, playing a series of single notes that accent the violins as they play the original Paganini theme (0:29). When the piano part becomes more involved (0:42), the oboes, clarinets, and bassoons also join in adding richness to the sound.

The piano takes the main theme at the outset of the second variation (0:48) with the horns and trumpets adding nasty-sounding accents. Throughout this section there is a bit of subtle dissonance that is replaced by the more flowing flute and clarinet accompaniment (1:01). In the third variation (1:08) the violins and flutes scurry rapidly while the piano has a lyrical, sustained line and the bassoon pipes in with piquant accents.

The fourth variation (Piu vivo) (1:33) is faster and livelier and teams the piano initially with the violas and then the oboes and flutes (1:40). The English horn provides the contrasting sustained line in a brief, wonderful solo (1:45). The fifth variation (2:04) has the piano dominating as the orchestra adds only occasional accents. In this section one can hear why the piano is called a percussive instrument; the racing, fast episodes are all pointed, almost like bursts of water hitting aluminum. Again there is contrast as the sixth variation (2:31) is much calmer, the piano quiet and mysterious as the strings provide a lush, sustained musical bed. As this variation evolves, some of the winds play occasionally, and when the variation nears completion, the English horn adds its plaintive voice (3:17) increasing the mysterious quality.

The seventh variation (Meno mosso, a tempo moderato) (3:25) slows the pace as the piano plays a series of steady, stately chords, weighty but not pompous, augmented by the low voices of the bassoons and cellos. A bit of strain creeps in (3:48) as the variation evolves into a firm, powerful march highlighted by the horns (4:03). Ironically this heavy variation ends with a light, graceful five-note comment by the flute and a single note in the violas, cellos, and basses. The eighth variation seems to burst out from the quiet (4:24) and returns immediately to the faster speed as the piano starts out propulsively while the bassoons and horns alternate powerful accents with the violas, cellos, and basses. This develops into a controlled frenzy as the flutes and oboes speed through rapid passages (4:37) snapping angrily.

The ninth variation (4:58) continues the fierce attack without pause, beginning with a series of jerky bursts, the musical equivalent of sporadic machine-gun fire heightened by the use of a tambourine, triangle, and snare drum. The piano ends this variation with one single timpani beat to accent the final chord. The angry, militaristic mood continues into the tenth variation (5:30), as the clarinets lead a heavy, steady march that builds inexorably toward a ferocious explosion (5:44) led by the percussion and bass drum. As quickly as it came, the explosion eases (5:55) as the sound becomes lighter with the piano racing accompanied by the high voices of the piccolo, flutes, bells, and harp. This ethereal atmosphere disintegrates into a series of phrases scattered through the winds while the piano plays on. The variation ends with the piano and bells quietly chiming a single note.

Quiet, trembling strings open the eleventh variation (Moderato) (6:24) introducing a languorous, dreamy piano phrase. This moment is reminiscent of turn-of-the-century French impressionist music, especially when the flutes add their sultry, sustained tone. The tonal colors reach their peak when the flutes and English horn play a sinewy phrase (7:03) supporting a flowing piano solo. A sexy, ethereal mood takes over when the piano is joined by the harp (7:24) before the piano plays alone to end this variation.

Out of the silence the twelfth variation (Tempo di Minuetto) (7:45) begins, the second violins slowly unveiling an uneven series of pizzicatos. The piano sleepily joins this unsteady minuet (7:54) sounding somewhat hungover, as if a drunken stupor had not had a chance to wear off. The clarinet adds a steady, sustained line (8:01) that is copied by the horn (8:10) contrasting with the piano's jerkiness. The cellos then become prominent (8:19) by taking the sustained phrase and making it soulful and lush. The oboe and clarinet add brief languorous phrases copied by the horn (8:49) just before the piano's unsteady minuet ends with a final chord played with the harp.

The strings, as if trying to restore order, begin the thirteenth variation (Allegro) (9:01) powerfully with the piano adding steady accents. Then the piccolo, flutes, and clarinets join the strings but play phrases twice as fast, creating instability (9:20). A rapid, upward phrase from the piccolo, flutes, and clarinets with powerful support from the horns, trumpets, trombones, and tuba leads directly into the fourteenth variation (9:30). A definite pulse is established in the horns, second violins, violas, cellos and basses while the flutes, oboes, clarinets and first violins play propulsively, driving the pace. The piano, accompanied by the brass instruments (9:46) increases the military-sounding nature of this section. It is powerful and fierce but somehow not violent. Gradually the energy wanes (10:04) leaving the piano alone to race on to the fifteenth variation (10:15), which starts as a jazzy piano solo with an improvisational quality. The strings and woodwinds add support (10:45), the cellos emerging with a lovely, sustained phrase that contrasts with the piano's more angular filigree. The piano's race is accented by the horns' quiet, yet angry snaps (11:13). But the piano dominates, finishing its fast scramble ending the variation with a single chord that seems to resolve all conflicts.

Tentative violins quietly begin the sixteenth variation (Allegretto) (11:22), introducing the piano accompanied by the clarinets and bassoons. A listless, mysterious quality is heightened when the oboe (11:33) and later the English horn (11:46) add a sinewy, Middle Eastern tone. This large symphonic work takes a detour through some chamber music as the horn and piano (12:00) play a haunting section with a solo violin. Gradually other instruments are added making the sound richer yet still intimate. The harp becomes more important, eventually ending the variation with the violins with a sense of foreboding. From this eerie ending the piano begins slowly (12:53) starting the seventeenth variation. Distant trumpets and horns playing sustained notes that swell and recede (13:03) cut through the piano's ongoing rumble. The mood brightens (13:33) as the woodwinds accompany the piano's steady climb, their notes swelling and receding while the piano rolls on. The pace slows (14:13) as the strings tremble beneath the piano's continuing roll. A final, sustained swell from the cellos as the piano plays on ends this strange variation.

The eighteenth variation (Andante cantabile) (14:37) is the most well-known part of the entire Rhapsody. The cellos' sustained note carries into the new variation introducing the piano now playing a thoughtful rendition of the theme (14:43) that seems as if the pianist is making it up as he goes along. The sound becomes more lush and romantic as the violins and cellos augment the piano (15:26). Then as the other instruments join, the sound steadily builds to a rhapsodic climax (16:07); here, thinking of the image of candles burning on a shiny black piano while a fire roars in the background is impossible to avoid. As this variation grew, so it shrinks with the instruments dropping out until the piano is left alone (16:54) quietly ending this fabulous variation.

A short, fast few seconds (Vivace) (17:29) bridges to the nineteenth variation (17:34), a jagged exercise for the piano accompanied by pizzicatos. The result is an angular, disjointed rendition of the theme with the pianist going up and down the keyboard, the strings plucking along, and the clarinets and horns occasionally accenting. The violins race furiously as the twentieth variation (18:04) starts out livelier than what has come before. The piano then determinedly joins, seeming to announce the beginning of the gallop, an image that is reinforced when the horns mimic the piano's call (18:10). The furious pace continues growing wilder with the addition of the other instruments, and it races right into the twenty-first variation (18:42). Again the pace quickens as the piano dominates, seeming to want to break away and race ahead from the rest of the orchestra, but it is held back by the firm accents played by the horns and trumpets.

Quicker and livelier still, the race drives on right into the twenty-second variation (19:09). Now the piano is the steadying force while the timpani quietly brews some trouble. The theme is now scattered about the string instruments; if one thinks of this variation as a puzzle, the piano provides the frame while the other instruments drop the pieces within its borders. The pace broadens (19:41) as the swells seem to be warning of trouble brewing, a feeling heightened by the brass instruments (19:54) preceding the piano's next rhapsodic fantasy (19:57), accompanied by sustained cello phrases. The piano, entering another technically demanding passage (20:15), flows up and down the keys like cascading water while the brass and strings alternate passes at the main theme.

The strings and snare drums lead the orchestra into a section (20:34) bridging to the next piano solo (20:43), and shortly thereafter the beginning of the twenty-third variation (21:00). The piano starts out alone, mysteriously creeping through the theme until the orchestra copies the solo line highlighted by chiming bells. There is an almost raucous quality that disappears when the piano takes over (21:31), interrupted by occasional orchestral interjections.

The twenty-fourth variation (21:49) starts with the piano, flutes, bells, and harp creating a magical, almost giddy sound. But the mood turns angrier just briefly as the piano and strings growl (22:10) and get louder. A return to the giddy opening of the variation leads to a fierce, strong outburst (22:38) driven by steady pulses and dynamic cymbal crashes. The piano breaks into a demonic passage (22:50) accented by the orchestra and the ringing of the triangle (22:56). There is a final explosion (22:59) and an immediate stop. Then the piano, like one last afterthought, tosses off a final turn of the main phrase.

PIANIST GARY GRAFFMAN:

"*It provides so much to relish. The inventiveness of the variations, the lush melodies, the wonderful orchestration, the inspired piano writing, and the intricate way the whole piece fits together like a jigsaw puzzle invite us to enjoy this music on many levels—intellectually as well as emotionally. But in the end, the most important thing is that it's just irresistibly pleasurable listening.*"

COMPARATIVE RECORDINGS

GRAFFMAN/BERNSTEIN/NEW YORK PHILHARMONIC
CBS MYK 36722   TOTAL TIME: 23:00

An exciting performance that manages to highlight the differences among the variations without chopping the rhapsodic nature out of the work. Bernstein and the Philharmonic are wonderful partners to Graffman's stupendous playing. The analog sound holds up well in the transfer to CD.

RUBINSTEIN/REINER/CHICAGO SYMPHONY
    ORCHESTRA
RCA RCD1-4934   TOTAL TIME: 23:07

One of the greatest performances ever recorded! Rubinstein plays this work in a lush, romantic style that oozes with silky tones, while Reiner and the Chicagoans play with precision and warmth. Though recorded in 1956, there is nothing outdated about the sound.

RACHMANINOFF/STOKOWSKI/PHILADELPHIA
    ORCHESTRA
RCA 6659   TOTAL TIME: 21:55

Since in this case the composer was one of the great virtuoso pianists of his day, this recording is not only an interesting historical document but a fabulous performance by the forces that gave the world-premiere performance. The monophonic sound pales in comparison, but anyone interested in this work should hear this recording.

IF YOU ENJOYED THIS PIECE . . .

Rachmaninoff composed four piano concertos, each one a masterpiece. However, it is best to start with the **Second Piano Concerto** with its lush Romanticism and Russian passion. Then, move on to Rachmaninoff's symphonic output beginning with the **Symphonic Dances** and the **Second Symphony.**

RAVEL
*B*OLÉRO

When Dudley Moore and Bo Derek starred in the movie *10*, her character's habit of making love while listening to Maurice Ravel's (1875–1937) *Boléro* took what was then a fairly well-known piece of orchestral music and turned it into a megahit. The work's record sales soared to unprecedented levels. The truth is, *Boléro* is not a great composition. Its single melody, heard over and over again, is pleasant and evocative at best. *Boléro* is, however, a fascinating, hypnotic work that provides a wonderful instrument by instrument dissection of a large, Romantic orchestra. Ravel referred to *Boléro* as his only masterpiece. However, he went on to say the piece contained no music. Certainly an overstatement in both cases, yet with some truth.

Ravel composed *Boléro* in 1928. While technically a twentieth-century work, its sexy melody is firmly rooted in the late-nineteenth-century Romantic era. Among the other important music composed in 1928 was Gershwin's *An American in Paris*, and Weill's *Threepenny Opera*. In 1928, Hecht and MacArthur penned *The Front Page*, and D. H. Lawrence wrote *Lady Chatterley's Lover*. Hoover was elected president, and the USSR began the first of its five-year plans. It was the year that saw the first scheduled television broadcast, the discovery of penicillin, the invention of the Geiger counter, and Amelia Earhart's first transatlantic crossing.

In many ways *Boléro* can serve as a guide to the post-Romantic orchestra. In addition to large string sections, Ravel used flutes, piccolos, oboes, oboe d'amore, English horn, various clarinets, bassoons, a contrabassoon, horns, soprano trumpet, trumpets, trombones, tuba, saxophones, timpani, snare drums, cymbals, tam-tam, harp, and a celesta. Repeated hearings will make it easier to pick out the role each instrument plays in the overall work, and to hear the way the melody changes when played by the different instruments.

To have a really clear picture of what this work is about, try to see the video that was done of a performance featuring Zubin Mehta and the Los Angeles Philharmonic. It guides the eye to where the musical action is occurring in the sections of the orchestra.

REFERENCE RECORDING: ERATO 2292-45766 BARENBOIM/CHICAGO SYMPHONY ORCHESTRA
TOTAL TIME: 15:50

The snare drums begin *Boléro*, setting the pulse that will incessantly be maintained for almost the entire piece. The opening is quiet and distant, yet firm and precise. The only accompaniment is provided by occasional viola and cello pizzicatos in the background. The flute unveils the melody (0:11). It is quiet, intimate, silky, and very sexy. Once the entire melodic phrase is played through, the first flute stops, and the second flute joins in (0:54) copying the rhythmic pattern established by the snare drums. This pattern serves as a bridge to the next solo interpretation of the melody, played by the first clarinet (1:00).

In the bridge to the next solo, the first flute replaces the second, accompanying the snares, and the harp adds its rich colors to the viola and cello pizzicatos. The solo is taken by the bassoon (1:50), which sounds even sexier than the flute or the clarinet.

Even though it plays at the upper end of its range, it contrasts with the next solo played by the soprano clarinet (2:41) and its even higher range. This solo has an exotic quality evoking the image of Scheherazade and sultry Arabian nights.

The next bridge is more interesting than the previous ones as the saxophone, second violins, and basses combine for a rich sound leading to the oboe d'amore solo (3:31). Its sound is warm, and in a lower range than the previous solo instruments. During this solo listen for the addition of the bassoons assuming the snare drums' rhythmic pattern conveying a more stately feeling. This mood is carried into the next bridge as the first violins and horns are added.

Throughout the first few sections the volume has been increasing slowly with the addition of more and more instruments. Now, for the first time, the melody is played by two instruments in unison as the flute and trumpet parallel each other (4:22). The trumpet, with its more piercing timbre, dominates. The next solo (5:12), played by the tenor saxophone, is jazzy and ultrasexy, moods continued by the high range of the sopranino saxophone solo (6:04) descending seamlessly into the soprano saxophone solo (6:40) that completes the phrase.

The next transition provides the first real sense of building or layering as more instruments join the snare drums, leading to one of the oddest expositions of the melody. This time the solo instruments are two piccolos, the first horn, and the celesta (6:54). The harmonies in this combination sometimes sound a bit strained, and unusual, especially when played against the now quite forceful background. During this solo try to pick out the bells of the celesta chiming through. The oboes, oboe d'amore, clarinets, and horns make up the next solo team (7:45), playing over a background forceful enough to begin to appear to be the foreground.

Trombones hardly seem sinewy, but when the first trombone slides into the next solo (8:36), the brazen sound oozes with burlesque sexiness. When this solo ends (9:21), the bridge becomes dramatic, increases in volume, and grows more propulsive. It now feels like the movement may be leading to some kind of climax. The bridge continues into the background as the flutes, piccolo, oboes, horns, clarinets, and tenor saxophone take up the melody (9:26). This time through it assumes a boisterous quality, becoming ever brassier and bolder.

At last the violins take the melody (10:15) supplying it with a regal, joyful quality. While they lead, the upper wind instruments parallel them. However, be sure to note how the phrasing is different between the winds and the strings; the winds play a longer line, while the violins provide more detail in their phrasing. The next pass at the melody (11:05) has the second violins joining the firsts. However, since each section of violins is divided into two parts, there are, in effect, four distinct violin lines being played, increasing the density of the sound. The melodic line is expansive and broad and does hide the accompaniment despite the formidable strength of the snare drums and timpani in the background. While the strings continue to lead in the next melodic pass (11:54), try to pick out the trumpet now playing with them.

Increasing in size like a rolling snowball, the forces playing the melody in the next section (12:45) include everyone except the bass clarinet, bassoons, contrabassoon, horns, trumpets, second and third trombones, tuba, harp, basses, timpani, and snare drums. Despite the size of this force playing the melody, the even balance between foreground and background is a tribute to Ravel's skill as an orchestrator. Of course, with this number of instruments involved it is not surprising that the next transition (13:30) verges on the raucous and leads to a brass-dominated melody. With each passing note the intensity grows and becomes increasingly abrasive (14:24). What was once sexy and subtle has built steadily to become brassy, overpowering, and relentless.

Suddenly the pattern is broken (15:08) and the melody does not follow the path established. Instead, the phrase ascends, led by the brass instruments, spiraling upward, out of control. When the blares from the trombones (15:30) repeatedly punctuate the propulsive, inexorable snare-drum pattern, it is clear that the power can no longer be contained, and what started in a mild, controlled manner degenerates into an ugly, blaring blowout. The climax is brief and powerful, as the final seconds verge on cacophony and then collapse into exhaustion.

PRINCIPAL PERCUSSION OF THE CHICAGO SYMPHONY ORCHESTRA, GORDON PETERS:

"*Nestled between the violins, cellos, and the maestro, I await the preparatory beat igniting a fifteen minute thread of hypnotic triplet rhythms. The flute is the first to dance atop the repetitious two-measure snare drum rhythms. Then come the other woodwinds in single file including the saxophones. Next the horn, trumpet, and trombone take their turns—all with a strong, insidious pizzicato orchestral accompaniment, building to one of the longest crescendos in the symphonic literature—a hypnotic ballet of early minimalism that seems to never end. And I have the luxury of 'front and center,' the focal point of all these intoxicating sounds. The pyramid of instruments, harmonies, and overtones sweeps you away. This is Ravel's Bolero! I start it and luxuriate in a tornado of rhythms and decibels, succumbing to a glorious modulation and ultimately a fireworks of bass drum, gong, and cymbals.*"

COMPARATIVE RECORDINGS

BARENBOIM/CHICAGO SYMPHONY ORCHESTRA
ERATO 2292-45766   TOTAL TIME: 15:50

The sound of the Chicago Symphony, especially the caliber of all the solo players, makes this a great recording. The buildup is well controlled, and the clarity and detail makes this an exellent recording for understanding how Ravel used the instruments.

MUTI/PHILADELPHIA ORCHESTRA
EMI CLASSICS CDC-47022   TOTAL TIME: 17:09

As with Chicago, the Philadelphia musicians play the solos magnificently. This is a sexier, more Latin, hot-blooded performance with a slow build under Muti's superb control, and the explosion at the end has a let-loose quality that is riveting.

SLATKIN/ST. LOUIS SYMPHONY ORCHESTRA
TELARC CD-80052   TOTAL TIME: 16:18

Slatkin is a skilled interpreter who brings an exciting overview to the piece, and this exceptional recording shows clearly why the St. Louis Orchestra has secured its place among the elite orchestras of the world.

IF YOU ENJOYED THIS PIECE . . .

Boléro is a unique work and it is hard to find a real match for it. If the wildness appeals to you, try Ravel's strange orchestral work **La Valse.** If it is his distinctly French sound that you like, listen to **Le Tombeau de Couperin** or his great ballet **Daphnis et Chloé.**

ROSSINI

*W*ILLIAM TELL OVERTURE

Although Gioacchino Rossini (1792–1868) composed his opera *William Tell* when he was just thirty-seven years old, it was to be his final stage work, and practically his last composition. Even though still very young he decided to "retire," despite being the most popular composer of the day.

Written more than a decade after his two comic master-pieces, *The Barber of Seville* (1816) and *La Cenerentola (Cinderella)* (1817), *William Tell*, or as it was originally titled in French, *Guillaume Tell*, received its world premiere in Paris at the Académie Royale de Musique on August 3, 1829. Contemporary reports vary as to how the opera was received by the public, but in general the press reports were favorable.

It is interesting to note that as Rossini prepared to retire, Chopin was just getting started on his fabulous career as a pianist and composer making his Vienna debut, and Mendelssohn was reintroducing the musical world to the beauty of Bach's *St. Matthew Passion*, which had been neglected for more than half a century. In the United States, 1829 saw the inauguration of President Andrew Jackson, while in France, Victor Hugo wrote his novel *The Last Day of a Condemned*.

The opera *William Tell* is not nearly as popular today as Rossini's earlier comic operas, which are part of the standard repertoire of most of the world's opera houses. In fact, *William Tell* is rarely performed anymore. Ironically, however, thanks to pop culture, the twelve-minute overture is one of the most popular and recognizable pieces of all classical music, for it is the *William Tell* Overture that contains the famous *Lone Ranger* theme!

Fortunately, the overture stands on its own and in fact has become a standard component of the symphonic repertoire. The overture is in four distinct sections and in many ways is like a tone poem that musically tells a story, a style used to great effect by many of the Romantic-era composers who followed Rossini.

Even though the overture was originally written to be performed in an opera-house pit, it uses fairly large forces, another reason for the piece's success on the concert stage. The orchestra includes piccolo, flute, oboes, English horn, clarinets, bassoons, four horns, trumpets, three trombones, timpani, triangle, bass drum, cymbals, and strings, with the cellos playing a particularly important part.

REFERENCE RECORDING: RCA VICTOR 61497
FIEDLER/BOSTON POPS ORCHESTRA
TOTAL TIME: 11:47

Don't expect the *William Tell* Overture to begin with the fast, popular melody with which it is identified! The outset is slow and contemplative and features five solo cellos. The initial theme is played by the first solo cello, alone and totally exposed. The melody evokes an awakening, or a sunrise, seeming to unfold and rise up slowly. The line is broken only by a brief comment from the four other solo cellos (0:09) before it resumes. This section is chamber music, albeit a strange ensemble consisting of a quintet of cellos. This pattern of solo answered by the other voices continues as the other cellos and the basses add their voices (0:42) layering the sound.

The main solo cello line is written high in the instrument's range, and since it is so exposed, it is even harder to play. The only non-cello instrument in this exposition is an extremely quiet timpani roll (1:25), which rumbles in the distance. Another timpani roll (2:35), this time more present, sounds like thunder and precedes the last few moments of the cellos' introduction. The section ends with the first cello holding an extremely high sustained note.

Suddenly (3:15), the second violins and violas take over. They scurry, tremulous, like a racing wind, the first signs of a brewing storm. Between phrases, the wind instruments play short three-note sections that sound like the first raindrops of the storm; piccolo, flute, and oboe go first (3:22), followed by the clarinets and bassoons (3:28). With each passing phrase, the volume and intensity increase ever so slightly, eventually becoming nervous sounding (4:00), with the rumbling timpani heightening the effect.

With the explosive entrance of the horns, trumpets, trombones, and especially the bass drum (4:19), the storm breaks out, raging furiously, as the upper wind instruments mimic the shrieking winds. The storm howls on, the repeated bass-drum beats never letting up, while more turbulence is created by the blaring, angry horns (4:58). When the three-note raindrop theme returns (5:29), the storm begins to subside, quieting down gradually with instruments stopping while others play more softly. A flute solo emerges from the ravages of the storm (5:49), peeking out cautiously at first, playing over the distant rumbling. Eventually (5:59), the flute is the only instrument playing, and its lovely little phrase leads to the Overture's next section.

Now (6:10) we are transported to a lovely pastoral setting. The storm has ended and we are left with a pleasant, peaceful mood created by a beautiful English horn solo. Eventually the flute copies the English horn theme (6:25). Then, over a series of resonant pizzicatos, the flute and the English horn engage in a dialogue of alternating phrases (6:41) sounding much like a bird and a dove might. When they join together (7:11), each playing its little melody, the triangle adds a charming chime. During this section, note how the flute sounds like a little bird chirping and flitting around, while the mellower sound of the English horn evokes the image of a slower, less flighty bird.

This bucolic picture is shattered by a sudden trumpet call (8:42) that cuts through sharply. It's rousing. It's exciting. It's dynamic. It's the *Lone Ranger* theme, and you'll be hard pressed not to yell out, "Hi ho, Silver!" There is no holding back now, as this section launches at a fast clip. Simply put, we're off to the races. As thrilling as the initial trumpet blast is, the addition of the horns (8:45) blaring the call adds color and richness. The visceral excitement is almost overpowering, especially when the timpani are also added (8:48).

When the calls are completed (8:53), there is a split-second stop. Then, the strings, two horns, clarinets, bassoons, and timpani shoot off into the theme, which will bring to mind the phrase "And they're off!" It is fairly quiet at first, but when the piccolo, flute, oboes, and the other horns join (9:00), it gets slightly louder. The addition of the cymbals and the triangle (9:06) yields a more raucous quality. The violins, flying through their phrases, are steadied by the rock-solid horns (9:16) bridging back to a resumption of the "And they're off!" theme (9:22). Though fast and exciting, this section must be kept under control, so that when it does explode (9:34), the explosion sounds meaningful.

During this entire section it is fascinating to see how much happens in short periods of time; in a matter of seconds the mood can shift and whole parts of the orchestra might be added or taken away. Note for example how the mood shifts from confidence to a bit of mystery (9:45). Then, just as suddenly, there is a new outburst of raucous excitement (10:06) as the rest of the orchestra pops back in.

The "And they're off!" theme returns (10:17) at the same high speed, but now with more fury and volume. In its next guise (10:35) this clichéd theme reverts to the way it was heard originally: fast, but quieter and controlled, just waiting to break out in an explosion, and Rossini does not disappoint, creating the best outburst yet (10:45), led by the tiny piccolo, whose high-pitched whistle cuts through the entire orchestra.

As the overture nears its conclusion, it goes through a series of rapid changes. First, it pulls back and quiets down just slightly (10:51), only to rebuild again, complete with ringing triangle and crashing cymbals. Then it retreats again (11:09) and builds steadily, only to ease up for one more reprise of the "races" theme, played initially by the wind instruments (11:20) and then with the strings. Suddenly, everything comes to a complete stop (11:24). Everyone has a split second to catch his breath. Then a loud explosion led by the bass drum leads to the Overture's raucous, unison conclusion. Although hackneyed and clichéd, the reason the William Tell Overture has become a cornerstone of the repertoire becomes clear during the final moments, when the power and excitement of the music are sure to thrill most listeners.

CELLIST RALPH KIRSHBAUM:

"Having been shot myself by an arrow at age six, I have great sympathy for William Tell. Now when I hear that beautiful cello solo at the beginning, it makes me glad to be alive!"

COMPARATIVE RECORDINGS

FIEDLER/BOSTON POPS ORCHESTRA
RCA VICTOR 61497   TOTAL TIME: 11:47

A legendary performance captured on a "Living Stereo" record and beautifully transferred to CD. The reading is exciting. It is clear that this piece was a staple of the Boston Pops under Arthur Fiedler.

KUNZEL/CINCINNATI POPS ORCHESTRA
TELARC 80116   TOTAL TIME: 12:20

A first-rate, exciting performance made even better by the superb digital sound. Kunzel and the Pops are the latter-day version of Fiedler and his band.

NORRINGTON/LONDON CLASSICAL PLAYERS
EMI CLASSICS 54091   TOTAL TIME: 11:53

If visceral excitement is what you enjoy, then this brilliant
performance is for you! Plus, there is a chance that this is closer
to the way Rossini heard the music. All that aside, it is a good
performance with great sound.

IF YOU ENJOYED THIS PIECE . . .

While few pieces have the visceral excitement of the *William
Tell* Overture, many have that Rossini flavor, which moves from
piece to piece. Of particular interest would be the overture to
The Barber of Seville and the famous aria *"Largo al Factotum"*
from the same opera. There are also **six string sonatas** that have
become quite popular that have some of the *William Tell* style,
without the excitement.

SAINT-SAËNS
CARNIVAL OF THE ANIMALS

Camille Saint-Saëns (1835–1921) was not only a talented composer, but also a superb pianist who began his career with a recital in Paris when he was just nine years old. As a composer his best-known works are the opera *Samson and Delilah*, his Third Symphony, known as the *Organ* Symphony, and the delightful suite the *Carnival of the Animals*, a *Grand Zoological Fantasy for Orchestra*. In each brief movement of this suite, Saint-Saëns wittily depicts another zoological creature, filling the piece with humor evident to musicians as well as to those with an untrained ear.

The *Carnival of the Animals* is scored for two pianos with central roles, strings, flute, piccolo, clarinet, xylophone, and harmonica. There are different versions of the work, as it can be performed by a chamber ensemble with one player playing each part, or by a larger orchestra using full sections of violins, violas, cellos, and double basses. Further, there are wonderful poems written by Ogden Nash that are often read as narrative descriptions between movements. (For our purposes we have chosen an orchestral version without any narration.) Depending on what animal Saint-Saëns was portraying, he used different combinations of instruments, thus the players used vary from movement to movement. Saint-Saëns also included several musical quotes, borrowing from other composers as well as himself, which will be highlighted as they appear in each piece.

Saint-Saëns composed the *Carnival of the Animals* in 1868, the same year he wrote his Third Symphony. It was also the year Henry James wrote *The Bostonians*, Robert Louis Stevenson wrote *Dr. Jekyll and Mr. Hyde*, Seurat painted *Sunday Afternoon on the Grande Jatte*, and Rodin sculpted *The Kiss*.

REFERENCE RECORDING:
TELDEC 2292-46155
PEKINELS/JANOWSKI/PHILHARMONIC
ORCHESTRA OF RADIO FRANCE
TOTAL TIME: 19:30

I. INTRODUCTION AND ROYAL MARCH OF THE LION: Andante maestoso   (1:47)

A brief, excited two-piano introduction precedes the strings, portraying the waking lions. The lower strings, double basses, and cellos are repeatedly answered by the violas and violins in a pattern that builds gradually growing faster, louder, and more frenetic. The two pianos play rapid scales, the first piano going up the keys as the second goes down, followed immediately by a unison chord. Then everything comes to a sudden stop.

The second piano begins a stately march (0:29) echoed by the first piano. They are replaced by the strings (0:37) playing a pompous melody; it is regal and heavy, broken up by occasional piano interjections. This continues until the second piano plays what can be best described as a *roar* (0:58), a sound often repeated, until the strings and pianos reverse roles (1:17), the pianos playing the march and the strings providing the *roars*. There is an almost oriental sound to this section diminishing the pomp somewhat and yielding a more exotic quality. A distinct *roar* from the first piano and the double bass (1:39) precedes the movement's abrupt end.

II. HENS AND COCKERELS: Allegro moderato   (0:41)

Pianos, violins, violas, and a clarinet are the instruments used in this depiction of clucking and pecking. The tone is light, and the pace moderately fast, as the second piano starts out with a distinctly plucky figure, soon copied by the violins. The jumpiness is modified by smoother passages beginning with the violas, on to the second violins, and finally to the first violins preceding a jagged clarinet entrance (0:21). The edgy quality of this movement is heightened by occasional dissonances. An extended first-violin solo (0:25) leads to the movement's end, and a chord played in unison by both pianos.

III. WILD ASSES: Presto furioso   (0:39)

This very fast movement is a tour de force for the two pianos, and they are the only instruments playing! The message here seems to be "Practice your scales," since that is virtually all the pianists have to play. They race up and down the keyboards; their challenge is to stay together. It is exciting, furiously paced, and it ends abruptly with two chords.

IV. TORTOISES: Andante maestoso   (1:41)

To portray these slow-moving creatures Saint-Saëns uses only the first piano and the strings. The piano establishes the steady, slow pulse as the strings play the melody in unison (0:09), and here we see the composer's sense of humor coming through, because to portray the tortoise he drastically slows down the famous "Can Can" from Jacques Offenbach's opera *Orpheus in the Underworld*. This usually fast, well-known melody normally evokes images of frolicking dance-hall girls kicking up their legs, daringly lifting their skirts. But in Saint-Saëns's strange adaptation it is steady, slow, and heavy. (Try to speed up the melody in your mind and see if you can remember the original version.) Interestingly, the tone changes somewhat when the piano's easygoing pulse goes through some fascinating harmonic changes (0:49 and 1:05). The movement slows down (1:22) and just fades away.

V. THE ELEPHANT: Allegretto pomposo   (1:23)

Here Saint-Saëns sarcastically gives the elephant a waltz, a dance even the best-trained circus elephant couldn't conquer! In this strange movement scored for just the second piano and the double bass, he again borrows from another composer, quoting the "Dance of the Sylphs" from Hector Berlioz's oratorio *The Damnation of Faust*. The melody is all in the bass, as the piano provides the second and third beats of the three-beat waltz. The bass changes the melody slightly (0:32), and when the piano varies its accompaniment playing a series of florid passages (0:59), the tone becomes somewhat lighter. As hard as it may be to imagine, the normally heavy bass combined with the piano creates a truly charming, humorous mood.

VI. KANGAROOS: Moderato   (0:38)

This is another movement scored for just the two pianos, who flit over the keys creating a musical impression of hopping around. The two pianos alternate, each playing its passages at uneven paces. The second piano has the final say, and its quiet last chord fades away.

VII. AQUARIUM: Andantino   (2:08)

This is an eerie, haunting movement, used with great effect in the Richard Gere movie *Days of Heaven*. It is scored for pianos, violins, violas, cellos, flute, and the harmonica. The pianos provide a sound evocative of gliding through water, while the flute and strings play the melody, and the harmonica, though difficult to pick out in the sonic blend, provides an off-the-beat pulse. The melody leaves a distinct feeling of an uneasy calm heightened when the pianos play a downward passage (0:25), seeming to portray dripping water, over sustained notes in the strings.

There is a brief pause before the initial melody returns (0:38), and the first sections are repeated. The flute's tone becomes deeper and more hollow (1:17), followed by a split-second pause and a series of upward glissandos played by the harmonica (1:29). The steady dripping of the water (1:48) followed by the flute, and then the pianos, ends this peaceful movement.

VIII. PEOPLE WITH LONG EARS:
Tempo ad libitum   (0:56)

Scored for just the two sections of violins, this movement is filled with musical "hee-haws." The first violins establish the pattern of a very high, short note followed by a sustained, low note. Be sure to notice how the violins may speed up or slow down, somewhat at random. This is because Saint-Saëns (in the tempo marking) indicates this movement should be ad-libbed, so there is no even pulse. It ends with a sustained low note in the first violins that drifts off.

IX. THE CUCKOO IN THE WOODS:
Andante   (2:15)

This movement uses just the two pianos and the clarinet. The rich sonorities of the pianos start out, soon disturbed by the annoying clarinet, playing the role of the cuckoo with a repeated two-note interruption (0:03), a quirky contrast to the serious-sounding pianos. The pianos have a comforting sound, a mood broken by some unusual harmonies (0:46) that belong to the more dissonant music of the twentieth century. When the pianos begin playing different lines (1:00), the tension mounts, the eerie nature comes to the fore, and the clarinet interruptions become further apart. The dissonances, heard in the pianos near the movement's end, are resolved in the warmth of the final chord.

X. AVIARY: Moderato grazioso   (1:19)

Shimmering violas and violins begin this portrait of the birds. While the strings provide an airy background, the flute enters (0:05) with a fast flight of fancy. The pianos' entrance (0:24) provides the chirping, fitting in neatly with the flute's flitting! Everything is delicate, and in the flute's solo one can hear the bird stopping occasionally, just for a second, to catch its breath. A quick run up the scale by the flute ends the flight.

XI. PIANISTS: Allegro moderato   (0:48)

Clearly Saint-Saëns was having some fun here including pianists among his zoological assemblage and directing the performers to act like debuting artists: nervous and filled with excesses! He scored this movement for the pianos with occasional string interruptions. When the pianos start, it is clear the composer was mocking the hours of boring keyboard exercises every piano student must endure. The speed of the exercises changes (0:35), but their tedium does not diminish even when the strings get more involved and the pace increases. Three unison chords and an abrupt cutoff leave us hanging in midair.

XII. FOSSILS: Allegro ridicolo (1:13)

This movement picks up right where the previous one left off. Featuring the xylophone, along with the pianos, clarinet, and strings, this movement steals the melody from Saint-Saëns's own *Danse Macabre*. While in that piece the xylophone represents the dancing bones of skeletons, here it represents the bones of fossils. The speed is fast, but does not race. After the xylophone and pianos have established the melody, the violins play a sustained phrase (0:19) under short piano notes, eventually becoming busier and busier. Out of these intricacies emerges the second piano (0:22) with the melody we know as the "Alphabet Song" or "Twinkle Twinkle Little Star," but which Saint-Saëns knew as "Ah! Vous Dirai-Je Maman."

Suddenly, out of this cheerful moment the xylophone reemerges with the *Danse Macabre* melody (0:29). Then another change of melody occurs as the clarinet (0:44) solos with the piano accompaniment, as Saint-Saëns briefly borrows from Rossini's opera *The Barber of Seville*. During this section listen for the strange accompaniment the xylophone provides. One final pass at the *Danse Macabre* (0:57) leads to the movement's curt ending.

XIII. THE SWAN: Andantino grazioso (3:21)

This musical portrait of a swan features a solo cello accompanied by the pianos. The first piano provides a steady flowing accompaniment, while the second only interjects occasionally. The solo cello (0:06) is the image of grace, elegance, and romantic calm. If any music is picturesque, this is it. While the mood remains peaceful, there is a slight increase of intensity (1:35), but it quickly dissipates. The pace slows (2:25) as sustained notes and interesting piano phrases end the movement.

XIV. FINALE: Molto allegro (1:37)

For the final movement, Saint-Saëns uses the whole orchestra together for the first time and often refers back to melodies he used in earlier movements of the work. The opening is the same as the very first movement, only faster and more excited. After the brief introduction, the piccolo, clarinet, and the first piano launch into a melody (0:11), laughing almost uncontrollably. The second piano replaces the first for the second phrase (0:20).

A xylophone note interrupts (0:26), and the pianos embark on their infernal scales over chugging strings. The strings double their pace (0:39) making everything more frantic. Then the violins and second piano (0:44) play the laughing melody, which quickly spreads to the rest of the orchestra (0:52). The frenetic pace continues, and we hear a recap of the "Hens and Cockerels" (1:03), followed by a return visit to the "Kangaroos" (1:11). Soon the "Long Ears" reappear (1:25), and then the wild xylophone leads the rest of the orchestra to this delightful piece's hurried ending.

ACTOR AND NARRATOR WERNER KLEMPERER:

"Carnival of the Animals with the Ogden Nash narration is the ideal blending of words and music. Nash makes the perfect communicator from Saint-Saëns to people of all ages, mixing lyrical poetry, satire, and humor to perfection."

COMPARATIVE RECORDINGS

PEKINELS/JANOWSKI/PHILHARMONIC ORCHESTRA OF
    RADIO FRANCE
TELDEC 2292-46155   TOTAL TIME: 19:30

This is a wonderful, lively, well-played performance that shows off the music all by itself. The playing is exceptional, especially by the duo pianists. The digital sound crystallizes the instruments, making it possible to hear each solo line, even the elusive harmonica.

BERNSTEIN/NEW YORK PHILHARMONIC
SONY CLASSICAL SFK 46712   TOTAL TIME: 30:48

The value of this older recording is Bernstein's interesting and educational narration as he explains clearly what Saint-Saëns was doing in each section. However, there is a great deal of talk between music sections, diminishing the section-to-section flow of the whole work.

LABEQUES/PERLMAN/MEHTA/ISRAEL PHILHARMONIC
EMI CLASSICS 47067   TOTAL TIME: 27:15

This is an absolutely delightful recording highlighted by the joyful playing of Katia and Marielle Labeque, and the fun-loving narration of the Nash poems by Itzhak Perlman.

IF YOU ENJOYED THIS PIECE . . .

Carnival of the Animals is a unique work in the Saint-Saëns canon, but if his basic musical style appeals to you, the **Organ Symphony** will be a thrilling listening experience. His opera **Samson and Delilah** is also a good work, filled with lush, Romantic melodies and the sexy, famous "Bachanale."

SCHUBERT

Quintet for Piano, Violin, Viola, Cello, and Double Bass in A Major, D. 667

TROUT

Franz Schubert's (1797–1828) creative output would have been considered immense if he had lived a long life. But when you consider that he lived only thirty-one years, his output is staggering, if not downright impossible. Among his greatest achievements are the wealth of songs that flowed seemingly effortlessly from his pen, and among the literally hundreds of songs is one titled "The Trout" (*"Die Forelle"*). This charming song served as the basis for the fourth movement of Schubert's *Trout* Quintet and in turn gave the Quintet its memorable name.

Schubert wrote the song in 1817, and at the urging of one of his musician friends, he composed the Quintet in 1819, scoring it for the unusual combination of piano, violin, viola, cello, and double bass. Though filled with classical-style melodies reminiscent of Haydn and Mozart, the Quintet does give musical suggestions of the Romantic era about to begin. One might consider the Quintet, and much of Schubert's music in general, as a bridge between the classical and Romantic eras. This duality was evident in the poetry and drama of the epoch as well; in 1819, Byron wrote *Mazeppa*, and Victor Hugo wrote his *Odes*, while Goethe, Keats, and Shelley were also active. In art, 1819 saw the completion of Turner's *Childe Harold's Pilgrimage* and Géricault's *The Raft of the Medusa*.

Schubert's *Trout* Quintet was not published during his lifetime, but has become one of the most frequently performed pieces in the entire chamber-music canon. In addition to having an interesting instrumentation, the Quintet is unusual because it has five movements, whereas most chamber compositions of the Classical era have three or four movements. (Only the late Beethoven string quartets have more movements.) One of the most important elements of this composition is the way the instruments seem to converse; one will state the theme and the others will respond, like a fine conversation.

REFERENCE RECORDING:
EMI CLASSICS 47448
LEONSKAJA/MEMBERS OF THE ALBAN BERG QUARTET/HÖRTNAGEL
TOTAL TIME: 38:35

FIRST MOVEMENT: Allegro vivace   (13:38)

A dramatic opening chord immediately grows soft and is followed by a delicate piano solo filling the sonic void. Then the strings take over with quiet, sustained notes slowly unfolding this mysterious introduction, with the one constant being the low note rumbled by the double bass. The viola and piano set off on their own (0:19), the violin and cello occasionally interjecting. These interjections become more frequent as everything gets busier and more intense until the violin breaks out from the rest of the group and firmly establishes the melody (0:47) over a strong pulsing string accompaniment with the piano throwing in sporadic comments. Then the piano and violin reverse roles, the piano taking the melody, the violin providing the interjections (1:08).

After a brief frenetic section the cello plays a lyrical, sentimental melody echoed by the violin (1:48). The piano plays all alone (2:25), quietly and calmly brightening the mood, and reintroduces the strings (2:41) as the violin takes the melody. Mysterious brooding takes over (3:04) but is interrupted by an explosion of happy sounds (3:19) as the strings play a jerky series of accents against the fast-paced, fluid piano line eventually assumed by the violin. A series of exchanges between the strings and the piano lead to the five instruments becoming one unit racing toward two chords (4:15) preceding a repeat and a return to the movement's forceful opening chord.

Following the repeat (8:35), the viola, cello, and double bass set a jerky pulse as accompaniment for the violin's quietly unfolding lyrical melodic line. Then, the double bass sleepily plays the melody (9:11) as the piano adds some delicate filigree, gradually reenergizing the pace.

Everything comes alive (9:42), filled with strain as the quintet is split into three distinct units: the violin and viola, the cello and double bass, and the piano. Here, unit one strains at the melodic line, while unit two plods heavily through some difficult passages, and unit three is split with the right hand providing filigree over the left hand's steadier accompaniment. This is an intense, busy section with lots going on at all times. Slowly the strain resolves as the viola, cello, and double bass establish a steady pulse while the violin and piano alternate comments (10:05).

Out of nowhere, there is a forceful chord (10:31) and we are returned to a reprise of the movement's opening. During this section try to pick out the jazzy accompaniment played by the double bass in the background. As before, the cheerfulness dissipates and turns sad (11:51) until the piano solo (12:11) restores the original mood before turning the melody over to the violin (12:25). A sudden burst of bravado (12:38) increases the intensity before the strings restore the lyrical line (13:16), and a final burst of force (13:24) brings the quintet together for a journey to the two chords ending the movement.

SECOND MOVEMENT: Andante   (7:02)

The viola, cello, double bass, and piano set the mood for this gracious stroll, the melody initially taken by the piano while the strings provide the steady, flowing accompaniment. The peaceful mood is altered (1:04) as the violin, viola, and cello play a steady series of notes that contrast with the more rapidly paced piano line. With each phrase, the contrast increases the tension and moves us further away from the movement's contented beginning. The tension eventually yields to sadness (1:22) with the viola and cello playing a soulful melody accented by the violin's series of two-note hiccups.

The mood turns happy again (2:01), the piano retaking the melody and the strings providing the accompaniment. This cheerfulness is short-lived as the violin mimics the piano (2:27); something verging on the tragic is brewing but cannot get to a full boil, and instead of turning sad, it resolves into a delicate, yet aristocratic piano melody with strings providing the rich background (2:55). However, any energy the movement may have had is now lost as it winds down into a quiet, sustained hold.

As if suddenly snapping out of a snooze (3:27), the movement resumes its elegant stroll, the piano leading a gorgeous series of exchanges among the instruments. A hint of tension returns (4:32) and again some trouble seems to be brewing, developing into a reprise of the viola and cello's sad lyrical line with the violin's hiccups (4:49). A quick shift in mood (5:29) takes away the sadness as the piano quietly leads while the violin and viola provide a steady pulse. The violin steps forward, mimicking the piano (5:58), and once again the sense of strain returns. But, as before, it does not develop, returning instead to the elegance of the stroll (6:27) with the piano playing the melody. The energy wanes gradually as the movement ends sleepily.

THIRD MOVEMENT: SCHERZO: Presto   (4:04)

Like a brisk wake-up call, the violin and viola launch into this exceptionally fast movement. The quick four-note phrases cut through with jagged edges, highly energized as the piano adds its percussive power. The movement's second section starts with the piano playing the four-note theme (0:23), answered immediately by the violin and in turn the viola; all of this occurs in a split second! Four comparatively heavy notes distinctly played by the cello and double bass relaunch the movement's opening theme. The second section of the movement is then repeated (0:57).

Following the repeat (1:32) the bounciness of the movement disappears, replaced by a new, lyrical line played initially by the violin and viola. (This is the Trio section of the Scherzo.) Even when the piano copies the melody, it retains its tenderness, a quality heightened when the viola and cello play the melody just before the first part of the Trio is repeated (1:44). When the Trio continues (1:54), the piano starts out, soon joined by the violin and viola, and then the cello and double bass. The quiet tenderness is briefly disturbed (2:11) by a loud, forceful interjection quelled by the strings. The Trio ends with the violin and piano playing alone (2:27), leading to a repeat of the Trio's second section, followed by a return to the brisk beginning of the entire Scherzo reprised without repeats until the beginning of the Trio.

FOURTH MOVEMENT: THEME: Andantino   (7:29)

This is the movement that uses the melody of Schubert's song "The Trout" as its base and gives the Quintet its name. It is a delightful theme and series of variations on that theme musically conveying the images written about in the song's lyrics. If possible, be sure to read the text of the song; it will enhance your appreciation of this movement.

The theme is established by the violin accompanied only by

the other strings. Try to pick out the double bass with its usual heaviness replaced by a charming lightness—like an elephant trying to tiptoe! Throughout this exposition the piano remains silent. However, when the first variation (1:02) begins, it is the piano that takes over the theme as the violin, viola, and cello provide the graceful accompaniment while the double bass plays some resonant pizzicatos adding a jazzy quality. (One can almost see the trout swimming around, darting through the water.)

In the second variation (1:57) the middle voices, the viola and the cello, take the theme with occasional help from the piano. It is easy to miss the theme here since the violin is given a series of fast, flowing notes that tend to attract one's attention. But this is little more than musical decoration that distracts from the main event. In the third variation (2:56) the piano takes over the carefree flitting of the violin as the melody falls to the cello and double bass.

The fourth variation (3:48) is an absolute shock, as a sudden, violent storm replaces the idyllic atmosphere that has dominated thus far. A series of loud bursts from the piano followed immediately by the same from the violin and viola dissipates this musical storm (3:55); the music becomes sunny with the violin providing a gentle melody. For a while the storm and calm alternate as the piano and violin have an exchange of musical comments (4:19) seeming to giggle at each other. Their chatter is replaced by a romantic, lyrical passage played by the cello (4:28). The sad mood is continued into the fifth variation starting out with the strings playing alone, the cello particularly tender. The piano copies (4:58) the cello, then passes the theme on to the violin (5:54). The pace is steady and slow; gone is the earlier exuberance. Suddenly, when the energy seems to have completely run out, the pace picks up (Allegretto) and becomes jaunty as the violin and piano start out on their own, skipping along at this new, faster speed (6:14). The cello then becomes involved (6:25) taking the theme from the violin as the piano sits out. Finally, the violin and cello join together for the graceful theme as the piano flits along (7:08). Gradually, the energy wanes again, though now the mood stays happy, and the movement ends sleepily, with a feeling of great contentment.

FIFTH MOVEMENT: FINALE: Allegro giusto
(6:15)

The final movement of the *Trout* Quintet can be best described as fun! It is a charming, lightheaded romp that opens with a loud chord quickly replaced by a delicate melody played by the violin and viola with a bouncy, jocular accompaniment from the double bass. Even when the piano replaces the violin and viola, the music retains its totally carefree quality.

The movement's opening chord returns (0:30), but this time after the initial phrase, the five instruments join for their first unison (0:37), louder and strong. After another brief outburst the piano continues alone (0:55) before alternating with the strings growing softer and more delicate with each passing phrase. Ultimately the strings take over and slow down the pace, lengthening the musical line. But quickly the piano jumps back in (1:12) with its bouncy energy.

The strings add mystery (1:29) while the piano plays a delicate, airy commentary that fits in between the strings' repeated phrases. It seems as if something is brewing throughout this section as the intensity swells and recedes, until it pulls back (2:31) leaving just the violin and piano. This temporary calm is disturbed by an excited eruption (2:46) that ends as quickly as it appeared. The piano calmly restarts the movement (2:52) introducing the other instruments, who join for a quick, exuberant romp to the end of the phrase. (Here there is an optional repeat to the beginning of the movement. The repeat is not observed in this recording.)

Another loud chord as in the beginning (3:05) restarts the music and leads to a reprise of the opening section of the movement followed by a unison, forceful outburst (3:43). (Much of what is heard in the final minutes of the piece is a recapitulation of the earlier section.) The brewing mystery returns (4:35) followed by some wonderful filigree in the piano accompanied by the violin, viola, and cello taking the melodic line (4:55).

The filigree transfers to the violin alternating with the viola (5:21), and the cello and double bass add a steady pulse while the melody is concealed in the piano. The intensity increases gradually, leading to an excited unison (5:53) contrasted with a delicate piano solo (5:59) before all the instruments join for the joyful romp to the final chords.

CELLIST ZARA NELSOVA:

"Perfectly played chamber music is achieved by listening to each other. The important element is not only knowing your own part, but in learning everyone else's part. In this way you can achieve a perfect balance.

"In the Trout Quintet there is an exquisite cello solo in the variations of the fourth movement. This is surely one of the most beautiful of Schubert's compositions."

COMPARATIVE RECORDINGS

LEONSKAJA/MEMBERS OF THE ALBAN BERG
    QUARTET/HÖRTNAGEL
EMI CLASSICS 47448   TOTAL TIME: 38:35

An absolutely delightful recording stressing the equality of the instruments as they have their musical conversation. The sound is especially superb because it brings out the richness provided by the double bass.

O'CONOR/MEMBERS OF THE CLEVELAND
    QUARTET/VANDEMARK
TELARC CD-80225   TOTAL TIME: 36:46

A first-rate performance filled with youthful exuberance, each part played with virtuosity. Excellent sound helps to clearly define each part while yielding a fine, rich sonic blend.

CURZON/MEMBERS OF THE VIENNA OCTET
LONDON 417 459   TOTAL TIME: 35:16

This recording is great because of the superb artistry of Clifford Curzon, whose interpretation is exquisite in every way. His style is matched by the fabulous musicians of the Vienna Octet, who must have his music in their blood. Despite being recorded in 1958 the transfer to CD is acceptable.

IF YOU ENJOYED THIS PIECE . . .

The first thing to do is listen to a recording of the original song *"Die Forelle"* and hear what Schubert used as his starting point. Then move on to the wealth of Schubert's chamber music, beginning with the **piano trios, the String Quartet No. 15, the Quintet for Strings,** and the fabulous **Octet for Strings and Winds.**

SCHUBERT

$\int$ YMPHONY NO. 8 IN B MINOR

UNFINISHED

Franz Schubert (1797–1828), one of history's most prolific composers, had little trouble writing his first six symphonies and in
fact completed the last of these in 1818. His seventh symphony,
little more than a series of sketches, remained undeveloped, and
his Eighth Symphony was begun on October 30, 1822, when
Schubert was twenty-five years old. By sometime in November
the first two movements of the symphony were completed, and
the composer had made an outline of a Scherzo that was to follow. Unlike most "unfinished" works, this one was not stopped
because its creator died; for some unexplained reason Schubert
set the score aside and never completed it. Of course, since there
is no definitive explanation, we can only assume the work is
incomplete. However, it is possible that Schubert felt the two
movements made a complete statement all by themselves.

Almost one year after beginning the Eighth Symphony,
Schubert gave the score of the two movements to one of his
friends, who kept it for forty years. The symphony finally

received its premiere in Vienna on December 17, 1865, some forty-three years after its composition.

To fully appreciate this unusual symphony it is necessary to think of it in terms of when it was composed, for while it bears the marks of a Classical symphony, it is in many ways closer to the Romantic style and joins other works as advance guards of the Romantic era. In 1822, Stendhal wrote *De l'amour*, Delacroix painted *Dante and Virgil Crossing the Styx*, the Sunday *Times* of London was founded, and in Vienna an eleven-year-old piano virtuoso named Franz Liszt made his concert debut.

Schubert's *Unfinished* Symphony is scored for flutes, oboes, clarinets, bassoons, horns, trumpet, three trombones, timpani, and strings. It is important to note how Schubert uses the entire orchestra by frequently spreading a melodic phrase across several groups of instruments.

REFERENCE RECORDING: NIMBUS NI 5274
GOODMAN/HANOVER BAND
TOTAL TIME: 23:17

FIRST MOVEMENT: Allegro moderato   (13:23)

The symphony begins mysteriously with only the cellos and basses playing. They are soon joined by the other strings, with the violins playing a fairly fast but quiet series of repeated notes. The first melody is played by the oboes and clarinets (0:22) soaring over the furtive violins and the stable pulse provided by the lower strings. This pattern is broken by a sting (a short interjection that starts loud then immediately gets quieter) from the bassoons, horns, and third trombone (0:34). The interruption is followed by an immediate return to the initial pattern, each phrase increasing in intensity, the volume building gradually and steadily.

When it seems it can build no further, the development comes to a sudden stop (1:03) and there emerges a calmer sustained phrase played by the bassoons and horns. This bridges the movement to one of the most famous melodies in the symphonic literature (1:13), played initially by the cellos with accompaniment by the clarinets, violas, and bass. (The following lyric has been set to this extremely pleasant melody: "This is the symphony that Schubert wrote but never finished.") The violins then pick up this melody (1:29), but it soon deteriorates and a split-second pause is followed by a quick change in mood to the ominous (1:46).

The happier melody tries to reestablish itself in a series of phrases played by the violas and cellos alternating with the violins (2:03), while the winds provide a more sustained contrast. Again the tension increases, leading to a series of strings played by the entire orchestra (2:23). Listen in this section for the power of the trombone adding darkness to the orchestral color. Out of the darkness the "famous" melody emerges, now divided among the various sections of the orchestra (2:37). Another harsh sting (2:54) is followed by pizzicatos and sustained notes in the oboes, clarinets, bassoons, and horns gradually growing quieter. This is followed by a repeat of the entire beginning of the movement. (During a repeat of this length it is interesting to try to identify places where the conductor does something a little differently.)

The harsh sting ending the first section is heard again (5:57) followed by the quieting down as described earlier, except this time there is a distinct chord change (6:06) that alters the mood. Out of this, the cellos and basses emerge with the movement's opening phrase (6:13) played even softer than before. Then the violins take over (6:27) joined by the bassoon. Together they are developing something new that grows out of an ever-increasing tension heightened by the ongoing rumble provided by the cellos and basses. This entire section is a series of buildups and brief eruptions followed by quick calming, all leading to one large explosion (7:44) led by the brass section, especially the trombones.

Suddenly the violins and violas take off at a furious pace while the trombones and the other winds play a forceful, rock-solid series of sustained notes (7:54). The contrast is thrilling and filled with conflict and leads to another series of stings (8:22) and retreats. A haunting, brief duet for the flute and oboe (8:54) leads to a recapitulation of the movement's opening from the point where the violins and violas first entered, and the same beautiful woodwind passages (9:07) rebuild the tension and lead to the stings (9:56).

The movement seems to run out of energy and in fact stops (10:44) until the stings return and the tension starts to rebuild. Following a particularly tragic-sounding interjection (11:54), the cellos return with a recapitulation of the movement's opening phrase (12:04) joined by the violins, clarinets, bassoons, and oboes. A continuous rumble provided by the timpani heightens the tension; the only appropriate description for this section is struggle and pain. Total exhaustion overwhelms everything, and three distinct, loud chords are followed by a tremulous chord getting softer and softer, eventually fading away, ending the movement.

SECOND MOVEMENT: Andante con moto
(9:54)

The second movement begins like a gracious stroll, easygoing, yet not quite carefree. A brief introduction provided by the horns and bassoons leads to the strings assuming the lead and developing the melody. The mood becomes bolder (0:59) and less gracious as the strings provide a steady pulse under the fanciful wind instrument lines. But the winds take over (1:22) and return to the gracious opening.

A clarinet solo (2:00) is made somewhat uneasy by the off-the-beat pulse played by the violins and violas. The calm is broken by an angry outburst (2:55) developing into a struggle highlighted by the first violins (3:09) playing against the second violins and violas. As suddenly as the calm was broken, it returns (3:22) with the strings playing alone, save for periodic interjections from the flutes, oboes, and bassoons. As the wind instruments' comments become more frequent, they lead into a recap of the movement's opening, complete with the bassoon and horn introduction (4:18).

A stately pulse in the strings accompanying the soaring winds (5:18) again takes away the movement's graciousness. As before, this leads to the off-the-beat pulse in the violins and violas and an oboe solo (6:20) taken over by the clarinet (6:53). However, this calm is interrupted by an angry explosion (7:14) and a return to the earlier struggle and conflict. The first violins (8:56), now playing quietly, begin the calming, leading to some exquisite wind solos, especially for the horns, and the symphony's extremely peaceful conclusion.

FOUNDER AND ARTISTIC DIRECTOR OF THE HANOVER BAND, CAROLINE BROWN:

"Most people have heard of Schubert's Unfinished *even if they haven't actually even heard the music! For orchestral players the music is perhaps in danger of seeming over-familiar, and so to perform it on authentic instruments of the period came as a remarkable experience. So many of the textures suddenly seemed much clearer and transparent and the ravishing melody in the first movement for the cellos—my instrument—sang through as if we were encountering it for the first time. The sudden outbursts of drama also came like bolts from the blue and the music emerged as if a coat of varnish had been removed."*

COMPARATIVE RECORDINGS

GOODMAN/HANOVER BAND
NIMBUS NI 5274   TOTAL TIME: 23:17

Played on instruments of the period, this is a beautiful reading that avoids the museum quality so prevalent in many period-instrument recordings. The sound is exceptional and shows off the brass instruments and their important part in this symphony.

REINER/CHICAGO SYMPHONY ORCHESTRA
RCA RCD1-5403   TOTAL TIME: 23:54

A dramatic reading filled with passion and detail. The
Chicago Symphony under Reiner treat this work with great love
and shows why it can be considered a Romantic work. The wind
playing is superb.

KERTESZ/VIENNA PHILHARMONIC ORCHESTRA
LONDON 417 680   TOTAL TIME: 27:30

This is a slow, stately reading of this symphony, taking a very
Middle European approach. There is nothing unusual or particularly dramatic about the performance; it is just a good addition to
a collection.

IF YOU ENJOYED THIS PIECE . . .

The symphonies in the Schubert canon that precede this odd
work are, for the most part, delightful classical works filled with
gorgeous melodies. The **Ninth Symphony,** known as the **Great,**
is one of the true masterpieces in the standard repertoire and
should be listened to repeatedly. Also, be sure to sample some of
Schubert's exquisite **songs,** his later **string quartets,** and the
Incidental Music to Rosamunde.

SMETANA

THE MOLDAU (VLTAVA)

A Symphonic Poem From the Cycle

Ma Vlast (My Homeland)

Painters have done it with canvas and oils; poets have done it with adjectives, pen, and ink; filmmakers have done it with lighting and different lenses; Bedřich Smetana (1824–84) did it using music and an orchestra. "It" is compellingly portraying the life of a flowing river, from a mere spring to a powerful, large body of water. In his symphonic poem *Vltava (The Moldau)*, Smetana uses the orchestra to take us on a fabulous journey down the river, following its path from rivulet to major waterway as it passes through the Bohemian countryside. It is a wonderfully evocative work filled with nationalistic sentiment, and though part of a cycle of works, this symphonic poem stands on its own and is often performed by itself in concert and on recordings.

The six symphonic poems in *Ma Vlast (My Homeland)* are musical portraits of Bohemia, each one depicting a different natural wonder. *The Moldau* is the second of the poems in the cycle, telling the story of the river from its inception as a stream, on its journey through a forest complete with the sounds of the hunt, past a rustic wedding, a quick visit with the *rusalkas*, the mythological Czech water nymphs, into the roaring rapids of St. John, past the Vysehrad, finally joining the Elbe River north of Prague.

Smetana, who spent most of his career conducting, had composed his nationalistic opera *The Bartered Bride* in 1866, decided to write his first symphonic poem, *Vysehrad*, in 1874, and went on to complete the second poem, *The Moldau*, on December 8 of that year. The year 1874 was an important one for music, as four pivotal works, each imbued with national flavor, were completed: Mussorgsky's *Boris Godunov*, Johann Strauss's *Die Fledermaus*, Brahms's *Hungarian Dances*, and Verdi's *Requiem*. It was also the year three men were born all of whom would play crucial roles in the history of the next century: Herbert Hoover, Winston Churchill, and Chaim Weizmann.

The Moldau is scored for piccolo, flutes, oboes, clarinets, bassoons, horns, trumpets, trombones, tuba, timpani, triangle, cymbals, bass drum, harp, and strings. In this brief work Smetana painted a fabulous portrait of the river, with each landmark on the journey clearly audible, making this a delightful excursion through southern Bohemia, the composer's beloved homeland.

REFERENCE RECORDING:
DEUTSCHE GRAMMOPHON 427 340
LEVINE/VIENNA PHILHARMONIC
TOTAL TIME: 11:58

A solo flute, hesitantly at first but growing steady, starts the flow of the stream, gentle, calm, and cool, with only occasional plucks from the harp and violins as accompaniment. As it weaves its way, the stream gradually picks up energy, and when the clarinet joins (0:25), the music gains volume, but without ever losing the sense of the flow. A triangle chime (0:57) introduces the cellos, violas, and second violins, who assume the role of the ever-increasing current, the sound now warmer, fuller, and richer, like bigger waves on a widening river. All of this steady growth is the introduction to the main theme played by the flute, oboes, bassoons, and first violins (1:03); now the streams have matured as the Moldau flows into the Bohemian countryside. This famous melody is bittersweet, filled with longing, ebbing and flowing, swelling and receding, mimicking the current of the river. This simple melody is taken from a folk song, and variations of it had been used in other nationalistic works prior to Smetana's. It may also sound familiar because of its similarity to the plaintive melody of the "Hatikvah," and because it has been used in several American television commercials!

The waters grow rougher, brought to life by the sharp accents of the horns (1:42) mixing with the rumble of the timpani and the excited ringing of the triangle. The flow that started the piece continues unabated, its swells rushing propulsively forward, moving it sonically from the background to the fore, then back again, the swirling violins making it choppier. From this agitation the main theme emerges (1:57), now more energized, passionate, and louder.

A loud outburst (2:48) led by the horns, trumpets, and timpani ushers the river, and us with it, into the forest as the excited sounds of the hunt are everywhere. Amid the splendor of the hunt as represented by the horns, be sure to notice how the strings continue the flow of the river in the background. The bittersweet longing of the main theme is gone, replaced by this absolutely joyful music. As the river flows, we leave the sounds of the hunt, the thrilling horn calls gradually becoming distant as the sound diminishes and fades into a quiet calm.

As the violins and violas set the steady (3:39), jaunty pace, we encounter a charming rustic wedding, the simple dance theme played by the clarinets, bassoons, and strings (3:42), delicate and jovial. The celebration becomes more lively (4:08), highlighted by the addition of the timpani, yet no matter how raucous, it always maintains its humble, tender dignity. As it grew in excitement, so it shrinks, eventually leaving only the cellos and basses (5:00), like the last guests remaining at the end of a party.

Quiet, eerie, sustained notes from the oboes, bassoons, and clarinets (5:05) bridge to the next section, a supernatural visit with the water nymphs playing happily in the moonlit river. Slowly the flutes start the flow of the water (5:24) as the strings glisten in the background. Then the clarinets playfully roll like gentle waves as the violins and violas shimmer (5:31); a chilling iciness turns magical when the harp adds its gentle grace (5:38), the pace constantly slow and relaxed, an endless flow of lush sound. Try to notice the increased richness the tuba, horns, and trumpets cause (6:54) even though their regal sound is nothing more than background color. However, these instruments steadily grow in importance, and when the sound swells (7:36), the trumpets cut through calling us back to reality, getting faster and faster.

Abruptly, most of the instruments stop (7:51) leaving the rapidly flowing flutes and clarinets and the rumbling timpani to lead to a return of the central bittersweet theme (8:00). The choppiness and rougher waters return (8:25) again led by the horns, but now the river has grown and the volume is powerful. Then, racing, the river flows more violently as we enter the churning waters of the St. John's Rapids (8:50), their strength and power captured by the horns and trumpets coupled with the rumble of the timpani and the bass drum. The flow that had been so dominant to this point is now chopped up into a series of more jagged string passages, while the high pitch of the piccolo adds its shrill cry to the fury. Each phrase increases the intensity; the river grows wilder and wilder as the sections of the orchestra blast angrily at each other, especially when the cymbals crash loudly into the fray (9:28). The apex of the rapids are reached (9:51) and passed; the fury immediately subsides, leaving a quiet murmur that evolves into an excited rush as the Moldau flows onward (10:03). Now the main theme is joyful; gone is the bittersweet undercurrent, replaced by an excited, fun-loving outburst exuberantly played by the whole orchestra as the river flows happily and freely. Listen especially for the thrilling accents provided by the trumpets (10:21).

Out of this sonic brilliance a new theme emerges (10:32); proud and noble, it represents Vysehrad, the high rock standing at the entrance of the river into the city of Prague. This national symbol is the focus of the first symphonic poem in the *My Home-land* cycle, and to invoke its majesty here, Smetana reuses the theme from the opening of that piece, now made powerful and glorious by the rich sounds of the brass instruments and the excited ringing of the triangle. When the brass instruments pull back (11:24), the strings continue to flow along propulsively while the winds and horns provide a rich, sustained background. Calm waters start to appear; the excitement spent, just the violins remain (11:41), slowly, quietly flowing, seeming to bob up and down, like very gentle waves. They fade and stop (11:51), the sonic void quickly filled by two loud chords, the final stop on this beautiful river's journey.

MAESTRO JAMES LEVINE:

"*By far Smetana's best-known work among concertgoers,* The Moldau *is a brilliant example of 'tone-painting' and is immediately understandable even on first hearing—the flowing river, the moonlight, the rushing rapids, all these things and many others are explicit in the music and recognizable as the piece develops. The 'big tune' near the end, however, which represents the legendary fortress Vysehrad towering over the banks of the river, will only make its full effect on those people in the audience who know the entire cycle of six tone poems, Ma Vlast ('My Country'), of which* The Moldau *is the second movement. This wonderful cycle begins with this very melody, scored unforgettably for two solo harps, and is one of my very favorite works in the orchestral literature—well worth investigating and, sadly, all too rarely programmed in its entirety. It is an utterly thrilling depiction of Smetana's love for his native Bohemia, the manifold beauties of this country and its illustrious history.*

"*When I performed the work in Vienna, which resulted in this live performance recording, two representatives from the Czech government came from Prague to give me their Smetana Medal for presenting the whole piece to the Viennese public; a couple of years later, I had programmed it with the Berlin Philharmonic, and the concerts (coincidentally as it happened) took place just at the time that Czechoslovakia, and the rest of Eastern Europe, was being freed of its Iron Curtain. The atmosphere at those concerts was indescribable!*"

COMPARATIVE RECORDINGS

LEVINE/VIENNA PHILHARMONIC
DEUTSCHE GRAMMOPHON 427 340   TOTAL TIME: 11:58

An unbelievable recording that will make you think you have just traveled on the Moldau. Every detail and nuance is captured perfectly, and the playing of the orchestra with its silky sound is exquisite.

SZELL/CLEVELAND ORCHESTRA
CBS MASTERWORKS MYK 36716   TOTAL TIME: 12:49

A classic recording led by the maestro who was very much at home with this music. Here, too, the details come through with incredible clarity, and the playing is excellent. The sound is fine.

KUBELIK/BAVARIAN RADIO SYMPHONY ORCHESTRA
ORFEO C 115 842 H   TOTAL TIME: 11:47

Though somewhat difficult to find, this recording is worth seeking out because of Kubelik's excellent interpretation and the fine orchestral playing. The sound of this 1984 performance is fine.

IF YOU ENJOYED THIS PIECE . . .

Begin by listening to the **five other symphonic poems in the cycle;** each will introduce you to another Bohemian wonder. Then listen to the symphonic excerpts from Smetana's opera **The Bartered Bride.** If the Slavic spirit appeals to you, sample some of the symphonic poems of Dvořák and his exciting symphonies.

STRAUSS, J.

ON THE BEAUTIFUL BLUE DANUBE, OP. 314

Johann Strauss the younger (1825–99) is the musical personifica-
tion of the splendor and elegance that was Vienna during the latter half of the nineteenth century. His hundreds of waltzes, each
one filled with lilting, infectious melodies, will make you want to
rise gracefully from your seat and glide across an overpolished
dance floor. Strauss, after all, was not called the Waltz King for
nothing! While most of his more than five hundred works are
enjoyable diversions, the waltz titled On the Beautiful Blue
Danube is an exquisite jewel perfectly conveying the regal beauty
and formality of the capital of the Austro-Hungarian Empire. In
a way it is fitting Strauss died just before the twentieth century
began; his brand of courtly elegance captured by his waltzes
would have been out of place in the mechanical, industrial, high-
pressure world of the 1900s.

Composed in 1867 when Emperor Franz Joseph ruled the
Empire with pomp and style, On the Beautiful Blue Danube is
probably the best known of Strauss's works, its recognizable
melodies used often in television commercials and cartoons.

Some of the other creations of importance dating from 1867 are Ibsen's *Peer Gynt*, Cézanne's painting *The Rape*, Twain's *The Jumping Frog*, and Marx's *Das Kapital, Volume I*. The year also saw the birth of the musician who would go on to be one of the most important conductors of the second quarter of the twentieth century, Arturo Toscanini.

In this waltz Strauss takes us on a musical journey over the calm waters of the Danube River using an orchestra of flutes, piccolo, oboes, clarinets, bassoons, four horns, trumpets, trombone, tuba, timpani, percussion, harp, and strings. Also keep in mind that this waltz is actually a series of shorter waltzes combined to create one long, seamless composition. The key to this entertaining music is that it must be light and delicate, always knowing it was meant for dancing, not just listening. Further, a well-played waltz will seem to speed up and slow down; there should be a freedom to the three-beat pattern creating an elegant sweep. Allow the piece to transport you back through time to a long-gone era when things were not so rushed and one could enjoy an evening of waltzing in sumptuous surroundings. Perhaps, to truly capture the mood, precede your listening with a piece of Sacher torte topped with whipped cream!

REFERENCE RECORDING:
EMI CLASSICS ENCORE 67788
BOSKOVSKY/VIENNA JOHANN STRAUSS
ORCHESTRA
TOTAL TIME: 9:18

I. INTRODUCTION: Andantino

Shimmering violins introduce a slow, romantic horn solo setting the mood; the development is leisurely, totally unrushed. Then the bassoons, cellos, and basses join the lone horn (0:10) adding great richness to the sound, growing more luxurious when the theme is taken by two horns (0:15). Think of each phrase as a gentle wave, the biggest of them (0:33) leading to a pullback, slowly quieting the surges as the cellos play the theme.

Suddenly, the pace picks up excitedly as the waltz tempo begins (1:01), the flute and piccolo cheerfully dominating, rushing to a split-second pause followed by the oboe and first violins playing a gracious melody (1:09) made more so by the charming chime of the triangle. Gradually the pace slows, leading to three distinct notes from the bassoons, and pizzicatos in the cellos and basses and a pause (1:21). After the silence we are politely ushered into the first waltz (1:27).

II. WALTZ I

Here it is, the exquisitely elegant melody of the waltz, but if you are at a concert, please do not get up and dance; just sway gently in your seat! The waltz is first stated by the bassoon, horn, first violins, and cellos with the other instruments providing gentle pulses as accompaniment. The melody flows easily as it moves steadily, slowly gaining momentum and strength, especially when the trumpet, trombone, and snare drum add their more powerful sound (1:47). The violins increase the intensity, never losing the light, joyful quality (1:54) as they get carried away with the excitement of the waltz. When the phrase is completed, a new airier, even more delicate section begins (2:03) dominated by the upper voices: the flute, piccolo, oboe, clarinets, and first violins, supported by resonant pizzicatos in the cellos and basses. This last section is repeated (2:17), ending the first waltz.

III. WALTZ II

The second waltz begins (2:32) with the horns and bassoons primarily providing the pulse as the first violins negotiate a fairly fast, free-flowing passage and the woodwinds accentuate the lightness of this section, which is repeated (2:48). Following the repeat (3:03) the harp assumes the free-flowing passage as the flute, trumpet, first violins, and cellos begin a languorous melody filled with moonlit romance. Six distinct, yet gentle notes played by the trumpet, horn, violas, and cellos herald a repeat to the beginning of the second waltz (3:19).

IV. WALTZ III

Following the repeat we glide right into the third waltz (3:36); this one lacks some of the romanticism. Still lush and rich in sound, there is an air of polite formality evident even when the pace accelerates, seeming to race slightly out of control (4:09), the energetic flow unabated.

V. WALTZ IV

A short bridge highlighted by the snappy roll of the snare drum (4:23) temporarily breaks the seamless flow before the waltzing resumes (4:28), gently opened by the clarinets, bassoons, and first violins. This new theme is easygoing and relaxed, qualities exaggerated during the repeat (4:49). The dreamy nature disappears in one excited beat (5:05) instantly whipping it into a more lively, energetic mode led especially by the flute, oboes, and first violins growing louder and more excited with each phrase. This section is repeated (5:21).

VI. WALTZ V

The fifth waltz begins rather stiffly (5:36), with a strong introduction provided by the sonorous bassoons, horns, and trumpets preceding a dainty response from the flute, piccolo, and first violins. A one-breath pause (5:46) introduces a delicate, softer waltz bringing back all of the earlier elegance and charm. But the horns, trumpets, and snare drum snap us back (6:17) to the energized dance; the image of smartly uniformed military officers guiding their beautifully dressed partners across the floor is unmistakable. Listen for the beats played by the trombones and tuba adding power to the dance, and the way they emerge with a brief solo (6:31).

VII. CODA

The power is dissipated as we enter this new, gentle section (6:45); the pace is still fast, but the energy is lower as if trying to take a quick break from all the excitement. The violins glide into a two-note phrase (6:57) answered by the more jagged two notes of the horns and the second violins and violas playing pizzicato. (Note the charming sound the contrast of "smooth" followed by "angular" creates.) This is a brief respite, and the gracious flow of the waltz resumes (7:02) with a recapitulation of the elegant second waltz. A mood shift leaves the flutes and first violins to lead into a mystery-filled section, the flow of the waltz no longer evident. But the gentle grace of the dance returns (7:31) as the clarinets, bassoons, first violins, and cellos easily resume the waltz, the energy growing with each passing phrase, building to a supercharged release that comes to a stop and is left hanging in midnote (7:57).

Slowly at first, the bassoon, horn, first violins, and cellos drift back into the waltz reminiscent of the horn's very first solo at the beginning of the piece. Gradually the dance returns to its full speed and power (8:28) and then abruptly stops, cut off in midphrase (8:34). The cellos and horn fill the void, dreamy and quiet as the violins shimmer in the background, each phrase filled with longing echoed by the flute and oboe. The trumpet elegantly copies the solo phrase (8:52) alternating with the flute. A sudden acceleration (9:05) rushes to the waltz's excited conclusion with the snare drum dominant.

PRINCIPAL BASS OF THE NEW YORK PHILHARMONIC, EUGENE LEVINSON:

"Whenever I play the Blue Danube, *I am transported back to my first visit to Vienna. As I passed by a statue of the young Johann Strauss with his violin in hand, I could feel my pulse quicken. Just thinking about the charm and elegance of Strauss and his music makes me feel like a young music student again.*

"More important than any single note is the overall impression created by the orchestra as a whole. You should be able to hear the Danube river and imagine the crystal blue of its waters. I still get goosebumps each time I play the piece."

COMPARATIVE RECORDINGS

BOSKOVSKY/VIENNA JOHANN STRAUSS ORCHESTRA
EMI CLASSICS ENCORE 67788   TOTAL TIME: 9:18

There is something very special about this recording, due in no small part to the Austrian charm and native elegance Boskovsky and his Strauss orchestra bring to the party! The CD sound is excellent.

KLEIBER/VIENNA PHILHARMONIC
SONY CLASSICAL SK 45938   TOTAL TIME: 9:45

Led by one of the most underrecorded conductors, the Vienna Philharmonic sparkles in this fantastic performance. It seems as if the Viennese musicians must walk in time to the waltz!

VON KARAJAN/BERLIN PHILHARMONIC
DEUTSCHE GRAMMOPHON 437 255   TOTAL TIME: 9:53

A slightly older recording, but it is interesting to hear this music in the hands of an orchestra that can be machinelike in its precision. A fascinating comparison, and an excellent recording.

IF YOU ENJOYED THIS PIECE . . .

There are hundreds of Strauss waltzes to listen to, each with a distinct style and all imbued with the great charm and delicacy of Old World Vienna. Of special interest, try **Wine, Women, and Song, Voices of Spring,** and **Tales of the Vienna Woods.** If you want something more substantial, try Strauss's delightful opera **Die Fledermaus.**

STRAUSS, R.

*A*LSO SPRACH ZARATHUSTRA, OP. 30
(THUS SPAKE ZARATHUSTRA)

When Stanley Kubrick chose the opening moments of Richard Strauss's (1864–1949) *Also Sprach Zarathustra* as the music for the staggering beginning to his epic motion picture *2001: A Space Odyssey,* he took a great piece of late-Romantic symphonic music and catapulted it into the pop-music category. Anyone who has seen the movie remembers the image of the sun rising and the apes pounding in time to the powerful soundtrack matching the visual images moment for moment. In Strauss's wildest dreams he could not have imagined the popularity his half-hour-long composition would attain.

Composed in 1896 and based on the mammoth poem by the philosopher Friedrich Nietzsche, *Also Sprach Zarathustra,* Strauss's fifth symphonic tone poem, was not intended as a musical representation of Nietzsche's work. Rather, Strauss saw his work as an homage to Nietzsche and a musical evocation of the evolution of man—a daunting goal but one well executed by the dramatic range of the music. Parts of the work are staggeringly powerful while others are tender and sweet; simply put, Strauss's manipulation of the large orchestra is fantastic, as he sometimes breaks it up into small groups and sometimes uses all of his vast forces as one powerful unit.

Strauss conducted the world premiere of the work on November 27, 1896, a few weeks after William McKinley was elected the twenty-fifth president of the United States. It was also the year of the creation of the Nobel Prizes and of the first modern Olympics, fittingly held in Athens. Puccini's immortal opera *La Bohème* premiered as did Anton Chekhov's play *The Seagull;* along with Strauss's work these oeuvres became an integral part of twentieth-century culture.

Also Sprach Zarathustra is a complex piece with frequent changes in instrumentation, pacing, musical coloration, and every other element that goes into great music. Therefore, do not try in your first few listenings to pick out the details because there are far too many. Instead, listen for the larger changes, the overall shape and structure of the work, and the sudden shifts in mood and tone. The symphonic poem is divided into nine sections, but do not expect distinct beginnings to all the sections because many times the music does not stop, instead continuing on uninterrupted. Strauss's orchestra is huge; among the instrumental highlights, listen for how he uses the six horns (one of his favorite instruments), the four trumpets, the three trombones, the large percussion section, the two harps, and the organ. Most of all, allow this music to fill your mind with brilliant, dramatic images.

REFERENCE RECORDING:
RCA LIVING STEREO 61494
REINER/CHICAGO SYMPHONY ORCHESTRA
TOTAL TIME: 31:48

PART I: SUNRISE   (1:31)

You will not actually hear the very beginning of the work because it is little more than an extremely low-level rumble provided by the contrabassoon, basses, bass drum, and low pedal note from the organ. Slowly the volume increases to where the rumble is, if not heard, at least felt! Then from this musical abyss, the trumpets (0:13), as if slowly waking, call out. As they are joined by the other wind instruments, their sound swells and then recedes, leaving only the timpani to pound out its steady, determined beats. What you have just heard is the beginning of *2001!* As the rumble of low notes continues, the trumpets again call out (0:31), now more confident, and the pattern repeats right through the timpani beats. A third time the trumpets call out (0:50), now louder and still more confident; a third time the sound swells, but this time the entire orchestra joins, highlighted by a cymbal crash and the incessant ringing of the triangle. It is loud, viscerally thrilling. This brief but tremendously powerful beginning ends with the organ and bass drum holding their taut lines after the rest of the orchestra has stopped. Then the organ cuts off, leaving the still-rumbling bass drum to fade away.

PART II:
OF THE PEOPLE OF THE UNSEEN WORLD
(3:10)

Following a brief pause the cellos and basses quietly and mysteriously begin to rumble, joined by the bass clarinet and organ; a pervasive creepy quality casts images of darkness. The horns play alone (0:38), distantly calling out as if trying to break through the gloom, before a few of the strings, led by the violas (0:53) and supported by the organ, start a tender melody; the interplay of the strings in this section is exquisite. Gradually more of the string instruments and the horns join, creating a layered, incredibly rich, passionate sound. After reaching the apex (2:36), the instruments begin to drop out; the intensity reduces and the sound diminishes, leaving the viola to play the final phrase.

PART III: OF THE GREAT LONGING   (1:45)

The viola's last note from the previous section is sustained right into the beginning of this one. A burst of excitement provided by the cellos and bassoons followed by the violins is heightened by an uplifting, rapturous harp passage (0:04), sustained by the soaring violins, flutes, and clarinets. The intensity wanes and turns to mystery as the second violins tremble beneath the piquant notes of the English horn (0:17). The tremble continues as the organ quietly intones the musical phrase for the word *Magnificat* (0:30) just before the horns emerge with a beautiful solo (0:37) blending directly into a viola passage filled with longing. The regal calm is shattered by the cellos and basses (1:01), the mood becoming almost violent as the trumpets angrily copy the phrase played earlier by the English horn (1:10). The excitement and strain increase steadily, building to a frantic race to the end of the section.

PART IV: OF JOYS AND PASSIONS   (1:50)

The start is explosive, launching with a rumble from the timpani while the strings continue to dominate. Try to pick out the short bursts from the harps; they add tremendous excitement. A seductive, wild fury develops, highlighted by the demonic phrases played by the violins and cellos (0:37); like a snowball rolling down a hill, the fury gains momentum and flails about wildly. Through this the brass instruments try to establish some order (1:15), angrily blasting through the maelstrom. There is some calming, although the passions still run high, but the brass wins out and the bassoons, contrabassoon, trombones, and tuba seem to cast a pall over the wildness, like a stern grandfather scolding an unruly child (1:34). Gradually, an unsteady quiet emerges as the sound fades away.

PART V: DIRGE   (2:16)

From the remains of the fourth section, the oboe emerges, mournfully crying out a melody echoed by the English horn

(0:12). The uneasiness now manifests itself in a slight disso-nance, as if the parts of a puzzle do not quite fit together. The sadness is pervasive, intensified by the strain in the strings, inter-rupted by the trumpet bravely announcing three steady notes (0:44), a dramatic contrast to the strings. But the sorrow prevails despite the distant ray of hope provided by the fifth and sixth horns and a bassoon (1:05). Worn-out, the constant strain diminishes and almost fades into silence, but the clarinets dream-ily revive the movement (1:44). The revival is short-lived as a brief viola solo (1:52) followed by a cello solo leads into an extended chord that quickly fades away.

PART VI: OF SCIENCE   (3:58)

The sorrowful nature continues almost inaudibly at first with only some of the cellos and basses playing. The pace is slow; gradually more cellos and basses join in, adding to the murmur of sound. The entrance of the bassoon (1:10) and the bass clarinet seems bright in comparison with the darkness of the cellos and basses. The violas, divided into groups, join their lower-voiced counterparts (1:19), adding to the buildup, like a dark, musical quagmire slowly growing. The violins (1:34) add their higher voices, increasing the layers of sound and the intensity. Only the entrance of the clarinets and bassoons (2:02) seems to enliven the mood at all.

A sudden burst of excitement (2:23) tears us out of the turgid heaviness; the contrast makes this new section seem frenzied due in part to the low-high tonal contrast as now the dominant sound is the soaring, ecstatic notes of the flutes and violins. The excitement grows as the flutes, oboes, and clarinets squeak with giddiness, a mood accentuated by the very high tremolo of the violins. Quickly the squeaks fade (3:00) revealing the distant trumpet with its three steady notes echoed by the oboe (3:08), leaving a new mysterious quality that is highlighted by the harp. Something seems to be brewing, but it is reluctant to emerge until a split-second pause (3:46) leads to an outburst led by the violins, flutes, and clarinets. From here there is a frantic flight and this section is left hanging, seemingly incomplete as it ends.

PART VII: THE CONVALESCENT   (5:02)

After a split-second pause the seventh section begins dramatically with two contrasting sounds working together; all at once the cellos, basses, and trombones loudly pronounce a series of heavy, plodding notes while the clarinets, bass clarinet, and second violins rip into fleeting passages. This contrast results in an angry fury raging unabated as more instruments join, taking either the plodding heavy line or the fast, wicked line. When the trumpets take the heavy line (0:28), they seem more determined to establish order, but they cannot and the fury races on endlessly. With each passing phrase the mood grows more animated and wild. Suddenly, out of this frenzy comes a full-force blast (1:18) as the entire orchestra joins together including the organ and bass drum, whose rumbling should make the ground shake! This unbelievably powerful moment will be recognizable; it is a recapitulation of the famous theme from the beginning of the entire tone poem, now in a mature, full-blown guise. At the end of the theme the orchestra remains silent as if exhausted by this outpouring of power.

The cellos' tremble breaks the silence (1:34) introducing the horns and bassoons playing a dark, creepy melody heightened by the addition of the contrabassoon. Throughout this murky section the orchestra seems to meander aimlessly as if trying to find its way in heavy fog. The flutes emerge (2:43) chirping wildly like out-of-control birds, their twittering continuing incessantly despite a vicious blast from the trumpet (2:48) slicing through. The woodwinds, inspired by this strange behavior, add their own quirky phrases making this section strange, giddy, and funny. Again the trumpet piercingly calls out (3:05), just as the violins add their sounds to this bizarre conversation now resembling a musical impression of all the animals in the zoo animatedly yammering simultaneously. This is brought to an end by a quiet cello solo emerging from the twittering (3:32) and copied by other strings. Order returns as the mood turns cheerful and builds to a joyful outburst (4:13) highlighted by the ringing of the triangle. Throughout, the trumpet calls continue to pop up as the excitement grows almost to an uncontrollable level filled with all the wildness from before, until it loses energy and fades away leaving the flutes and clarinets (4:57) twittering at each other.

PART VIII:
DANCE SONG AND NIGHT SONG   (7:36)

The twitter continues, now joined by the trumpet quietly and slowly playing the three notes of the work's dramatic opening. The first violins copy the trumpet, and the two instruments toss the three-note phrase back and forth, faster and faster until the violins eventually keep it and a solo violin emerges with the dance melody (0:21), jaunty and graceful. Then the oboes, accompanied by the rich sound of the harps, copy the melody making it bouncier (0:33) and introducing solo violins now playing a Gypsylike version of the dance (0:38). This is happy, "feel-good" music that wallows in its glee and becomes sentimental (1:09) like dance-hall music might be. But the joy cannot be sustained forever, and the oboes and clarinets (1:43) subtly remind us of the tension that had existed. This unsettles the picture and hints of brewing trouble as the frantic quality returns, but out of the uncertainty the solo violin boldly reestablishes the dance melody (2:01). The happy mood is heightened by the addition of the clear chiming of the glockenspiel (2:56) playing along with the strings and harps. When the wind instruments enter (3:14), the pace slows, becoming expansive, relishing the joy of the moment although still with an occasional hint of strain.

The flute and oboe join for a calm, charming duet (3:45) accompanied by an intimate group made up of the bass clarinet, the harp, a solo violin, and two cellos. The horns and trombones add weight (4:02) and seem to gurgle quietly while a solo violin weaves its passages. There is a sense that trouble is again on the horizon as the piece meanders. But the strings set the direction (4:44) with a sinewy, relaxed sexiness that languishes in the richness of the sound.

A hint of darkness returns (5:03) provided by the cellos, bassoons, and contrabassoon. Slowly, piece by piece, the excitement rebuilds as Strauss scatters solos throughout the orchestra until a sonic explosion (5:43) reveals a thrilling, yet controlled outpouring of rapturous melodies. Occasionally the wild excitement subsides and becomes more dreamy and peaceful, but the intensity of the passions remains evident. With each pullback there is a resurgence that increases the power, especially when the timpani, horns, and trombones loudly call out (7:15) followed by another explosion, this one including the cymbals (7:22). This is the wildest outburst of all and it flies directly into the work's final section.

PART IX: NIGHT WANDERER'S SONG   (4:40)

The frantic wildness continues, now intensified by blaring dissonances and loudly tolling bells all going on while occasional blasts from the trumpets still cut through. Gradually the power and excitement dissipate, the pace slows, and the volume diminishes. Like clouds parting to let the sun shine through, the struggle resolves (1:00) as the harp introduces a tender string passage. Though calm, a bit of sorrow lingers in the midst of this lush music. The bassoon and violins enter into an intimate dialogue (1:35) seeming to speak of forgiveness. Eventually the violins take over, and they quietly remove all the strain, leading to the harp (2:35) evoking a musical image of the stairs to heaven mysteriously appearing.

The final minutes of this incredible work are magical. Intimate and tender passages that quietly swell and dissipate create an absolutely ethereal atmosphere that conjures up images of the tender endings of fairy tales. The final chords fade away into a heavenly void, leaving an eerie silence. Three virtually inaudible pizzicatos played by the cellos and basses close the curtain on *Also Sprach Zarathustra*.

PRODUCER JACK PFEIFFER:

"At one point during recording I asked Reiner if the brass were in the proper proportion, and Reiner answered that yes, they were because (and this is quoting Strauss himself), 'I never look encouragingly at the brass section.' "

COMPARATIVE RECORDINGS

REINER/CHICAGO SYMPHONY ORCHESTRA
RCA LIVING STEREO 61494   TOTAL TIME: 31:48

Even though this recording was made in 1954, few, if any, subsequent ones have equaled its beauty and a clarity that allows the listener to be overwhelmed by the massive power of the piece while still able to appreciate the details of the orchestration.

PREVIN/VIENNA PHILHARMONIC ORCHESTRA
TELARC CD-80167   TOTAL TIME: 34:51

An excellent performance with extraordinary sound. The interpretation is a little more on the romantic side, tending to allow phrases to unfold slowly. The members of the Vienna Philharmonic sound incredible.

KEMPE/STAATSKAPELLE DRESDEN
EMI CLASSICS 64346   TOTAL TIME: 33:00

A classic recording by a conductor well known for his Strauss interpretations. Though recorded in 1973 the sound is excellent and allows the listener to hear all the details. There is nothing extraordinary about this recording, but it makes an excellent addition to a collection.

IF YOU ENJOYED THIS PIECE . . .

Strauss's symphonic tone poems are all quite beautiful, especially **Ein Heldenleben** and **Don Juan.** However, Strauss's greatest music was written for the voice, so be certain to listen to his exquisite **Four Last Songs** and his operas, especially **Der Rosenkavalier, Ariadne auf Naxos,** and **Salome.**

STRAVINSKY

L E SACRE DU PRINTEMPS
(THE RITE OF SPRING)

Few, if any, pieces of music have shocked the world the way Igor Stravinsky's (1882–1971) *Le Sacre du Printemps (The Rite of Spring)* did when it premiered on May 29, 1913. The story of that first performance is legendary and helped secure the work's place as a pivotal piece in the history of music. The world premiere was held at the Théâtre des Champs-Élysées in Paris, danced by Diaghilev's Ballet Russe conducted by Pierre Monteux, with choreography by Nijinsky. On that opening night riots broke out as the audience was startled, some negatively, by the radical sound and vision being unveiled before them. Right from the start, laughter, catcalls, and shouting erupted, so loud the music couldn't be heard; however, the visceral excitement and staggering brilliance of the ballet overcame the initial reaction and placed the score into the mainstream. It is a critically significant piece of twentieth-century art.

In 1913 the fox-trot raged across America, Woodrow Wilson was inaugurated as the twenty-eighth president, the federal income tax was begun, and Grand Central Terminal in New York

City opened. It was also the year three critical works of literature were published: Freud's *Totem and Taboo*, Thomas Mann's *Death in Venice*, and D. H. Lawrence's *Sons and Lovers*.

While listening to *The Rite of Spring* keep in mind it is a ballet and was not intended as a piece of concert music, although it is often played as such and is a favorite of orchestras and conductors everywhere. Stravinsky's correspondence from the time of the work's premiere indicates the need for an orchestra of 105 musicians including quintuple woodwinds (i.e., five oboes), eight horns, five trumpets, three trombones, two tubas, five timpani, and an extremely large percussion section. Percussive, rhythmic, and propulsive are all apt descriptions of the music, as it is filled with a variety of sounds capturing the barbarity of nature, possibly inspired by the composer's impression of the violent Russian spring.

The story told in *The Rite of Spring* is beautifully synopsized by the work's subtitle: *Pictures of Pagan Russia*. Briefly the tale told is "Part I—The Adoration of the Earth" in which at the bottom of a sacred hill Slavonic tribes gather to celebrate spring. A witch tells fortunes followed by a wild dancing game ending in exhaustion, with more ritual games played between the members of two tribes. Old wise men arrive interrupting the festivities, the sage then kisses the earth, and the first part ends in a frenzied dance.

In "Part II—The Sacrifice" young virgins dance at the foot of the hill to choose the victim to be "honored" by being sacrificed. She dances her final dance as the other maidens glorify her. The wise men return to witness her dance, ending with the sacrifice of the chosen.

Stravinsky's own words will best serve to send us into the wild world of *The Rite of Spring*. In 1912 he wrote: "I want the whole of my work to give the feeling of the closeness between men and the earth, the closeness between the lives of men and the soil." Keep this vivid image in mind as you experience the visceral excitement of Stravinsky's music and its less than gentle vision of spring.

REFERENCE RECORDING:
MUSICMASTERS 67078
CRAFT/ORCHESTRA OF ST. LUKE'S
TOTAL TIME: 30:05

PART I—THE ADORATION OF THE EARTH
(14:10)

I. INTRODUCTION

A soulful, earthy bassoon solo quietly and slowly unfurls, meandering, its hollow sound eventually joined by the bass clarinet and clarinet creating a mild dissonance. The sound grows steadily as other wind instruments are added, remaining dark and uneasy, like the calm before a distant storm. This free-flowing section, void of any jagged edges, develops slowly as the winds blend together, sometimes dissonant and sometimes harmonious. The first break in the flow is the pizzicato interjection of the violas and second violins (0:57) adding a piquant quality. The flutes (1:10) distantly chirp as the other wind instruments chime in commenting with sounds reminiscent of zoo animals—a collage of unusual sounds.

A trill in the first violins (1:25) momentarily creates a tonal calm before leading to a newly propulsive section (1:33), energized and more determined, but no less dissonant. Suddenly, a cheerful oboe solo pops out (1:57) of the sonic morass, its melody becoming more pointed when assumed by the high voice of the soprano clarinet (2:02). The basses add a rumble to the already muddy background (2:09), sliced through by the soprano trumpet like a laser of light in a cloudy sky. The activity increases, growing busier and more complex; then just when it seems to have reached a boil, it stops suddenly, interrupted in midphrase (2:30), the silence filled by the lonely bassoon sullenly recapitulating the piece's opening theme, interrupted by the violins playing a rhythmic pizzicato (2:40), like a series of rapid clock ticks. An eerie, mysterious chord (2:51) is sustained as the violins renew their pizzicato pulses leading directly into the second section.

II. THE AUGURS OF SPRING; DANCES OF THE YOUNG GIRLS

The second violins, violas, cellos, and basses assume the beat established by the first violins, creating a violent, steady pulse made even uglier by occasional blasts from the eight horns. (This section may sound like the battle music used in any of the outer-space war movies from the 1970s and 1980s.) The English horn and two bassoons interject (0:07), mumbling like trolls busily jabbering together until the propulsive anger returns (0:11), now more animated. A bassoon trill (0:21) introduces the excited violas shuddering wildly as the mood verges on cheerful. But again the propulsion resumes (0:33), guttural and primitive, leading to a split-second pause (1:07) and a violent outburst that includes the trumpets blurting out what sounds like a musical "Ha-Ha!"

As the violins scratch (1:18), the wild pace restarts, scattered, jerky, and unsettled until the horn emerges (1:29) with a tuneful melody, quietly echoed by the flute. Slowly the energy rebuilds, little excited phrases popping up amid the excitement as a celebratory mood takes hold, heightened by the happily chiming bells (2:04). The frivolity is interrupted (2:12) by a sudden quiet, tinged with mystery and anticipation; building gradually and growing wilder and faster with each passing phrase, the music seems to want to race away, held down only by the occasional pounded beats of the timpani, moving inexorably to the third section.

III. RITUAL OF ABDUCTION

The wildness stops for just a second, the ferocity instantly returning with the angry beats of the bass drum followed immediately by the alarmed, shrill cry of the soprano trumpet (0:03). We are thrust into a wild, orgiastic scene, furiously fast and almost uncontrolled. The wind instruments try to establish a steadier beat (0:32), but the pace remains fast, even when the horns' calls stand out above the fray. No one can gain control; the untethered nature of the movement is always dominant, especially when the strings begin to fly furiously through some passages (0:56) interrupted by occasional, angry thrusts. A quiet, haunted trill in the flutes emerges (1:09) and sustains until the end of this section, continuing uninterrupted into the next.

IV. SPRING ROUNDS

The flute's trill carries over, contrasted by the haunting tone of the soprano clarinet and bass clarinet tranquilly intoning the start of the ritualistic spring dancing games. Gradually the sound fades, replaced by weighty beats in the strings (0:24), making movement burdensome until the oboe and bassoon add a lighter quality (0:34). But despite their efforts the heavier pulses keep returning, often filled with subdued sorrow. A trill in the piccolo and soprano clarinet (1:11) seems to twitter over the heaviness, erupting (1:42) with a timpani crash, the pulses more forceful, increasing the strain and the dissonance. Brutal and painful, each passing phrase intensifies the struggle until it is so weighted it cannot go on (2:18); a breath leads to the piccolos and flutes flying into a skittish frenzy joined by the strings. The wildness is stopped cold by a ferocious beat (2:34), from which the trilling flute calmly emerges and fades into the dance's end.

V. RITUAL OF THE RIVAL TRIBES

The trombones, tubas, timpani, and bass drum shatter the calm with a musical "Splat!" introducing the horns, bassoons, cellos, and basses beginning another wild dance (0:03). A bouncing timpani solo (0:17) heightens the visual imagery as the sections of the orchestra snipe at each other, exchanging crisp outbursts. The oboes and clarinets play a brief solo (0:32), their contrasting sounds creating sonic discomfort, quickly replaced by steadier, propulsive passages dominated by the strings, horns, and bassoons (0:39). The muted trumpets (0:43) launch a graceful melody copied by the violins (0:48), its cheerful, almost elegant theme seeming out of place amid the work's brutal force. But this is only a brief respite as the anger and ferocity resume (0:55), wildly excited as the brass instruments blast out repeatedly while the strings carry on their propulsive rhythmic patterns. A series of steady bass-drum beats (1:30), starting out in the distance covered by the fury of the orchestra, continues relentlessly, growing more present with each phrase and continuing right into the next movement.

VI. PROCESSION OF THE SAGE

The beats continue, suspended on sustained horn chords, punctuated by periodic tam-tam crashes, and growing angry, developing into incessant hammering (0:20) now louder and more percussive, sounding like a brass marching band gone totally out of control. When there is no room left for the sound to grow, the pounding stops suddenly (0:39) and fades away.

VII. THE SAGE

An eerie, mystery-filled, sustained chord quietly begins this brief section played by the bassoons and supported by almost inaudible timpani beats. An equally eerie sustained chord intoned by the strings (0:19) presents itself and quickly fades away.

VIII. DANCE OF THE EARTH

A wicked explosion launches the final section of the work's first part; percussive and furiously fast, the bass drum rumbles while the brass instruments blast away like fierce gunfire. Explosion after explosion pounds, relenting just a bit as the bass clarinet tries to emerge with a solo (0:25) as the strings continue to fly. But there is to be no calm, as the power rebuilds led by the staccato, rapid-fire trumpet maintaining the frenzied pace, growing louder and louder. A series of vicious sneers from the brass instruments (0:59), like angry slaps, punctuate the endlessly flying strings, building to one final explosive beat (1:04) that stops the flight in midphrase. It fades away, ending "The Adoration of the Earth."

PART II—THE SACRIFICE   (15:55)

I. INTRODUCTION

The horns quietly sustain their notes as the flutes and clarinets steadily play a moderately paced, flowing phrase, creepy and eerie with a distinctly hollow sound. The sound becomes strained, seeming to be weighted down, and led by the strings, grows lethargic (0:44). A difficult-to-hear, high violin solo (1:04) tries to pierce through the murky sound, but disappears into the other instruments' sound. The violas have more success (1:21) with a comparatively harmonious, yet sad theme filled with resignation.

A brief pause (1:30) precedes the trumpets sadly playing alone, their tone funereal as some of the violas and cellos join in while a bit of a rumble begins in the background. This section is more intimate, using only part of the orchestra's massive forces. A haunting chord (2:21) appears, sounding like the music for a movie about a lost world, its nightmarish quality impossible to mistake. Sustained flutes introduce and support a beautiful theme for the horns (2:57), continuing the steady flow. As they fade away, the cellos and basses establish a rich base over which the horns and bass clarinet play a ponderous phrase; the sound is muddy and remains so through a brief solo for the cellos (3:24) ending this section.

II. MYSTIC CIRCLES OF THE YOUNG GIRLS

There is no pause as six violins tenderly open this section accompanied by cellos and basses; the melody is sinewy, almost sexy, and flows seamlessly. An abrupt pizzicato (0:22) starts the clarinets wobbling until the shimmering violins, buzzing like busy bees, introduce a soulful flute solo (0:29). The clarinets take over (0:40) followed by the oboe and bassoon (0:52), the sound gradually increasing and growing more dissonant. But when the violins and bass clarinet copy the flowing melody (0:58), it sounds gentle, filled with compassion.

In midphrase the flowing melody suddenly stops (1:07), replaced by the pizzicatos in the violas and cellos and a quiet, sustained note in the horns, introducing two flutes and two violins joining for a strained passage that becomes heavier and heavier. The horns try to lighten the mood (1:41) plaintively singing out the melody, echoed by the flutes and violins creating a lush resonance. Another rendition of the theme is played by three oboes and three cellos (2:12), followed by an angry interjection from the horns and a brief pause. Then, the theme starts to return, but it is disoriented, still sustained but muddled by extraneous sounds, finally stopped by a single burst from the trumpets and horns (2:40), the first salvo in a rapidly accelerating series of thrusts. Steadily they get faster and louder, building to a wild eruption (2:53) with violent pounding; eleven ferocious beats played by the timpani, bass drum, and strings end the section and launch us directly into the next.

III. GLORIFICATION OF THE CHOSEN ONE

Wickedly fast and accentuated by vicious blasts from the percussion, the excitement has reached a fevered pitch; ugly yet erotic, it blasts incessantly and leads to a particularly strident passage featuring the strings and horns (0:21). The pounding of the bass drum further heightens the fierce power (0:30) like forceful blows standing out amid the chaos. The volume recedes suddenly (0:38) as the strings play angry pizzicatos; wicked and nasty, they are steady and propulsive, qualities intensified by the addition of the wildly dancing timpani. The pace and intensity increase, the pounding becoming more frequent as the chaos spreads. It stops abruptly.

IV. EVOCATION OF THE ANCESTORS

A single "Splat" played by the bass clarinet, two horns, two tubas, cellos, basses, and timpani quickly fades away. The horns, trumpets, and all the woodwinds join trying to establish a joyful theme (0:02), but they are interrupted by an angry response. Undaunted, they start again (0:14) but cannot sustain the drive as another eruption (0:22) leads to a sustained note in the bass clarinet, and one more attempt, this time by the bassoons and contrabassoon, restarts the once cheerful pulsing. It succeeds, and a swelling eruption (0:34) briefly returns the brass to the theme they started at the section's outset. It disappears, the bassoons and contrabassoon collapsing in a heap as quiet pulses played by the tambourine, timpani, and bass drum bridge into the next section.

V. RITUAL ACTION OF THE ANCESTORS

The eerily steady pulse continues unabated introducing the English horn (0:10); the combination of tambourine beats and soulful English-horn solo creates a Middle Eastern sinew, like a snake charmer's music, an impression intensified by the addition of the flute (0:22). Gradually, as if totally exhausted, they fade away, replaced by the bassoon slowly playing two-note phrases while the flute plays a faster-flowing line (0:46). The trumpets, way off in the distance (0:58), seem to be marching unevenly against the steady, mechanical pulse in the foreground. The violins blend in, shimmering steadily, leading to a ferocious outburst (1:27) led by the horns; while the steadiness remains, it is clearly getting wilder.

The fury suddenly subsides (1:37), the brass instruments'

power dissipated, as the woodwinds nastily snipe at each other, growling. Big, steady beats from the percussion and timpani (2:02) dominate this louder part contrasting with the flying flutes and violins. Then, dramatically, the horns blast through intensifying the beats, evoking the image of a horrifying pagan celebration. It is visceral, never relenting, pounding beat after inexorable beat.

As if pushed off a precipice, the sound disappears (2:20), leaving only the distant pulse and a mysterious-sounding phrase filled with sexy smoothness from the flute (2:28) echoed by the clarinet (2:39). A series of flutters in the clarinets quietly ends the section in a disjointed manner.

VI. SACRIFICIAL DANCE (THE CHOSEN ONE)

The final episode is begun by a single chord snapped by the strings. Then, the fury and wildness return as the strings, horns, and percussion snipe wickedly, egged on by the pounding of the timpani. Suddenly the ferocity abates (0:27) leaving a quiet creeping that moves unsteadily and then becomes the background for the trombones angrily blurting out (0:39); it is a momentary outburst, but the steady pulses continue. Then the soprano trumpet, soprano clarinet, and piccolo bite through (1:00), sneering nastily, seeming to stick out their tongues. It is fiercely angular and leads to the entire ensemble angrily pulsing (1:14), each beat moving us closer to a chaotic eruption that ends abruptly (1:26).

Now the trombones sneer (1:34) as others respond in kind, while the violins begin a whirling, rapid passage, wildly erupting in a single beat that cuts off (1:49). The timpani resumes the rhythmic pounding as the strings lead the vicious sniping; but somehow, despite all the energy, it never seems to get going. Not to be deterred, the timpani starts an even wilder dance (2:16) bouncing rapidly from drum to drum as the brass instruments add their angry accents; now it is unstoppable, the sacrifice going forward in all its wicked glory. Having grown louder and wilder, the dance relents momentarily (2:51) with a series of thrusting beats pounded by the timpani and brass, before resuming uncontrolled.

The upper voices, except the violins, drop out (3:18) leaving the more guttural lower voices to sustain the fury led by the constant timpani. After a few miniature eruptions, the power relents (3:45) as the eight horns dominate this section of strength conservation; something is brewing as the eruptions become more frequent and the pace gets faster and faster. Abruptly everything stops (4:12) except the flutes, gently gliding upward. One final, chaotic outburst ends the sacrifice, the incredibly powerful sound left to decay into the void.

MAESTRO ROBERT CRAFT:

"I think no one would claim any immediate influence of The Rite of Spring *on the music of the 1990s, or at any rate on the newfangled new music, except in the sense of an ancestor which, like a prize bull, has inseminated the whole modern movement. Composers, including Stravinsky, have tended to regard it as a dead end (bang rather than whimper), but that has protected its originality.*

"It contains as much of the genius of its age, of the ethos of the twentieth century, as any one creation, and it has already demonstrated resilience to fashion."

COMPARATIVE RECORDINGS

CRAFT/ORCHESTRA OF ST. LUKE'S
MUSICMASTERS 67078   TOTAL TIME: 30:05

A fabulous recording led by the man who worked closely with the composer and knows every detail of the piece. The visceral excitement and incredibly fast pace will nail you to your seat.

DUTOIT/ORCHESTRE SYMPHONIQUE DE MONTREAL
LONDON 414 202   TOTAL TIME: 34:59

A gorgeous performance by an ensemble and conductor who seem to have an affinity for this music. Each instrument comes through clearly, and the performance allows the listener to savor the piece.

SLATKIN/ST. LOUIS SYMPHONY ORCHESTRA
RCA VICTOR RED SEAL 60993   TOTAL TIME: 35:07

Another excellent recording, this one led by Leonard Slatkin, whose championing of twentieth-century music is well documented. His reading of this score is imbued with passion, and his orchestra meets every challenge.

*I*F YOU ENJOYED THIS PIECE . . .

Few works have the power and excitement of **The Rite of Spring,** but Stravinsky's other ballet scores will conjure up fabulous images. Start with **The Firebird;** its thrilling ending will leave you openmouthed. Then try the less powerful but absolutely delightful **Pulcinella.** After enjoying these pieces, sample some of Stravinsky's less often performed compositions such as the oratorio **Oedipus Rex,** the **Symphony of Psalms,** and the **Symphonies of Wind Instruments.**

TCHAIKOVSKY

1812 OVERTURE, OP. 49

Peter Ilich Tchaikovsky (1840–93) may be best known for the few minutes of overpowering bombast that concludes his *1812 Overture*. Given that the work is usually accompanied by fireworks, it has become a composition whose musical qualities are often not noticed. While the visceral excitement of the piece's ending is memorable, the earlier sections are filled with the more beautiful and passionate melodies. Actually, its full title is *1812—Ouverture Solennelle*, or *Solemn* Overture, hardly a title that sounds like it belongs to a fifteen-minute piece best known for its explosive cannon shot!

Tchaikovsky composed the Overture to celebrate and remember the victory of the Russian army over Napoleon and the invasion of 1812. The piece was written in 1882 for the Moscow Exhibition of Arts and Crafts. It premiered on August 20 of that year as part of the consecration of the magnificent Cathedral of the Redeemer in the Kremlin built as a remembrance of the military events of 1812. The Cathedral was dynamited by the Bolsheviks after the 1917 Revolution, but fortunately the Overture has survived and thrived. The year of the Overture's premiere saw Edison build the first hydroelectric plant in Wisconsin, Wagner compose *Parsifal,* and the founding of the Berlin Philharmonic.

The orchestra required for the *1812* Overture is huge. Some of the more unusual instruments to watch and listen for are English horn, bass trombone, tuba, tambourines, triangle, bells, a military band, and a cannon. Also, Tchaikovsky drew heavily on nationalistic themes to represent the warring nations. The more recognizable will be the French anthem *"La Marseillaise,"* which appears several times throughout the work. Also, be aware of the tremendous dynamic range in the piece, from the ultraquiet to the deafeningly explosive. While the Overture is a great piece for celebratory, outdoor concerts, because of its dynamic demands it is also a perfect work to show off the sound of an excellent audio system.

REFERENCE RECORDING: RCA VICTOR 60739 TEMIRKANOV/LENINGRAD PHILHARMONIC AND LENINGRAD MILITARY ORCHESTRA (LIVE CONCERT PERFORMANCE)
TOTAL TIME: 15:44
TIME WITH APPLAUSE: 16:18

The *1812* Overture can be listened to as a musical depiction of a series of skirmishes within a battle. The warring parties, Napoleon's French army and the defending Russian forces, each have their own themes. The French are represented by their national anthem, *"La Marseillaise,"* while the Russians are represented by a solemn hymn and by the work's most famous melody, which will be pointed out each time it appears within the piece.

For anyone who knows the *1812* Overture only in terms of its raucous finale, the solemnity of the opening moments will be a surprise. The beginning features the violas and cellos alone; their theme is the melody from the Russian hymn "Save, O God, Thy People." While only two sections of this huge orchestra are playing, the texture is rich and full, and while quiet, there should be no lack of sound or intensity. For a brief phrase of the prayer the flutes, clarinets, first horn, and bassoons (2:18) take over. Note the contrast of sonorities between the lower strings and the winds as they alternate passages before eventually joining together.

The solemnity is shattered by a single timpani beat (3:05), followed by the strings playing anxiously in unison, as the horns and woodwinds add their angrier voices. Another timpani beat (3:12) introduces a plaintive oboe solo. During this next section the pulse provided by the violins and violas is the one steadying force in what develops into a furious battle. With each passing phrase the intensity and ferocity increase.

Through the turmoil, the first militaristic horn calls can be heard (4:05) in the distance. The battle rages, complete with blaring trombones and crashing cymbals. Suddenly, for just a split second, everything stops (4:35), and the bassoons, cellos, and basses take over forcefully. Like a scolding grandfather, they seem to quell the turmoil.

In the distance, the distinct sound of the snare drum emerges (4:52) preceding the oboes, clarinets, bassoons, and horns gallantly playing the famous melody. One can almost see the soldiers on horseback elegantly riding in to save the day! To add some romance to the picture, the violins and violas join with a sinewy series of phrases (5:05) that contrast with and at the same time heighten the militaristic elegance of the horn calls. But, this momentary peace begins to disintegrate (5:24) as the horns grow angrier and the strings more anxious. Then, the battle subsides, seemingly played out, and the music comes to a complete stop (5:50).

Suddenly (5:52), the violins break into a fast passage copied by the rest of the orchestra. The brisk phrases are like sniping: short bursts of gunfire exchanged from one section of the orchestra to another. The "fighting" is fierce and fast. Amid this turbulence the horns play a new call (6:29), echoed and then firmly established by the bugle (6:36). This time though, the call is the French anthem, "La Marseillaise," and its theme is heard several times over. But its presence is fleeting. Chaos returns (6:58), and we are thrust into what sounds like a ferocious maelstrom. Over the shooting, played primarily by the cymbals and timpani, the "*Marseillaise*" returns (7:17), as the French again dominate the battle.

The mood changes drastically, becoming romantic and happier (7:41), as the violins and violas, accompanied by a steady series of chords in the woodwinds and horns, play a flowing, new melody. (Try to listen for the triangle chiming along in the background.) Melancholy sets in (8:12) until the flute, oboes, and clarinets take over the romantic melody (8:18), growing softer with each passing phrase. Soon, only the flute and clarinet are left, and quietly they lead to a new melody (8:52), played by the flute and English horn, its dancelike nature given a bohemian flavor by the addition of the tambourine. The oboe, clarinet, bassoon, violas, and cellos each play the dance melody briefly before it, like all the other melodies that have preceded it in the Overture, fades away (9:21).

The fast passages played earlier by the strings reemerge, and the trumpet quietly, but crisply, calls us back to the battle (9:29). The turmoil steadily rebuilds, with more instruments adding their voices in every passing phrase, until a series of explosions (9:55), like distant cannons, launch the battle into higher gear, complete with occasional refrains of the "*Marseillaise*." Eventually the battle dies down, and we hear a recapitulation of the romantic violin melody (10:50), which evolves into the bohemian dance tune, again with the tambourine adding appropriate flavor (11:24).

Quietly the horns sneak in the "*Marseillaise*" (11:38), interrupted by the violins and violas playing skittishly, like nervous animals before a storm. The snarling trumpet (11:53) indicates that the battle is rebuilding as more voices join the fray, increasing incessantly until it explodes (12:09) with the whole orchestra going at full throttle. The orchestra's upper voices, led by the violins (12:20), launch into a frenzy that gradually subsides. Suddenly (12:52), the military brass band blasts through, playing the Overture's opening hymn, only now its prayerlike solemnity is replaced by joyous grandeur, intensified by clanging bells and crashing cymbals. Though exultant, the pace is steady and pompous.

Everything gets loud and fast (14:20) as the orchestra boldly returns to the original militaristic theme heard after the hymn at the opening of the work. Now the image of the soldiers on horseback carries the added glory of the victorious army. Bells clang; cannons explode in a display of controlled cacophony. With all the melodies playing against one another, the sound is jubilant and thrilling, and the whole orchestra plays to the Overture's explosive unison ending, usually as fireworks burst overhead!

MAESTRO YURI TEMIRKANOV:

"If it is not to be played bombastically, my advice is not to play it at all!"

COMPARATIVE RECORDINGS

TEMIRKANOV/LENINGRAD PHILHARMONIC AND
LENINGRAD MILITARY ORCHESTRA
RCA VICTOR 60739   TOTAL TIME: 15:44

Recorded in concert at the Tchaikovsky Gala in Leningrad in 1990, this is a visceral performance. While not musically or sonically perfect, its Russian flavor and passion oozes through every note.

MUTI/PHILADELPHIA ORCHESTRA
EMI CLASSICS CDC-47022   TOTAL TIME: 15:24

A stunning performance that begins with the rich tones of the Philadelphia strings and never loses its intensity for a moment. The sound is spectacular and allows the listener to pick out instruments and particular phrases from the mass of sound created.

JANSONS/OSLO PHILHARMONIC ORCHESTRA
EMI CLASSICS 64291   TOTAL TIME: 14:33

This is an exciting recording filled with great clarity and intensity. Further, it has exceptional sound with the ability to blast you from your seat.

IF YOU ENJOYED THIS PIECE . . .

There are two compositions that follow nicely on the heels of the *1812* Overture. Tchaikovsky's **Fourth Symphony** has a comparable visceral excitement and explosive brass sections, while Beethoven's **Wellington's Victory** is a similar musical depiction of a battle. It, too, is not a great piece of music, but is fun to listen to.

TCHAIKOVSKY

SYMPHONY NO. 6
IN B MINOR, OP. 74
PATHÉTIQUE

Peter Ilich Tchaikovsky's (1840–93) last symphony, known as the *Pathétique*, is a large-scale work that is at once thrilling and heartbreaking. Written in 1893, it is among his very last compositions, and it is probably a reflection of Tchaikovsky's most personal feelings. In essence, it is, at least partially, an autobiographical creation. When listening to the more melancholy sections, it is impossible not to be moved by the pathos that fills every phrase. What is even more striking is that this primarily gloomy, extremely mature work was composed just one year after Tchaikovsky completed his delightful ballet *The Nutcracker* with its child's fantasy and cheerfulness.

The *Pathétique* is a Romantic symphony in the truest sense; it looks back toward the style of the latter half of the nineteenth century and gives no hint of the dissonance prevalent in the new century just seven years away. Ironically, the year of its composition was one that presaged the upcoming century, for it was in

1893 that Henry Ford built his first car, and Karl Benz built his four-wheel car. It was also the year that saw the completion of Verdi's last opera, *Falstaff*.

The Sixth Symphony premiered in St. Petersburg on October 28, 1893, with Tchaikovsky conducting. One week later Tchaikovsky died. Further, it is believed that he may have committed suicide, possibly from intentionally drinking unboiled tap water and thereby contracting cholera. Keeping in mind that he was possibly suicidal as he composed the work makes listening to the Sixth Symphony an extremely intense experience. Listen for how Tchaikovsky uses the large orchestra to heighten the strain and conflict, a musical manifestation of his mental state.

REFERENCE RECORDING:
DEUTSCHE GRAMMOPHON 419 604
BERNSTEIN/NEW YORK PHILHARMONIC
TOTAL TIME: 58:31

FIRST MOVEMENT: Adagio—Allegro non troppo—Andante—Moderato mosso—Andante— Moderato assai—Allegro vivo—Andante come prima—Andante mosso   (22:34)

The first thing to notice about this movement is the series of sections delineated by changes in speed as indicated by the many tempo markings listed above. While the movement is segmented, a never-ending flow results in a unified composition.

The opening of the movement is somber and dark. It features the low instruments, the bassoon, cellos, and basses playing softly. There is a definite feeling of sadness, a very Russian sadness filled with strain and the image of bearing a great burden. This introduction continues until the Allegro non troppo begins (2:29). While this second section is faster, it is certainly far from a joyful romp. The initial melody is played by the strings and quickly imitated by the flutes and clarinets. There is an unsettled, nervous quality to this new phrase as it builds and expands until the horns punctuate it with a clear, militaristic call (3:20), followed immediately by a calming down. This ebb and flow continues until the next brass blast (4:25) and a harsh series of explosions and ultimately a musical pullback.

A brief cello solo leading to a viola solo (5:10) serves as the bridge to the next tempo change and the beginning of the Andante (5:30), a highly romantic section with the melody played by the violins and cellos. This is lovers' music, starry-night stuff! (Listen for the horns punctuating the background.) A flute solo immediately followed by the bassoon copying the phrase (6:50) begins the Moderato mosso section. Soon the clarinet joins the other solo instruments, while the strings provide the accompaniment.

When the strings stop playing, the woodwinds, after a split-second pause, play a short transition that leads to the Andante (8:10). Here the strings reprise the ultraromantic melody, while the winds and basses provide a steady accompaniment. The next tempo shift, to the Moderato assai, occurs in the midst of the soaring string passages (9:40) and is almost unnoticeable. A sultry clarinet solo (10:29) creates a false sense of calm soon broken by a violent explosion (11:34), the beginning of the Allegro vivo. The mood shifts from romantic to angry. There is a distinct sense of alarm; chaos prevails, highlighted by a series of almost vulgar brass blasts. Ironically, the lower brass instruments provide the first sign of order returning (12:40), as they play an almost solemn passage over the still-rumbling cellos and basses. Soon the anger seems to run out of energy, and a brief, uneasy calm lasts long enough to give the angry energy time to rebuild. When the brass instruments blare out their melody (14:00), the anger is fully restored. The militaristic trumpet calls (14:35) make the battle even more intense. The strain builds inexorably, and the trombones and tuba further heighten it with a series of sustained notes (15:30).

Seemingly brought down by its own weight, the chaos and strain finally fizzle out (16:57) as the Andante come prima section begins. Here the romance of earlier sections returns, only now feeling much less settled and relaxed. A lovely clarinet and flute solo (19:26) emerges, interrupted only by the persistent, yet distant thunder of the timpani. This exhausted calm leads to the final section, Andante mosso (20:49), ushered in by the strings all playing pizzicato as accompaniment to a beautiful brass passage. While there seems to be an element of jazz here, there is no mistaking the processional, regal quality of this section. The movement ends quietly.

SECOND MOVEMENT: Allegro con grazia (8:29)

This movement is airy and graceful, a dramatic contrast to the weighty struggle of the opening movement. The cellos play the melody first, followed by the winds. A fabulous section in which the strings play pizzicato against the flowing melody in the winds (1:48) brings the mood into the near-joyful realm. A further expansion of this mood occurs when the violins and horns contrast with slightly differing versions of the melody (2:16).

The energy wanes when the strings wind down and the timpani joins in with a series of steady, repeated notes (2:44). Throughout this section there are hints of a return of both the ultraromantic mood and the emotional strain from the first movement. The original, graceful melody from the beginning of the movement emerges (5:05) almost out of nowhere and recapitulates what occurred earlier.

A distinct winding down (7:15) is led by the oboes, clarinets, and bassoon. Here Tchaikovsky takes the orchestra apart and has phrases passed from one instrument to another. One last remembrance of the original melody (8:08) leads to the movement's restful ending.

THIRD MOVEMENT: Allegro molto vivace (9:52)

The flighty beginning, played primarily by the violins, belies the serious, militaristic movement that is to follow. The first hint of what is to come occurs in the oboe (0:13), then the brass and the horns; it is well disguised. But then there is the first explosion

(1:12) and the clear picture of what this movement is all about emerges. The energy builds and builds, seemingly unstoppable. Out of this swelling energy the clarinet emerges with a solo version of what is turning into the main melodic thrust (1:55). The strings pick it up (2:13), beginning another series of swells that pull back when the clarinet retakes the melody (3:08).

The constant building and retreating goes on, teasing, yet never fully unloading in a full-orchestra explosion. Each successive explosion lasts a little longer, and a dramatic timpani roll (5:24) leads to a full-scale buildup featuring the brass instruments. Then there is a forceful march (6:21) complete with crashing cymbals. This entire section is a tour de force for the brass instruments and leads to the biggest explosion of all (7:40), the formerly combative forces now unified in one overpowering march. The timpani plays the distinct rhythm of the march (8:55) leading to the raucous ending: four unified, aggressive beats played by all the instruments except the woodwinds.

FOURTH MOVEMENT: Finale: Adagio lamentoso—Andante   (17:12)

Filled with anguish, this is one of the saddest movements of music ever written. There is a tortured quality that makes the burden inherent in the opening movement seem lightweight in comparison. This is the musical depiction of deep depression; it is slow and ponderous.

The strings set the tone right at the outset; they wail the opening phrases, a musical expression of hopeless resignation. The flutes add a particularly haunting element throughout this exposition. The opening phrase returns (2:11), now with more intensity. A bassoon solo (3:31) serves as a bridge to a new phrase and mood (4:15), beginning with the horns playing a series of repeated notes. This new melody, somewhat less depressing in nature, is played by the clarinets, bassoon, violins, violas, and cellos. This part is more thoughtful, but soon the strain rebuilds and the intensity increases in a steady progression.

The release finally comes (7:15) in an emotional overflow erupting from the entire orchestra. Suddenly the pace quickens; the intensity eases and we are led into a repeat of the movement's opening (8:31) with its lamentation and resignation. Then the strain and conflict increase and the strings and brass vie for dominance; it increases as a rolling snowball grows until it becomes overpowering. Here it is important to listen for the ascending notes in the brass (11:00) cutting through the strings. When the opening phrase returns again (11:33), it is no longer just in the strings; now the winds and strings combine in what sounds like a final effort to break out of the bleakness that prevails. But this last-gasp effort disintegrates into total exhaustion; the struggle has ended.

A unison brass section (12:17) seems to sound the death knell. The final section of the movement begins with repeated notes in the basses (13:23) followed by a sorrowful new phrase played initially by the woodwinds and violins and then echoed by the violas and cellos. Slowly the instruments drop out as the movement grinds to its resigned conclusion. Throughout this section the repeated notes in the basses continue. Soon only the basses and cellos are left, like the last people to leave a funeral, their sound drifting off into the distance.

PRINCIPAL CLARINET OF THE NEW YORK PHILHARMONIC, STANLEY DRUCKER:

"There is a melody in the first movement played first by the violins and later the clarinets that you will remember and sing or hum; it was used as the theme for a pop song. The symphony's third movement contains one of the best marches ever written."

COMPARATIVE RECORDINGS

BERNSTEIN/NEW YORK PHILHARMONIC
DEUTSCHE GRAMMOPHON 419 604   TOTAL TIME: 58:31

Recorded in 1987 during Bernstein's frequent returns to the Philharmonic podium as Conductor Laureate, this is a well-played, passionate performance filled with Bernstein's excesses; unusual, to say the least, but it works.

REINER/CHICAGO SYMPHONY ORCHESTRA
RCA 5602   TOTAL TIME: 45:15

A crisp, much less passionate performance, but one that shows Reiner's masterful control and the fabulous brass section of the Chicago orchestra. Despite the recording's age, the sound is fine.

SLATKIN/ST. LOUIS SYMPHONY ORCHESTRA
RCA 60438   TOTAL TIME: 49:25

A surprising recording in that there is an absolutely Russian sound to this performance by an orchestra from the middle of the United States and an American conductor. Additionally, the feeling and sonic brilliance make this a recording worth adding to a collection.

IF YOU ENJOYED THIS PIECE . . .

Of Tchaikovsky's six symphonies, the last three are the best known and most often performed. However, the **Fourth** and **Fifth** Symphonies are more powerful and less sad than the *Pathétique*. Also if the Russian style appeals to you, listen to Tchaikovsky's brilliant **Violin Concerto,** and the clichéd but still wonderful **First Piano Concerto.**

VIVALDI

THE FOUR SEASONS

Critics have said that even though Vivaldi (1678–1741) composed hundreds of concertos, he was not a creative composer since all of his concertos sound alike. There is no doubt that his concertos follow a pattern in the baroque style, and when listened to one after the other, Vivaldi's compositions do become boring and repetitive. That said, the fact is that the violin concertos known as *The Four Seasons* are wonderful, evocative pieces that deserve to be an important part of the standard repertoire.

Composed in 1725, *The Four Seasons* is part of a set of twelve concertos known as Opus 8, bearing the overall title *Il Cimento dell'Armonia e dell'Invenzione (The Contest Between Harmony and Invention)*. In this set of violin concertos, Vivaldi sought to expand the limits of the baroque concerto form by composing descriptive music. In the case of the four concertos describing the parts of the year, Vivaldi used prefatory poems as literary guideposts for the music. In fact, he actually placed the text of the sonnets in the appropriate places in the music as cues. Thus, Vivaldi has left us a way to identify specific spots in the music, a musical expression of his vision of nature. Given the quasi-Romantic-era quality of this musical impressionistic view of nature, it is interesting to note that Vivaldi composed these concertos in the same year that Canaletto painted his precise, accurate, picture-perfect *Four Views of Venice*. It was also the year that saw Alexander Pope translate Homer's *The Odyssey* and Bach compose the *Anna Magdalena Notebook*.

While it is true that *The Four Seasons* sounds much like many other Vivaldi concertos, the music should be very recognizable as parts of these concertos have been used repeatedly in television commercials and as background music for movies, the most distinctive example being in the movie *The Four Seasons* starring Alan Alda and Carol Burnett.

The structure of the piece is four distinct violin concertos, with each concerto containing three movements. While any one of the concertos can be performed by itself, the four are usually performed as a unit. The orchestration calls for violins, violas, cellos, a bass, and a harpsichord. The solo violin part is not as dynamic or impressive as a Mozart or Romantic-era concerto, and the soloist often plays along with the first violins, occasionally stepping out for a solo. In order to fully appreciate Vivaldi's accomplishment, be sure to read the poetry before listening to the music. Then, listen for how the elements of nature are depicted and for the dramatic changes of mood, which Vivaldi accomplishes with very few instruments. In essence, Vivaldi's *The Four Seasons* should be considered a forerunner of Romantic poetry or the musical views of nature that Beethoven and Wagner composed later.

REFERENCE RECORDING:
EMI CLASSICS CDC 47319
PERLMAN/ISRAEL PHILHARMONIC ORCHESTRA
TOTAL TIME: 41:03

CONCERTO NO. 1: SPRING

FIRST MOVEMENT: Allegro   (3:11)

In this poem, we are presented with a vision of spring being welcomed by singing birds, gentle breezes, and flowing streams. Musically, the beginning has the whole orchestra, including the soloist, playing together as a joyful unit. The mood is cheerful and sunny. The first chirping bird is heard (0:30) played by the solo violin as other birds, portrayed by violins in the orchestra, add their happy voices. These bird conversations are interrupted by a repeat of the opening melody, again played by the whole orchestra (1:01).

Now the streams and breezes are portrayed by a flowing, softer unison series of phrases (1:09). Though fast, this section seems incredibly calm, and it is replaced by another refrain of the original, joyful melody (1:30). But, everything becomes frantic (1:37) and nervous as we are presented with a sudden blackening of the sky accompanied by thunder and lightning. To heighten the nervousness, the solo violin has a tricky series of fast passages (1:45). The storm subsides, and the violins return to the sweeter sounds of the birds (2:11). Slowly, evidently as the skies clear, the mood brightens and the soloist has one more lyrical solo (2:37) leading directly into a refrain of the movement's opening, quieter now than ever before.

SECOND MOVEMENT: Largo   (3:11)

This slow, lazy movement paints a musical picture of a flowery meadow, the peaceful rustle of leaves on branches, and a goatherd who rests with his dog. The violins establish the pulse, broken by occasional accents from the violas. This is all a moody, somewhat dark background for the beautiful, lyrical solo violin part (0:05). The key to the solo part is long, sustained phrases contrasted with the pulse. Here the soloist has the chance to add some personal touches through the use of embellishments.

Save for occasional increases in intensity, little changes in this movement. The trick is to keep the constancy interesting for the listener. At one point (1:23) the soloist pauses, allowing the accompaninent to become more prominent. But, this is short-lived as the soloist resumes (1:30) the sustained phrases. The violin solo stops (2:55) and the unceasing accompaniment carries quietly to the movement's end.

THIRD MOVEMENT: Allegro   (4:14)

To complete his image of spring, Vivaldi turns to the classic vision of a nymph and a shepherd dancing beneath the fair sky accompanied by the happy sound of a bagpipe. The movement's opening jumps out: joyful and bouncy with the whole orchestra playing together. The solo emerges (0:33) and literally dances, sounding more like a fiddle than a concert violin. It is a brief solo, however, as the full orchestra returns (0:58) with a slightly more somber version of the movement's opening.

The soloist's next turn (1:34) is jumpy. (Perhaps the nymph and shepherds have become a bit raucous.) During this passage, listen for the technical trick of having the soloist sustain one note while playing others that constantly change. When played well, it will sound like two violins playing at one time. Once these passages are completed, the pace quickens and the solo line seems to be laughing (2:13) as it bounces along. The orchestra and soloist reunite (2:38) and the mood becomes sadder (2:46) until the next solo (3:15). Here, with each passing phrase, we are lifted out of the doldrums, leading to a joyful recapitulation of the movement's opening (3:38) and its contentment.

CONCERTO NO. 2: SUMMER

FIRST MOVEMENT: Allegro non molto   (5:12)

Vivaldi's vision of summer begins with torpor caused by the blazing sun scorching the pine trees and causing living creatures, man and beast alike, to languish. The slow pace of the music portrays a struggle to move in the heat. The orchestra and soloist play in unison. The first section of the opening movement ends in exhaustion.

Suddenly (1:09), the solo violin takes off at a furious pace accompanied only by the harpsichord and bass. According to the poetry, this section represents the cuckoo raising its voice. Musically, the challenge to the soloist is to play this fast section at a constant pace so that it does not speed up and race out of control. Just briefly the rest of the orchestra joins in (1:37), echoing the soloist's melody and pace. But the racing ends and we are returned to the torpor of the opening (1:42). This is replaced by the next solo (1:57), representing the graceful songs of the turtle-dove and finch.

Summer's gentle breezes (2:29) are played by the violins and violas flowing easily. But these breezes become harsh north winds (2:44) whose fury is portrayed by the racing phrases. Once again the heat and slow pace set in (3:12). The next solo (3:24), filled with pathos, represents the weeping shepherd, who is worried about his fate at the hands of the fierce winds' return, illustrated by the whole orchestra (4:41).

SECOND MOVEMENT: Adagio   (2:31)

This movement is all about the shepherd, who rouses himself but is still afraid of the winds, lightning, and swarms of gnats and flies. It is a series of alternating slow and fast sections. The solo violin opens with a sustained line accompanied by a jerky, but steady and heavy pulse provided by the violins. The rest of the orchestra interrupts with an angry burst (0:20). This is the first of the fast passages. It is very short. This pattern is repeated three times in the movement, with the final section (2:14) being one last burst of fury, probably the swarming flies.

THIRD MOVEMENT: Presto   (2:57)

The shepherd's story ends sadly: his fears are justified as thunder fills the skies, bending trees and flattening crops. This is basically a musical version of a lightning storm, and its speed is immediate and constant. The orchestra begins together, and the violins launch into a battle (0:12) as the firsts and seconds alternate. The solo steps out (0:53) with a demanding, expressive passage that is in its upper range. The rest of the orchestra returns

(1:12) and plays a steadier, more down-to-earth passage, leading to a return to the movement's opening fury (1:33).

The next sections are filled with difficult violin solos alternating with fierce orchestral passages. The "dueling fiddles" return (2:14), snapping at each other. The final solo (2:37) is propulsive and brings in the rest of the orchestra for its last, fierce passage.

CONCERTO NO. 3: AUTUMN

FIRST MOVEMENT: Allegro   (4:51)

Autumn is welcomed by a spirited peasant dance in celebration of a fine harvest. The orchestra, playing in unison, captures the happiness. The soloist takes up the dance (0:28) playing two notes at once sounding like two violins, before the others rejoin (0:57). The celebration turns to imbibing; the peasants drink from Bacchus' cup (1:08) as the violin launches into a solo imbued with wild abandon. This eventually leads to a bit of a drunken stupor (1:59) as the solo line slows.

The orchestra takes over and recapitulates the opening dance (2:06). The drunken fantasy of the solo line returns (2:29) in a more free-flowing fashion, only to be replaced once again by the full orchestra and the original dance (2:56). The next solo ends the drinking and turns into a sleepy stupor (3:24) as the celebrant succumbs and drifts off. One final dance (4:25) ends the movement.

SECOND MOVEMENT: Adagio molto   (2:54)

The second movement is a musical portrayal of the sound sleep that is so inviting in this pleasant air and season. It is slow and sustained, a series of steady, calm chord changes. Save for the continuous rustling of the harpsichord in the background, there is virtually no movement here; all is still. Throughout, the solo violin plays as part of the orchestra. The final chord (2:30) fades into sound sleep.

THIRD MOVEMENT: Allegro   (3:00)

We're off to the hunt! It's dawn and the huntsman sets out with horns, dogs, and guns tracking his prey. At the outset, the strings, playing in unison, portray the stately gait of the horses. Despite an orchestra made up of only string instruments, it sounds as if there are hunting horns. The first solo (0:34) calls for the violinist to play a series of demanding double-stops. As in the other movements, the solo sections alternate with orchestral interludes.

The next solo (0:56) is even harder and includes a section that flows in an almost jazzy manner (1:07). One orchestra section (1:35) portrays the exhausted and scared prey, and then later (2:36) the animal is caught, as the solo violin slows down, somewhat sadly. But the successful hunt is celebrated (2:45) with one last reprise of the movement's regal opening theme.

CONCERTO NO. 4: WINTER

FIRST MOVEMENT: Allegro non molto   (3:31)

This is the most consistently beautiful of the four concertos. It opens with a steady series of short, staccato notes capturing the icy bite of winter. It builds slowly as instruments are added. The first solo (0:38) portrays shivering in the cold wind, and the whole orchestra (1:13) takes the role of stamping feet trying to stay warm.

We are returned to the iciness of the movement's beginning (2:04), before the violin takes the lead in a beautiful solo that includes an evocative portrait of chattering teeth (2:33). One final unison section brings back the stamping-feet melody (3:03), ending the movement.

SECOND MOVEMENT: Largo   (2:17)

This movement has been used in countless television commercials. It is one continuous violin solo over a steady accompaniment. The poem tells of the contentment that can be had by sitting by the fireside while rain pours steadily outside. The solo line is unmistakable, the mood is romantic, and while it is slow, there is a constant sense of motion.

The movement has two sections, and during the second (1:00) the soloist has time to improvise and add personal touches to the beautiful melody. A sustained trill (1:57) in the solo part quiets, turns into one unison chord, then fades away.

THIRD MOVEMENT: Allegro   (3:08)

Unlike all the other movements in *The Four Seasons*, this one begins with a violin solo. It is like a fantasy played over a sustained cello note. The poetry speaks of walking on ice, and the caution necessary to avoid falling. The orchestra's entrance (0:22) is timid, uncertain, but it builds as the poem deals with stepping forth with conviction (0:45). The subsequent solo (0:58) is fast but steady, running cautiously on the ice. With the full orchestra playing (1:41) the ice cracks.

Suddenly, everything slows down (1:55) as we listen for the cold winds to howl. For just a moment, everything is calm. Now the rage of the battling winds (2:29) is portrayed by a fast violin solo launching us into a frenzy that speaks of the joys that winter brings. An exciting unison section carries on to the end of the year's cycle.

ITZHAK PERLMAN:

"Both the orchestral and solo violin parts in Vivaldi's Four Seasons are early examples of program music. In this case there are actual poems describing the various movements in conjunction with the various seasons. Each movement then has as a result an introduction to the listener and enables the listener to understand how Vivaldi described the words in music."

COMPARATIVE RECORDINGS

PERLMAN/ISRAEL PHILHARMONIC ORCHESTRA
EMI CLASSICS CDC 47319   TOTAL TIME: 41:03

This is a beautiful performance featuring Perlman's sweet tone and expressive playing. It is a conventional reading, and an ideal introduction to these concertos.

KENNEDY/ENGLISH CHAMBER ORCHESTRA
EMI CLASSICS CDC 49557   TOTAL TIME: 40:13

This recording was the rage when it was released in 1989. It launched Nigel Kennedy into stardom, but is not a standard performance at all. This is the recording for people bored with the usual.

AGOSTINI/I MUSICI
PHILIPS 426 847   TOTAL TIME: 41:32

The Italian, conductorless chamber orchestra I Musici specialized in the music of Vivaldi, and this recording shows off their expertise. This is the performance by a group of soloists; it is traditional and enjoyable.

IF YOU ENJOYED THIS PIECE . . .

There is no shortage of recordings of Vivaldi violin concertos that will sound much like the concertos in **The Four Seasons.** But, if you want to go beyond the violin, listen to Vivaldi's concertos for lute and mandolin, and his **Gloria,** a stunning choral work.

APPENDIX A

GLOSSARY OF SELECTED TERMS

ACCELERANDO: Get faster

AD LIBITUM: A direction given to the performer to interpret freely, totally at liberty to vary the tempo ignoring the stricter markings

ASSAI: The Italian word for very; as in *Allegro assai*

BADINERIE: A dance movement in a suite of movements, usually jocular in nature

BOURRÉE: A dance movement in a suite of movements, usually fairly fast and bouncy

BREVE: Short; curt

CADENZA: A section most often in a concerto allowing the soloist the chance to play alone, often in a spectacular improvisational manner

CANON: A work in which the melody is delivered by one instrument or voice and is repeated by one or more other voices in turn before the prior voice has finished, thus creating an overlapping effect; for example the children's songs "Row, Row, Row Your Boat" and "Frere Jacques" are sung as canons

CANTABILE: Singingly

CAPRICCIOSO: Capriciously

CODA: The "tail" section of a movement seemingly appended at the end; usually slightly different from the main body of the work

COME PRIMA: As it was at first

COMMODO: Comfortably

CON: With

    CON BRIO: With vigor; with brio

    CON FUOCO: With fire

    CON GRAZIA: With grace

    CON MOTO: With movement or animation

    CON VARIAZIONI: With variations

CONCERTO: A work written for orchestra and one or more solo instruments

CRESCENDO: An increase in volume

DA CAPO: From the beginning

DELICATEZZA: With delicacy

ELEGIA: Elegiacally; elegy

ENERGICO: Energized

FEIERLICH UND GEMESSEN: Ceremonially and stately

FEROCE: Ferociously; wildly

FINALE: The final, last movement or section of a composition

FUGUE: A round in which the theme is started by one instrument or voice and is copied in rapid succession by one or more other voices, and then develops into a complex interweaving of melodic lines; it is much more complex than a canon and usually has a secondary theme

FURIOSO: Furiously

GIOCOSO: Jocularly

GIUOCO DELLE COPPIE: A game of pairs; two at a time

GIUSTO: Just; accurate; usually used to modify a tempo marking

GLISSANDO: A rapid slide through a scale; think of gliding

GRANDEZZA: Grandeur

HORNPIPE: A jaunty dance, originating as a sailor's dance, popular in England for a period beginning in the 1500s until the mid-1800s

INTERMEZZO: An interlude

INTERROTO: Interrupted

KÖCHEL (K.): The listing of Mozart's works as catalogued and numbered by a man named Köchel; used instead of opus numbers for his works

KRAFTIG BEWEGT: Moving with power

LAMENTO: A lament
LAMENTOSO: Lamentingly
LANGSAM: Slow
LEGATO: Smoothly, without interruption
LEGGIERO: Lightly, gently
LENTEMENT: Slowly

MAESTOSO: Majestic
MARCATO: Emphatic; marked; accented
MENO MOSSO: Less quickly
MINUET also MINUETTO/MENUET: A graceful dance in 3/4 time popular in seventeenth century France; the style and form of the music was used extensively throughout the baroque and into the classical era
MINUET AND TRIO: The form that evolved and became an integral part of classical era music; the structure was the minuet/trio/repeat of the minuet; the trio section was usually scored for a smaller ensemble and was generally lighter in texture than the surrounding minuet sections
MODO: Manner; style
MOLTO: Very
MUTED: Using mutes, instruments are able to make their sound quieter and more distant

NON TROPPO: Not too much

OPUS: Work; the cataloging of composers' works giving numerical order to their sequence of composition

PESANTE: Heavily
PIZZICATO: A direction to pluck with the finger rather than using the bow on the strings of a violin, viola, cello, or bass
POCO: A little
POLONAISE: A dance, originally Polish, that is very stately in nature and is moderately fast

POMPOSO: Pompously

RIDICOLO: Ridiculous

RONDO or RONDEAU: A movement form made popular during the 17th century in which there is a recurring section, refrain, alternated with, in its full form, at least three other varying sections

RUSTICO: Rustic

SALTARELLO: A fast dance of Italian origin; the root of the word is *saltare*—to jump

SARABANDE: A slow dance from the baroque era

SCHERZO: A generally fast movement of a work made popular during the classical era; it began to replace the minuet movement in Haydn's symphonies and was used more fully by Beethoven

SEMPRE: Always

SENZA: Without

SOLO: Alone

SORDINO: A mute used to quiet and alter the sound of string instruments

SOSTENUTO: Sustained

STACCATO: The shortening of a note, cutting it off before it can resonate. It usually creates a jagged, pointed effect with short, curt notes

STRINGENDO: With increased tension and actually getting faster

STÜRMISCH BEWEGT: Moving stormily, violently

SUITE: A group of movements put together as a unit; most often dance movements

TANTO: So much

TEMPO: The speed selected by the composer at which the work is to be performed. These markings are indicators to give the performer(s) guidance, but are always subject to interpretational freedom. The sequence of the most common tempo markings from slowest to fastest is as follows:

LARGO
LARGHETTO
LENTO
ADAGIO
ANDANTE
ANDANTINO

MODERATO
ALLEGRETTO
ALLEGRO
VIVACE
PRESTO
PRESTISSIMO

TRANQUILLO: Tranquilly, quietly
TREMOLO: Tremulously; a shaking or trembling caused on string
   instruments by the rapid repetition of notes
TRILL: An ornament that decorates a note with a fast alternation of it
   with the note just above it in the scale

VALSE: The French word for waltz
VIVO: Lively, alive

POSTLUDE

A LIST OF OTHER IMPORTANT WORKS OF INTEREST

Now that you have been introduced to some of the most popular and important compositions in the classical music repertoire, you may want to expand your library by listening to some of the other great works by these and other composers. As you build your compact disc collection keep the following suggestions in mind:

- Choose recordings from all price ranges; some of the best performances ever committed to tape have been reissued on CD and will thrill you.
- Choose performances by different artists; once you find some favorites you will be able to seek out other recordings by them of other pieces.
- Always remember when selecting recordings there is no right or wrong; pick works and performers you think *you* will like!

*S*OME ADDITIONAL WORKS

Albinoni:	*Adagio*—a slow, sad piece from the baroque era; an ancestor of Barber's *Adagio* for strings.
Bach:	*Toccata and Fugue in D minor for Organ*—this is

the "haunted house" music made famous by the
original *Phantom of the Opera.*
The Italian Concerto—a spectacular work for solo
piano or harpsichord.
The Saint Matthew Passion—one of the greatest
choral works ever composed; it becomes more
staggering with repeated hearings.
The Goldberg Variations—a single, simple theme
changed and modified in a fabulously inventive
series of variations played by a solo keyboard.

Beethoven: *The Moonlight Sonata*—a gem with one of the most
famous beginnings of any piece of solo piano
music.

Bizet: *The Carmen Suites*—orchestral suites based on the
melodies from Bizet's hit opera.

Borodin: *The Polovtsian Dances*—gorgeous and dramatic
dances from Russia; you may recognize the
melodies, some of which were used in *Kismet.*

Britten: *The Young Person's Guide to the Orchestra*—a wonderful journey around the orchestra from one of
the twentieth century's greatest composers.

Bruch: *Violin Concerto No. 1*—an ultra-Romantic, ravishing violin concerto.

Bruckner: *Symphony No. 4: The "Romantic"*—A traditionally
heavy piece of Romantic orchestral writing filled
with sonic spectaculars; great to show off a sound
system.

Chopin: Any of the *Nocturnes* for solo piano should be
experienced.

Copland: *Fanfare for the Common Man*—few pieces this
short pack the wallop of this very American composition.
Lincoln Portrait—a moving tribute for narrator and
orchestra.

Corelli: *Christmas Concerto*—the best known of this
baroque master's many concertos.

Dukas: *The Sorcerer's Apprentice*—it's hard not to see
Mickey Mouse in *Fantasia* as the star of this amus-
ing orchestral work!

Elgar: *Pomp and Circumstance Marches*—every gradua-
tion ceremony has used the most famous of these
pompous marches.

The Enigma Variations—a very melodic piece of English orchestral music.

Gounod: *Funeral March of a Marionette*—this was the theme to Alfred Hitchcock's TV show!

Janacek: *Taras Bulba*—a dynamic orchestral work with some great brass sections.

Joplin: *Piano Rags*—the main theme to the movie *The Sting* made these ditties popular.

Mascagni: *Intermezzo from "Cavalleria Rusticana"*—a passionate Italian interlude taken from the thrilling opera; it was used in the movie *Raging Bull*.

Mendelssohn: *A Midsummer Night's Dream*—the incidental music for Shakespeare's comedy; it has one of the two most famous wedding marches composed.

Monteverdi: *The Vespers of 1610*—the perfect introduction to the genius of early baroque vocal writing.

Mozart: *Eine Kleine Nachtmusik*—though overplayed and clichéd it is still delightful.
Sinfonia Concertante for Violin and Viola—an incredible piece; happiness and sadness all in one fabulous concerto.
The Horn Concertos—four melodic concertos for horn and orchestra.

Mussorgsky: *A Night on Bare Mountain*—an orchestral showpiece.

Pachelbel: *Canon*—made popular by its use in the movie *Ordinary People*, this is a short, calming work during which not much happens.

Praetorius: *Terpsichore*—Renaissance dances; they will transport you to a distant age.

Prokofiev: *Peter and the Wolf*—a wonderful story and the perfect way to learn the sounds of the instruments.

Ravel: *Pavane for a Dead Princess*—a short, tender piece with an exquisite horn solo.

Respighi: *The Pines of Rome*—lush orchestrations paint this musical landscape.

Rimsky-Korsakov: *Scheherazade*—1001 listenings will never dull this tale!

Schubert: *Winterreise*—an incredible cycle of songs for male voice and piano; intimate.

Schumann:	*The "Spring" Symphony*—a good Romantic symphony with nice melodies.
Sibelius:	*Finlandia*—rich orchestration will transport you to the North.
Sousa:	*Marches*—Americana at its best!
Tchaikovsky:	*The Nutcracker*—the perennial favorite; not just for children.
Vaughan Williams:	*Fantasia on "Greensleeves"*—a twentieth-century rendition for orchestra of the famous old English song; very calming, like a lullaby.
	Fantasia on a Theme of Thomas Tallis—sonic richness abounds!
Verdi:	*Il Trovatore: The Anvil Chorus*—you will recognize this one; it's been used in countless TV commercials.
Villa-Lobos:	*Bachiana Brasileira No. 5*—a haunting few minutes of sexy, sinewy sound.
Wagner:	*Lohengrin: Wedding March*—this is the other famous one, known as "Here Comes the Bride."
	Ride of the Walkyries—a relentless pace; a thrilling piece used in *Apocalypse Now*.
Weill:	*Threepenny Opera Suite*—an orchestral adaptation of some of the best-known songs from Weill's most popular work, including *Mack the Knife*.

ACKNOWLEDGMENTS

This book has been created with the help, encouragement, and support of all my family members and many cherished colleagues and friends. To each of you I offer my most sincere thanks; it could not have been done without you!

There are some specific people who deserve special appreciation:

My father, Maestro Julius Rudel, whose musicianship and artistry taught me to appreciate and listen to the great treasure of music.

My daughters, Rebecca Katherine and Susannah Elizabeth, whose visible excitement when hearing the music showed me why and how these great works get passed from generation to generation.

My editor, Dave Dunton—a constant pillar of support who suffered through my misgivings and was always there to remind me of our target; and to everyone at Fireside.

My mentor and friend Wallace Gray.

My dear friend and colleague Jeffrey Nissim.

David Reuben, whose counsel is always valued.

Gary Schonfeld and Ron Hartenbaum—for the office and the laughs.

Ann and Mark Kenyon—for the friendship and the house.

Peter and Jimmy for bothering me on the train!

Special thanks to Billy Joel—it is wonderful to hear how excited he is about the classics and have him share those feelings with others.

Also, great appreciation to Jane Arginteanu for working so hard to make the arrangements.

Special thanks to Don DeVito.

In addition, there are many publicists, press agents, record producers and musicians who worked to write and collect the quotes within each chapter. To each of you I owe a huge debt of gratitude, for through your efforts the musician's perspective has been made available to the non-musician.

Many record labels participated in making CDs available for my review, and there are some friends and colleagues at these companies who were of tremendous assistance. Thank you: Andre Becker, Peter Elliot, Bernice Mitchell, Laraine Perri, Linda Sterling, and David Weyner.

Finally, a most special thanks to my business partners, colleagues and staff. By putting up with me, each of you is in some way responsible for this book.

ABOUT THE AUTHOR

ANTHONY JASON RUDEL was literally born into the field of classical music. As the son of internationally renowned Maestro Julius Rudel, Rudel's formative years were spent in concert halls and opera houses throughout the world. His own music studies began with violin lessons at age six. He started his professional career at age nineteen as an on-air personality for WQXR FM/AM in New York, the classical radio stations of *The New York Times*. After graduating from Columbia College, Rudel became part of the management team at WQXR, ultimately rising to the position of Vice President of Programming. It was during those years that he began experimenting with ways of introducing new listeners to classical music.

After leaving WQXR, Rudel held a variety of positions in the music field ranging from director of an arts festival to record producer. In 1992, he began publishing *Classic CD* magazine, the first magazine to include a compact disc as an integral part of the editorial with each issue. He has served as a consultant to many arts organizations, and now continues to work on recordings. Further, Rudel is a frequent lecturer on music and often writes liner notes for new classical music recordings. His first book, *Tales from the Opera*, a compilation of fifty great opera plots told as short stories, was published by Simon and Schuster's Fireside Books in 1985.

Rudel is Vice President of Classical Programming for SW Networks. He lives in Westchester, New York, with his wife Kristy, and their daughters, Rebecca and Susannah.